The Writing Life

Historical & Critical Views of the Tish Movement

THE WRITING LIFE

Historical & Critical Views of the Tish Movement

edited by *CH Gervais*

with an introduction by Frank Davey

Black Moss Press

Copyright © 1976, *the authors.*

Published by *Black Moss Press,* RR 1 Coatsworth, Ontario. Orders, be they trade or institutional, may be directed to *Mosaic Press*, box 1032, Oakville Ontario L6J 5E9.

Graphics and cover illustration are by Craig Robinson of Leamington, Ontario. The cover is after a colour slide owned by Frank Davey; it portrays some members of the original *Tish* group at George Bowering's parents' home in Oliver, British Columbia, August 1961. From the left are an unidentified friend of Red Lane, Frank Davey, Red Lane (without shirt), George Bowering and Robert Hogg.

Typeset by *People Media Graphics* (Guelph) in Univers. Printed and bound by *The Porcupine's Quill, Inc.* (Erin). The stock is Zephyr Antique Laid.

ISBN 0-88753-016-8 (paper)
     0-88753-020-6 (cloth)

Contents

Preface *CH Gervais* 7
Introduction *Frank Davey* 15

1. Genealogy
Wonder Merchants: Modernist Poetry in Vancouver During
   the 1960's *Warren Tallman* 27
The Genealogy of *Tish Beverley Mitchell, S.S.A.* 70
Before *Tish*, from *Oral History of Vancouver*
   Brad Robinson 94
Stan Persky's Section from *Oral History of Vancouver*
   Brad Robinson 103
Black Days on Black Mountain *Frank Davey* 117
Lunchtime Reflections on Frank Davey's Defence of the
   Black Mountain Fort *Louis Dudek* 128
The Most Remarkable Thing About *Tish*
   George Bowering 134
Anything But Reluctant *Frank Davey* 136
The Vancouver Report *Carol Bergé* 143
Introducing *Tish Frank Davey* 150

2. Poetics
Rime, A Scholarly Piece *Frank Davey* 165
Notes on the Stack *Lionel Kearns* 172
Stack Verse . . . A Definition *Lionel Kearns* 177
Frank Davey *Elizabeth Komisar* 179
Tish: A Movement *CH Gervais* 193
Poetry and the Language of Sound *George Bowering* 208
How I Hear *Howl George Bowering* 216

Preface

The *Tish* poets, or the west coast Canadian writers of the early 1960s, fashioned for themselves a very authentic and significant activity in this country's writing. In a very real sense the amateurish-looking mimeographed magazine became a vehicle for probably the most cohesive writing movement in Canada.

The magazine, or "poetry newsletter", as it was termed, had its origins, as one will notice in the genealogical section of this book, in the creative writing classes at the University of British Columbia and the July 1961 lectures by Robert Duncan at Warren Tallman's home. Tallman was the catalytic force behind the birth of the magazine, even though, in the Brad Robinson interview with Gladys Hindmarch, the irony in this is pointed out that he was taken by surprise when he heard that five aspiring young university students of his had intended to edit a poetry magazine. The astonished professor's response was simply the rational observation that no inexperienced group of writers could initiate a literary magazine. Several years later, the same Tallman found himself writing a long, detailed essay for an American periodical (*Boundary 2*, State University at Binghamton 1974) describing the enthusiastic young poets as "wonder merchants" and a major Canadian writing movement.

The young writers were George Bowering, Frank Davey,

James Reid, Fred Wah, David Dawson and Gladys Hindmarch.

The organizational aspects of the little magazine are outlined thoroughly in the articles included in the genealogical section, especially in Tallman's "Wonder Merchants" piece, the interview with Hindmarch and Davey's own introduction to the reprint of *Tish 1-19* published by Talonbooks last year.

The important fact however is that what was initiated then in 1961 has come to be recognized as that unique force in transforming what Davey sees as our "cultural and literary consciousness." *Tish* had something to do with the shifting in our emphasis in Canadian poetry from the humanist tradition (F.R. Scott, Douglas LePan, Eli Mandel) which viewed the universe as "finite, orderly and manageable," to the stance by the universist that all things are "divine, mysteriously structured and essentially ungraspable." (*Tish 1-19*, Davey introduction)

That shift however shouldn't be minimized at all, for indeed it's a big moment in Canadian literary history. When the *Tish* poets opened themselves up to the influence of such experimenters as Robert Creeley, Robert Duncan, Allen Ginsberg, Michael McClure, Jack Spicer and Jackson Maclow, they were in effect welcoming what Tallman viewed as "language lessons."

The pervasive Yankee influence, attacked by some even now (Keith Richardson, Robin Mathews), however developed into something much more unique — "a modernism of their (*Tish*ites) own devising." ("Wonder Merchants", Tallman.)

"Interest," says Tallman, "in the American writers continued but the intensity began to fade as the energy centre shifted to what was happening in their own home town." The essays in this book deal adequately with this aspect later, but what I am wanting to emphasize here is that Tishites did in fact develop for themselves a poetry of their own kind. That style of writing is defined by Tallman as a language which concentrated "on the wonder that came bubbling up from within" or "proprioceptive" writing, verse which turns "to inner stars in their hidden courses." Where poets such as Dudek and Layton were exploiting the "self" as subject matter, Tishites travelled further to tell the story of their *life* — the life within them, that is, and not the daily newspaper brand of commonplace names.

Essentially then, what *Tish* did was to establish a concentrated rejection of the humanistic approach to poetry. The effect was the creation of a veritable movement in the true sense of the word.

Davey in the Komisar interview describes his activity as a writer, for example, as being concerned with not just writing, but the encouragement of others in order to "create a literary climate in which serious literature and a literature involved with language . . . (can) be created." This was basically the thinking of *Tish* generally. In speaking with Davey at his home in Toronto, during the compilation of the book's essays, he indicated that the view was pseudo-Marxist in the sense that one's own career came second to the concern for language. Attesting to this, he says eastern writers (Toronto-based) are individualists who speak about "the weather and sex" and the commonplace — everything, but writing; whereas, the westerner narrows his focus to the writing game and the details of language.

"Literary climate" is the clue. What *Tish* did was to launch "a ten year explosion of poetry in Vancouver . . . for what Raymond Souster has termed a 'new wave' of poetry across the country." (*From There to Here*, Frank Davey, Press Porcepic, 1974)

This so called new wave originated from a much more cohesive group than other movements, according to Davey. He may be right, for when one starts looking at earlier literary movements, such as the *McGill Fortnightly Review* (1928-29) and the *First Statement* group (1942-45), the differences in style, content and opinions are abundant and evident. In *Tish* the effort was concerted and closely-knit.

Its influence upon poetry across Canada is undeniable and considerable. Take for example, the development of *sound* and *concrete* poetry. If the back issues of *Tish 1-19* are scanned, one notices that the magazine's poetics may be responsible in some way for the poetry of bill bissett, Joe Rosenblatt and the Four Horsemen. Even renowned poet

Earle Birney acknowledges the vast changes in his own style in perhaps his most experimental book *rag & bone shop* (McClelland and Stewart, 1971) when he recognizes the significance of "bp nichol & his generation, for turning me on."

Nichol, although not one of the contributors to *Tish*, was in a sense the counter-part of its activity in Toronto where he delved into the visual and sound aspects launched by the magazine's poetics.

A feature of the *Tish* poetics is that throughout, the magazine discusses the idea of "breaking down structures" to allow one's voice to burst forth. This emergence, in other words, will bring with it one's total character or scope of influence (ie: Bowering's evangelistic Grandfather poem or Rosenblatt's bumblebee verse). With the total breakdown of words into pure sound, this element still exists, because the sound always finds familiar ground in old songs, jingles or word-games.

The record of this influence or scope is however documented here in what I see as a kind of literary history. The movement's roots are charted here through the assembly of all those salient articles which have been written *about* the *Tish* poets.

As I mentioned earlier, there are two sections to the book — the genealogical and character of the movement, and the poetics. The former tells the story of *Tish* and its editors, with commentary on its successes and failures, philosophies and style. Frank Davey dominates the section with three selections—the original reprint introduction to *Tish 1-19*, combined with a piece being used in a comparative anthology of poetry in British Columbia, and a *Tamarack Review* article on the Black Mountain influence, and a *Canadian Literature* article which defines the status of *Tish* as a little magazine in the line-up of others in Canada.

An article by Louis Dudek responds to Davey's assessment of Black Mountain with a piece which is central to the discussion of *Tish* poetics and influences. The Montreal poet seems to put into perspective the poetry scene in Canada at that period and clearly defines the progress made in the regional-based writing pockets in this country. A much more academic indictment of the movement is given by Beverley

Mitchell in an excerpted version of her M.A. thesis for the University of Calgary in 1972.

Tallman's Wonder Merchants essay which first appeared in *Boundary* is a crucial intensive piece for this book, because its backgrounding of the literary and cultural influences on the *Tish* movement is so complete that it has the effect of dispelling any suspicions about the American impact on Vancouver. The essay is also significant because of Tallman's position with the movement, since he was its central instigating force, and ironically, not by choice.

Two sections from an *Oral History of Vancouver* by Brad Robinson provide the reader with a conversational and lighter focussed look at *Tish* from the *inside*; Persky's interview being jocular and vivid, whereas Hindmarch's is much more informative and to the point. Carol Bergé's *Vancouver Report* is much the same thing, but is more *immediate* in that it is a gathering of notes actually made during the creation of *Tish*. I've also included Bowering's farewell to *Tish* which appeared in number 20, entitled simply "The Most Remarkable Thing About *Tish*."

In summary the entire section for the most part gives an over-view of the movement as literary history with the implications it holds for modern Canadian poetry.

The latter section, or the one devoted to poetics, is simply an application of the kind of things being spoken about in the first part of this book. Here we have Bowering dominating the focus with two articles — two of which immediately follow *Tish* ("Poetry and the Language of Sound" and "How I Hear Howl"). These deal, obviously, with sound, and Bowering's point is one made by Ezra Pound whom he quotes as saying: "poetry begins to atrophy when it gets too far from music." The projective poet (Olson, Duncan, Creeley) utilizes sound, he says, to record his own speech as a response to the poetic experience. These two articles are perhaps the most important discussion of *Tish* poetics in this volume, however the Komisar interview with Davey provides a kind of addendum to Bowering's view of sound. Here Davey speaks about the interpretation of literature as being what writers "*actually* put on the page." He also discusses the idea of "locus" or the place out of which a writer composes.

In a review recently of George Bowering's *The Catch* published by McClelland and Stewart, I referred to his "Autobiography" and "George, Vancouver" poems as being *georgegraphical* verse. The discovery aspect of the work is very much in the travel sense, but the exploration or search is of one's self. Tallman makes the point in "Wonder Merchants" when he says the *Tish* poets are writing about the *life* within them. Thus, Davey in this Komisar interview which is post-*Tish* says he too when he wrote *The Clallam* penned it as an emblem to personal loss.

Davey has another piece included in this section. It is entitled "Rime, A Scholarly Piece," which essentially makes a case for joining form to content through the Duncan inspired technique of "rimes of image." Lionel Kearns attempts a similar theory in his "stacked verse" pieces. These are not particularly major breakthroughs in Canadian poetics, but to understand the developments of *Tish*, they are significant.

Finally, there is a piece by this editor which attempts to divide *Tish*'s concern for poetics into two themes—the relation of the poet to his art and the relation to his "sense of place." The article which first appeared in *Alive Magazine* and was later published in a chapbook series by *Alive* takes to task many of the *Tish* poets.

Articles left out, which may have been included are those written on Creeley by Tallman in *Tish*, as well as several other pieces from the magazine, chiefly those by Davey ("One Man's Look At Projective Verse," *Tish* 5; and "The Problem of Margins," *Tish* 3). However, it was the intention to compile only those articles actually dealing with the movement of *Tish* — preferably following its activity from 1961-63.

In addition to this, it was my intention to provide a companion volume to *Tish 1-19*, thus it was imperative not to be repetitive.

However, because I also wanted the book to stand on its own, as an assessment of the *Tish* movement, I found it necessary to include two articles from the original magazine, as well as the reprint's introduction by Davey. Their inclusion, I think, does not detract from the use of the book as a mate to the Talonbook reprint.

The Writing Life, I think, can be viewed as a literary and historical document, because it gathers those insights into what it meant to be a writer on the west coast of Canada in the 1960s and presents the philosophical and even social elements of that time. The irony is that the *life* the *Tish* poets were concerned with, was that life *within*. Thus, it is my hope that in these essays a little of that life will be discovered and not just the activity of those times.

CH Gervais
Stevenson, Ontario

Introduction

Fifteen years after the founding of *Tish* magazine and the beginning of the Vancouver poetry movement, both are known more through legend and superstition than through fact. To a few, the *Tish* writers have been a group of "sterile" technicians "who reduce poetry to a contraceptive plaything" (Milton Acorn); to others they have been initiates into a "life-style" informed "with the fervour of a revivalist meeting" (G.V. Downes). To some *Tish* has been a branch-plant 'Black Mountain north' whose poets have made "a genuine new American poetry movement . . . into a jingoist religion" (Earle Birney), who write in a "goddamned new style foisted on the ignorant young by Olson" (Louis Dudek—an opinion which changed later). To these *Tish* has often been an instrument of U.S. imperialism, "an import from the U.S.A." (Dudek) whose leading critic, Warren Tallman, had "no interest in Canadian poetry except insofar as it can be considered an extension of the faddish American style of Williams, Olson, Creeley, which has no relevancy to our native literary traditions and sensibility" (Irving Layton), or even the instrument "of a particularly pernicious branch of U.S. imperialist writing, which calls for liberation through personal relation to place or 'locus'" (Robin Mathews). At times the imperialist and academicist myths about the *Tish* writers have been combined, as in Milton Acorn's branding

15

them (together with Northrop Frye) as "Imperialist Academics", "bourgeois-minded poets who are less concerned with passing on information than they are with hiding professional secrets". To calmer voices, *Tish* has been at the very least a conspiracy ("an in-group whose far-out gods are still Olson, Williams, and Creeley"—Al Purdy) or a clique which had unjustly 'captured' the B.C. literary scene and which posed some threat to other writers across the country (Purdy again: " . . . they [the *Tish* writers]'ll have an influence in Canada beyond anything I'll ever have. Because I have no influence at all . . ."). Or it has been an opportunistic "imitation" of fashionable U.S. styles—Purdy once again: "are they [George Bowering and others] influenced or do they think, my god, it would be a good thing to write this guy and see if he could help me out, make me a little more prominent myself? That's very cynical, eh?"

Such misunderstandings, suspicions, myths, apocryphal stories, suggest that *Tish* plays a large role in the Canadian literary imagination. These misunderstandings survive mainly because of ignorance—ignorance both about *Tish* poetics and its antecedents and about the contemporary B.C. writing community—an ignorance which the present collection should do something to end. There is, for example, extreme ignorance in Canada about the theories of Charles Olson, whose thinking had a decisive influence on the early years of the *Tish* movement. This ignorance is particularly harmful where it concerns Olson's ideas about composition and style. The notion that Olson attempts to "foist a style" totally misunderstands, contradicts, his actual teaching. To Olson, the language and form of a poem are *absolutely* relative to the particular poet, the particular circumstances (national, provincial, regional, local, temporal, personal—) in which its poet writes. He condemns derivativeness of style—condemns it more vigorously than Purdy or Mathews condemn the derivativeness they imagine Olson asks of his fellow-writers.

I fall back on a difference I am certain the poet at least has to be fierce about: that he is not free to be a part of, or to be any, sect; that there are no symbols for him, there are only his own composed forms, and each one solely the issue of the time of the moment of its creation, not any ultimate except what he in his heat and that instant in its solidity yield. That the poet cannot afford to traffick in any other "sign" than his one, his self, the man or woman he is.

("Against Wisdom as Such")

Far from encouraging imitative writings, Olson's poetic insists upon each writer's manifesting himself in language exactly appropriate to the person he is and to the physical and temporal circumstances in which he writes. This poetic, accurately followed, precludes the possibility of the kind of colonialist writing which Mathews and Acorn pretend to have been *Tish*'s goal. In actual fact, because of Olson's insistence on "particularism", Mathews, Acorn, and Purdy have in their comments about *Tish* done little more than trap themselves in a critical Catch-22. For if *Tish* writing is derivative and imitative, it cannot be faithfully based on Olson's teachings; if it is based faithfully on Olson's teachings, it is by definition not imitative and derivative. Clearly these critics misunderstand something.

Particularly galling is the implied myth in much of this criticism that any Canadian writing that is informed by a knowledge of non-Canadian writing is of necessity colonial. *Tish* writers are blamed for seeking masters ("I am not clear why any genuine writer should need . . . father-figures or idols"—G.V. Downes); they are blamed for reading non-Canadian contemporaries ("Ever since the Black Mountaineers invaded Vancouver the so-called *Tish* poets have had delusions of poetic grandeur"—Len Gasparini); they are blamed for seeking knowledge of the root-figures of English-language modernists—Pound, H.D., Hulme, Williams. By these criteria the English Renaissance would be not a national flowering but a colonialist debacle, the sonnet "foisted" upon its lyricists by Petrarch, terza rima forced on its satirists by Dante; the courtly love conventions of the sonnet would be continentalist "imports" from Cretien, Andreas Capellanus, and Petrarch; pastoral conventions would be impositions on Spenser from Theocritus and

Virgil—imperial Greece and Rome; Spenser's epic conventions would be intrusions from a yet more suspect, because more recent, source in Ariosto. Such criteria similarly imply disapproval of Eliot's learning from Laforgue and Baudelaire, Yeats' learning from Pound, Pound's learning from Browning, Gautier, and deGourmont. Literary history emphatically denies such implications. Language is not a national phenomenon; the best writing in any nation or culture can provide writers elsewhere with forms, structures, and visions which will yield them new articulations in their own context. Glwadys Downes, a scholar whose criticism of *Tish* is distinguished by being lacking more in generosity than in good sense, does acknowledge this. "The French in 1550 were as excited about their own language and the new classical and Italian forms as the *Tish* group were about Creeley and Ginsberg. They absorbed what they wanted and made it their own, as Tallman believes the *Tish* group has done."

The independentist or 'sturdy woodsman' concept of the Canadian poet, self-fathered and self-nourishing, that Acorn and Purdy imply in their comments on *Tish*, is an eastern-Canadian idea with no future. It denies the common ground that all writers share in language, and it denies the reality that all writing must not only be specific to its occasions but must make and hold its way both in the international world of writing and in the long traditions of cultural literatures. The most 'colonial' B.C. writers are not *Tish*-descendants such as Bowering, Marlatt, Gilbert, Bissett, or Kearns, who have used propositions from Dante, Blake, Pound, Stein, Williams, Olson, and others to develop idiosyncratic language-structures particular to the personal, psychological, linguistic, and existential realities of each writer. The Most 'colonial' are, ironically, the independentists often accepted by Ontario-based CanLit for their recognizable and familiar styles—Robin Skelton, Susan Musgrave, Pat Lane, Tom Wayman, the late Pat Lowther and Stanley Cooperman; these are colonial in the sense that their work could be written in any number of places by a variety of internationally interchangeable writers. The independentist stance is, paradoxically, an international stereotype, expressed in either proud or perverse rejection of human community. Humanists anywhere can adopt the roles either on non-accountable eccentric (Cooperman, Layton, Musgrave, Lane, Wayman) or of existential sufferer (Atwood, Lowther, Newlove).

It is the sense of *belonging* that is projected by *Tish* magazine, and by Vancouver poetry since *Tish*, that has been most incomprehensible, even unacceptable, to writers and critics in other provinces: the sense of belonging to a specific geography, of belonging to the political and social life of that geography, of belonging to both a local community of writers and an international community of writers, of belonging to (rather than possessing and *using*) language, of being *at home* in place, community, and language. The humanist's Crusoe-like fixation on independent man allows him only paranoid views of communal activity. Community to the humanist appears as 'in-group', 'fad', 'school', or 'clique'. The writers' sense of being co-workers in a common task of maintaining a directness of language and image that will illuminate for their community the many and shifting grounds of its life, together with the cooperations that occur when writers hold such a view of each other, appear to the humanist only as "incest". Writes Len Gasparini of *Tish 1-19*, "Literary incest was never more blatant."

No one will ever fully understand *Tish* magazine or B.C. writing since *Tish* who does not understand this concept of community. This concept assumes that man must find his place in the cosmos, in the physical geography of his place, in the social fabric of his human settlement, in the rhythmic and syntactic patterns of his language; that these patterns are liberating and sustaining rather than imprisoning. The B.C. writer's choice of basic philosophical assumption has not been the existential despair of Sartre and Camus (a frequent Toronto choice), but the "historical immersion" of Jaspers, the existential indwelling (*Wohnenlassen*) of Heidegger. From this view the world outside the self becomes not adversary, to be feared, attacked, used, or manipulated, but *environment*—to be lived in, So language becomes medium rather than tool. The act of writing becomes a "poetics of dwelling."

... a true poetics of dwelling is a *metron*, a pacing-off of the bounds of our habitation, and an embodiment of the rhythms of this walking in structures of language. Thus measured and given voice in poetry, the ground speaks to us, invites an authentic living, a *poesis*, poise among all things that are, to the eschatalogical possibility which yet lies on the horizon of the present....
> (John Bentley Mays, "Ariadne: Prolegomenon to the Poetry of Daphne Marlatt")

Fellow-writers become not competitors but citizens-in-language with common assumptions about their roles as servants of language and polis and with common goals of making the grounds of life in their community "speak" to all its inhabitants. While Toronto-centred writers band together to seek economic power, forming The League of Canadian Poets, the Writers' Union of Canada, the Canadian Periodical Publishers' Association, The Association of Canadian Publishers, B.C. writers band together to serve the local communities of place and language, to assist each other in making individually authentic articulations of that place to its people. The cooperative character of *Tish*, and of *Iron* the *B.C. Monthly, Blew Ointment, The Georgia Straight* after it, and of the related Coach House Press in Toronto, appear as "incestuous" to the Toronto imagination because this imagination is individualistic, mercantilist, and unable to comprehend a vision of selfhood discovered in the fabric of historicity and circumstance rather than in humanist arrogation over circumstance.

It is in the above context that Stan Persky's remark, in interview with Brad Robinson, that *Tish* is "the beginning of poetry in this particular place" must be read. Persky does not mean that there were no previous poets in Vancouver; he is aware that at least fifty years of poetry including Birney, Livesay, Fiamengo, and Webb preceded *Tish*.

... this is the beginning of poetry in this particular place. suddenly the city has an imagination. It didn't have one before, a collectivity. Suddenly people are writing as Vancouver poets.

He is speaking of poetry as the voice of a place of habitation, articulated by individuals back to that community. He is not speaking of individuals isolated in suffering (Webb) or detached by satiric perspective (Birney, "Damnation of Vancouver") who, having abandoned hope for their place, write for extra-provincial publication and audience. He is also not condemning by implication these earlier poets, as eager critics of *Tish* will no doubt want to pretend (as in Birney's characterization of the *Tish* movement as "a jingoist religion with saints and martyrs and persecution of heretics"). Because these poets produced work which Persky and most Vancouver writers since *Tish* have not found interesting for themselves, nor relevant to the international mainstream of modernist writing, does not preclude the possibility that this work has intrinsic value and accomplishment. Such imputations to the *Tish* movement— as Purdy's calling it a "limited school that says this is the best or the only way of writing"—constitute one further myth about *Tish*, a myth that is at least inaccurate and mischievous, and possibly paranoid.

Tish cannot be understood as a prescriptive school. It was a movement that espoused a poetry of individual articulation, place, and community. The magazine was "a poetry newsletter—Vancouver". The work it started was not a number of isolated careers—it was the work of a collectivity beyond its editors, which has continued the original attempt to give voice and imagination to the northern Pacific place. This is evident in both the names of many of their periodicals —*The B.C. Monthly*, *Scree*, *Raincoast Chronicles*, *The Georgia Straight*, *The Pacific Nation*, and in the political, sociological, and theological concerns by which these magazines transcend mere 'literary' focus. These periodicals have belonged not only to a community of writers but to a larger community that both includes and values writers. Similar evidence lies in the books which have followed *Tish*—Fred Wah's *Lardeau* and *Pictograms from the Interior of B.C.*, Daphne Marlatt's *Vancouver Poems*, *Steveston*, and *Steveston Recollected*, Bissett's *Of the Land Divine Service*, Gerry Gilbert's *White Lunch*, Bowering's *George, Vancouver*. These various successors to *Tish*—books, periodicals, presses—have often been related to local projects—to Radio Free Rain Forest; to Intermedia, a gallery-cum-production co-op; to the Western Front gallery; to the Reynoldston Research and Studies' 'Oral History of B.C.' (Marlatt's *Steveston Recollected*, Gladys Hindmarch's "Before *Tish*" interview, and the Persky-Robinson interview excerpted here were all parts of this project); and have directed themselves almost exclusively toward a B.C. readership.

Tish also cannot be understood in separation from the international movements—also not prescriptive schools—of which is it a part. These antecedents, like *Tish* itself, are para-literary; they view literature not as a thing in itself or as a way to individual renown but as an inseparable part of the social, cultural, and political life of its culture. The *Tish* movement has its roots in Matthew Arnold's view of the writer as cultural custodian, in Pound's view that the accuracy of a culture's language and the health of its arts are inextricably tied to the morality of its economic life, in Williams' sense of art as participating in the literal events of the artist's community, in Arnold's, Pound's, Williams', and Olson's emphasis on *prosody*: that on the writer alone rests the continued functioning of syntax and vocabulary as signifiers (rather than as obfuscators—as the commercial users of language would have it) of the community's life. This is the "main line" which Louis Dudek in "Lunchtime Reflections" traces to *Tish* from Imagism and from Williams' 'no ideas but in things', remarking that "this preference for the contemporary 'thing' . . . implies great honesty toward experience (such as we have in Creeley and in the Vancouver poets), also a will to purity in language, and integrity in the use of free organic verse forms." In Canadian poetry before *Tish* the most indisputable representative of this "authentic modern tradition" is Dudek himself. This tradition has been communal (Williams) and cultural (Pound) rather than individualistic; has been concerned with prosody (Joyce, Stein, Olson) rather than theme; has been local (Williams, Bunting, Yeats, Olson) or culturally historical (Pound, Eliot, David Jones) rather than nationalistic; and has viewed writing as a cultural 'office' rather than as a personal linguistic skill. Clearly such a tradition has little to do with such Canadian phenomena, however accomplished, as Jones' and Atwood's thematic criticism, Newlove's despair, Layton's extravagance, Macpherson's quatrains, Mathews' nationalism, or the lobbying of the Association of Canadian Publishers.

Tish was also rooted, like Pound, Eliot, Olson, before it, in the mainstream of Western philosophy, which in this century has passed through the anti-humanism of Wittgenstein, Whitehead, and Hulme, the radical pessimism of Sartre, the search for historical rootedness of Heidegger and Jaspers, and the assertions of phenomenological immersion of Merleau-Ponty and Bachelard. All of these plus Nietzsche, Kierkegaarde, Buber, Marx, Husserl, Unamuno were or became as familiar to writers with the *Tish* ambit as were the writings of Duncan, Olson, and Creeley; all became 'influences' on the kind of writing Vancouver writers would value. In 1961, the year of *Tish*'s founding, I underlined the following passage in Jasper's *Man in the Modern Age*:

> ... what is requisite is that man, in conjunction with other men, should merge himself in the world as a historically concrete entity, so that, amid the universal homelessness, he may win for himself a new home. His remoteness from the world sets him free to immerse his being. This remoteness is not achievable by an intellectualist abstraction, but only through a simultaneous getting in touch with all reality. This immersion is not a visible act of one who plumes himself on it, but is effected through tranquil unconditionedness. Remoteness from the world gives an inward distinction, but immersion, on the other hand, awakens all that is human in selfhood. The former demands self-discipline; but the latter is love.

This passage still expresses much of what *Tish* and Vancouver poetry since have been about: *community* ("in conjunction with other men"), *geographic historicity* ("a simultaneous getting in touch with all reality") *anti-humanism* ("tranquil unconditionedness"), *particularism* and *localism* ("historically concrete entity", "a new home") and a *disinterest toward* the kind of *paranoid individualism* its most querulous Eastern critics have practiced ("immersion ... awakens all that is human in selfhood ... love"). 'Love' is an abused word, semantically weakened by careless and neurotic usage, but it is an harmonic quality always present in the communal and the cooperative, in the orders of language, and in the dwelling-place and habitation. As the pages which follow testify, this word is yet another key to *Tish*.

Frank Davey
December 1976

Genealogy

Tish group at a party for George Barket at Earle Birney's in 1958. At the far right is Judith Copithorne, Lionel Kearns in background, and George Bowering in foreground.

Wonder Merchants: Modernist Poetry in Vancouver During the 1960's

Warren Tallman

1 The Yanks Were Coming

In February 1962 Robert Creeley read poems from *For Love* at a University of British Columbia Festival of Contemporary Arts. On his way from Albuquerque to Vancouver he stopped over for readings at Reed College and The University of Washington. Having something considerably other than a fashionable reputation at that time, he experienced some predictable reactions in Portland and Seattle: polite but puzzled attention from audiences motivated more by academic rituals than by anything resembling specific curiosity, leading to a similarly ritualistic scatter of applause, thank you - and - who do we get next week? Vancouver was different, a pleasantly rickety lecture hall, an overflow crowd, mostly students, prolonged surges of laughter when the poems were humorous ("Ballad Of The Despairing Husband"), muffled, scattering giggles when they were wry ("What should the young/man say, because he is buying/Modess?"), a felt attentiveness when they were compelling ("The Door"). This en masse spontaneity held through an hour of reading, pause, another half-hour of reading, pause, and another half-hour of audience-poet conversation. When the moderator wrapped it up at nearly six p.m. there were protesting hisses even though many of the audience had stayed past what in sprawled-out Vancouver can be some god-awful rides home. "It's been a long time," Creeley told them, "since I've experienced such energy and attention, and I'm very, very grateful." All of which spells out one starting point for the exceptional activity in poetry in Vancouver during the 1960's.

There is a puzzler here. Of the several hundred decidedly unacademic persons listening, not more than 25 knew Creeley's work in any meaningful way. *For Love* wasn't published until the next month and Creeley's other volumes were very fugitive indeed. More, a good many of the poems in *For Love* are not so simple as to provide instant access on first hearing. Then, as now, his brilliant syntax is often formidable. Yet the audiences' responses were not only enthusiastic, but intelligent, appropriate gestures at appropriate moments. I think one answer to the puzzle was something like Vancouver innocence — then. By 1962 audiences at Reed and The University Of Washington had acquired a perhaps too-knowing scheme of responses, certain touchstones for placing poets. Since Creeley's poems were not like Robert Lowell's, Theodore Roethke's, Richard Wilbur's, James Wright's or Kenneth Hanson's, and certainly not like standard-brand Auden, Thomas, Frost, Tate or Ransom, a certain bemusement must have settled in. In Seattle it needed a William Carlos Williams to break through the feeling that poetry readings were genteel social occasions. Williams did it by pushing the microphone away, sitting on the front edge of a long table, and reading and talking like a soft-voiced, passionate and impatient man who happened to be a poet. Creeley derives in good part from Williams and is also a man-poet rather than the other way around. But Williams' great lesson leads to individualism and disresemblances, one Williams to a Williams, one Creeley to a Creeley. So being over-prepared in many ways the audiences at Reed and Washington were not prepared at all.

Neither was the Vancouver student audience, but they were *ready* for Creeley's Modernism. A good many of them did know Frost, Auden, Thomas, Lowell, Roethke. But not as touchstones by which to locate an unfamiliar poetry. Because they were not caught up in a scheme of classifications they could respond directly to Creeley's qualities and quick-handed subtleties as a man via the amazingly succinct language into which, deceptively simple, he releases the complicated tensions and pressures which move in his poems. Unacquainted with any set rules for the game being played the audience was instantly and intensely aware that the player was somehow, humanly, superlative. And because Creeley is committed to relationships between persons in the here and now of life, their responses moved readily into the man as he read his poems, the ones that so expertly fumble his New England shyness into place, his wry humour, his wicked, devil-may-care wit, his complicated concern for others, the at times pounding, at times wistful, at times painfully honest emotions with which he projects those ways in which his surroundings tend to take him over. Because the students were open, receptive, and could perceive the man they went along willingly, with a fineness of attention to the poems. There was a kind of reversal in which they as actors in an impromptu drama provided an outstanding performance for the gratefully impressed audience of one. And among the several hundred who played out this part at least a dozen were energetic young poets of the Vancouver place.

But the poets differed from others in the audience since they already had many clues to the Modernism Creeley was bringing to town — source, San Francisco poet Robert Duncan. The latter gave readings at the previous Festival of Contemporary Arts, February 1961, to another more than capacity audience who provided the same direct, uncluttered attention to his presence as the man who happens to be the most rangingly articulate Modernist writer of mid-century North America, a kind of Picasso or Grand Piano to the possibilities. After his noon-hour reading, the poets in the audience asked would he read some more that evening. Because immediacy of surroundings, experiences and people is a source value for Modernist artists, particularly Duncan, he readily agreed. And as he read that evening he talked. And as he talked the whole field was activated. There was no easy understanding the cascades of information that came bubbling up. But there was no mistaking the enchantment. Relying on their ability to look with direct eyes at the man and his qualities as their most reliable guide to the poetry, the poets in the audience let him deeply in. How deeply and fully became clear three months later when school let out in May, and George Bowering, Frank Davey, David Dawson, Lionel Kearns, James Reid and Fred Wah (who would later become the editors of *Tish* magazine) formed a study group meeting each Sunday to discuss recent publications that Duncan had recommended: Donald Allen's *The New American Poetry*, 1945-1960; Charles Olson's *The Maximus Poems*; and Duncan's *The Opening of the Field*. What was Olson saying and implying in his essays, "Human Universe" and "Projective Verse"? Just how do you read or try to read his "The Kingfisher"? "The Songs of Maximus"? "Variations done for Gerald Van De Wiele"? or Duncan's "Poem Beginning With A Line By Pindar"? his "Structure of Rime" series? Creeley's kinetic syntax? and what about Corso, Ginsberg, Levertov, Spicer, Blaser, and other poets Duncan had lit up on his busy pinball machine at the centre of the Modernist cafe? All concerned were aware of having no workable answers to the possibilities he had turned loose.

With that kind of good sense that goes with direct eyes and open responses, they did a typically absurd but intelligent thing. The group of six expanded their numbers to 20, so there were both poets and interested friends of poets, subscribed $5 each and offered Duncan the $100 to appear in Vancouver and lecture at length on Pound, the Imagists, Olson and the *Maximus Poems*, his own "Structure of Rime" poems in *The Opening of the Field*, and, as it turned out, Creeley, Levertov, Ginsberg and early days with Jack Spicer and Robin Blaser during the Romantic "Berkeley Renaissance" of the mid-1940's. The absurdity. In 1961 round trip plane fare between San Francisco and Vancouver was $105. At that time, as during the previous 15 years since he had elected to be a poet and nothing but a poet, Duncan had been living on the approximately nothing a year such choices entail. Having good cause to respect money as that precious gold it is supposed to be — for Duncan a penny is a very real thing — he nonetheless let poetry make the decision, flew up by bus, gave three 3-hour lectures and stayed on for nearly a month of non-stop monologue on all aspects of Modernist art. Direct responding to direct. In any given city 20 persons passionately interested in poetry constitutes some kind of majority, which meant that during July and August 1961 the poetics of Modernist writing were very powerfully established in Vancouver. Having open sensibilities, with considerable wonder bubbling up in them, the Vancouver poets responded to a man who happens to be a Modernist, not simply by profession, but in all the fibres of his inner being. Talking Modernism he was Modernism.

Duncan's genius is so expansive that it seems at times to be geniuses. Start almost anywhere, say the Greeks, and move almost anywhere, say into modern times. Whether it is history, music, art, philosophy, psychology, or writing, he can summon information more actively and provocatively into mind on impulse than a working team of more systematic scholars could possibly haul into presence with caravans of books. His knowledge is never exhaustive, every sentence of Plato at his fingertips. It is more nearly a vast collection of lore, some familiar, some curious, some startling, with which he has furnished the huge house of his imagination, room, after room after room. Thus he is less interested to study ideas from times past for their own sake, more for the sake of itimations they bring into his mind, stimulating *his* ideas. One collects curious objects in order to transform with their presence other objects already in the room. His collecting treasures from the past and present less for their sake than for his is not arrogance but an outstanding instance of a poet following paths pioneered by Pound and Olson which have been leading poetry out of an age of perception into a new age of proprioception. Proprioception becomes the vital pivot within the poet upon which much Modernist art turns for its effects.

Perception is "to take from" implying attention to surrounding objects, events and others. Proprioception is "sensibility within the organism by movement of its own tissues." It's snowing. The eyes of perception take the snow in *out there*. The eyes of proprioception become an inner threshing floor on which a snowman will be enacted. The perceptive writer sees himself in the midst of the surrounding world as object. The proprioceptive writer sees the surrounding world in the midst of himself as subject — "sensibility within the organism." Duncan's most immediate prototype for this shift from outer to inner spaces is Charles Olson who first subjected himself to Gloucester, Massachusetts in order that he might *incorporate* that place into himself and thus become Gloucester. I have attempted previously to chart the process by which Olson managed this profound achievement (*Open Letter*, Summer 1972) and one passage still seems accurate:

> Each man's intellect is a sum of memories so Olson searches among documents, records, manuscripts, seeking from these specifics, closely considered, a mind of Gloucester. Searches out the phrasings, weightings and soundings of both the speech around him and that discernable in the writings of the place — the Pilgrimmes voice — that mixture as of Shakespeare and the Geneva Bible cast on a rock-ribbed coast. An ear of Gloucester. Works at sea, a deckhand, and on land, a postman, walks the streets, beaches and heights letting slow footsteps discern old roads, boundaries, property lines, building sites. Feet of Gloucester. Stands at named places looking out through his eyes where earlier men had looked out through theirs. Eyes of Gloucester. Names the original names, hunts out tales, legends, gossip, shipwrecks, accidents, skirmishes. Feel of Gloucester. Remembers childhood, ballgames at dusk, car rides, excursions, picnics, smell of Tansy, "I rolled in as a boy," ancient root plant. Self of Gloucester. Thus gradually, intermittently, but under steady pressure of a desire to root all roots in, Olson takes on in his form a form of that city.

Eventually the city looks out through his eyes, speaks through his voice, remembers through his memory, has its meetings in his person. Having no whisper of political influence at city hall, his voicings nonetheless were the politics of the place. L'etat, c'est Moi. But this king, a supreme individualist, argued that such was the proper *state* for all persons, each of us his or her own city.

But it isn't our cities per se that Olson revolutionized. Gloucester doubtless goes right on its charmingly tacky ways, as little aware that it shines and glitters in his writings as it was how alive it was while he was in life. It is writing, it is the self-contained and self-containing sentence that he helped tip over like an old fence that in falling released a stampede of possibilities. As every school child is falsely taught, the written sentence goes from subject by way of verb on over to object. But in the proprioceptive sentence *self* becomes the subject, the *writing* becomes all verb, and the *object* is life, to live. Because this definition of the sentence has crucial implications a closer look is in order. By subjecting himself to his environment of whatever kind the writer becomes the subject of all these, such as he is or is not. And what is his writing but notation for looking by way of image; thinking by way of word; hearing by way of sounds, stresses, junctures, silences; moving by way of syntax — the arrangement of the parts in time-space; feeling by way of all the above; and bodying himself forth by way of speech that rides out into the world on its precious breath of life via rhythms appropriate to the occasion. To look, to think, to hear, to move about, to act, to feel, to speak: that is, to live, preferably as Henry James advised, "all you can." The proprioceptive artists is reaching toward a mode of writing, modes, forms, which will let life take place. Such artists are under a life sentence, and *live* is the new grammar, syntax, law.

Hence Duncan's value for the Vancouver poets, arriving with his Portuguese cape and enchanted mind in a cloud of words, so given over to himself as subject — living it up — that he is the inveterate monologist of all that is happening in the ideas and poetry of those around him. Ask Duncan a question about Plato and you will not get a perceptive answer, which would be to focus on your Plato as the *object* of interest. The first impression is that he did not perceive your question and he has argued at times that he in fact does not perceive others. But proprioception is only a deepening, an internalization of perception. It is not *your* Plato that interests him, but *his*, the Plato-in-himself. Your question re-arranges that Plato so he immediately begins to pour out the re-arranged Plato-in-himself, often at great length. But if you can maintain attention (or, better still, relax and simply take in what he is saying) it will dawn on you at a certain point that his monologue *corresponds* to your question, opening it up into a much larger affair than you had dreamed when you put the question in the first place. Thus, he was not discussing Pound, Williams, H.D., Olson, Zukofsky, Creeley, Levertov, Ginsberg, or the Spicer and Blaser of Berkeley days — chief figures of his literary environment — perceptively, as objects. He was speaking of them proprioceptively, as assimilated into himself as subject. Duncan was talking Duncan, and *there* they all were — after his fashion.

Again, the prototype is Olson. When he so scathingly attacks his fellow Gloucester poet, Vincent Ferrini, in "Letter 5" of *The Maximus Poems* he is not attacking the friend who lives nearby in town. He is attacking proprioceptively, Ferrini-in-himself. Olson is warning Olson. Likewise his monumental discontent in *Letters for Origin* with Cid Corman-in-himself. Even as he lands on them like a huge slide coming down inside, his affection for them goes calmly on. Recognizing self as subject, Olson wanted *Origin 1* to feature in magazine form an approximately full image of himself as of that time. Hence the way his work is distributed throughout the magazine, like legs, arms, hands, eyes, face. But the main instance of Olson's proprioceptive know-how is his choice of Creeley to edit *Black Mountain Review*. By 1954, even earlier, he was aware of the Creeley-in-himself as the rock on which North American Modernism would depend. Like many another large man, Olson was inwardly soft despite the earthquakes that could take place. Creeley was, and still is, *adamant*. He once said (typical understatement) "I am so much where I am that I tend to take on the loyalties that are present in that place." As anyone who has read his notes, reviews and essays over the past 20 years knows, he has maintained an almost pounding insistence of steady emphasis upon the Modernists that *Black Mountain Review* brought into place. He is so much where Black Mountain was/is that he has tended to sustain the loyalties of that place. Actually, he is always so much where he is that he tends to take on and internalize almost everything that is present in a given place at a given time. When things begin to wobble, go out of line, or change direction, he has been known to act out. Thus in February 1963 in Vancouver, when George Bowering was still struggling to realize the possibilities of his life in poetry, Creeley leaped up suddenly, grabbed him by the shoulders, not a fight but a direct exchange. And because Bowering is so open a man, it went in, the exchange, and he has ever since possessed a Creeley-in-himself as an invariable for his Modernism. Just as, ever since "Letter 5" of *The Maximus Poems*, Ferrini has had a very hot Olson-in-himself indeed.

Duncan of course became a different kind of rock or jewel with his many-faceted messages concerning the language of proprioceptive writing: the open-ended sentence in his "Structure Of Rime" series, one of those poems that can go on telling its stories for years; the inner workings of vowel and consonant, stress, silence and juncture; the tone leading of vowels; the pleasures of disarrangement, dissonance, disparities; the rhyming of ideas and images as well as of sounds. And, above all, this subtilized articulation of words as magic, numenous, romantic, derived from the magic that can bubble up in the self as subject, defeating by transformation any bleakness in the surrounding environment. In this open, empty western region around Vancouver it was the sense of inner wonder Duncan chiefly taught. He told at some length the story of Berkeley days he shared with Jack Spicer and Robin Blaser in the mid-1940's when they were re-creating a middle-ages world of spells and charms in the Berkeley house where they all lived or visited, a meeting place for poetry.

Duncan's story took on fuller dimensions when Spicer arrived in Vancouver in February 1965 to read and returned in May to present three reading-lectures, and when Blaser arrived in February 1966 to read and returned that fall to take up residence in Vancouver where he now teaches at Simon Fraser University. Duncan had tended to argue that the numenousness of the world is also in the language, the god in the words. Spicer argued that the spiritual forces are from outside and use the poet's language as their medium.

Drolly fond of kitch-culture metaphors, he likened the spiritual forces to Martians sending their messages via the poet as though he were a radio broadcasting words chosen by the Martians. The poet's task in this process is to clear all merely personal static from consciousness in order that the messages be uninfluenced by personality. Possibly as an extension of the radio metaphor Spicer and Blaser saw the spiritual forces working not only with language as an alphabet for their messages but with continued stories or dramas as on radio — Hi Yo Silver, away. Hence their conception of the serial poem which passes from episode to episode until the tale is told, the play played out. If the poet happens to be an adept in Middle Ages lore, or Greek, or Egyptian, the Martians will naturally choose images and ideas from those periods in order to get the messages through. *Choosing* the Poet's brain.

Spicer's drollness was personal relief from his awareness that he was tempting and wrestling with the gods. Baseball was his favorite kitch version for the contest because the ball player has to be ready for a number of things to happen. Everything is in the readiness, and the action in baseball as in the language of the serial poem is reflexive, automatic, instinctive. The second baseman doesn't think of himself when he participates in a double play. It's the ball, the elusive, shuttling sphere. And the poet must be concentrated like an athlete on the play of images and words, moving the language around reflexively, rhythmically and with maximum economy as he fields the message coming through. Which is why such serials could never get onto commercial radio or into ball parks. They seem discontinuous and unscheduled. The poet knows only what is taking place at the moment it takes place and must wait for the next event, idea or image to occur. The more fully involved he gets the more he is at the mercy of the poem. Instead of writing it in any conventional sense, he simply participates in the writing just as the poem participates in a larger drama. In a baseball series no player can control what happens. But often a single player will emerge as somehow the centre of the overall energy being exerted. Crucial opportunities are attracted to him and he often becomes the hero or goat, or, as sometimes happens, both. Likewise the serial poet. Errors can be made which drive the gods away, stopping the poem. In the work of Spicer, Blaser, and a number of Vancouver poets who have taken over variations on the serial poem as their most characteristic form, the poems tend to work by way of keenly experienced images, and events which follow from the images. Boat trips, gardening, trees, moths, a sequence of days, fights, injuries, Tarot cards —whatever compels energy that then moves toward meaning—and the writing is somehow "among" these images and events, participating as long or often as the energy lasts or recurs. The fact that the form of the poem reaches toward direct energy sources and thus the numenous is perhaps why it has had appeal for George Bowering, Gladys Hindmarch, David Dawson, Frank Davey, Daphne Marlatt, Brian Fawcett and Stan Persky. The latter came to Vancouver in 1966 and has lived here since. A close friend and publisher of Spicer and Blaser, Persky is in himself an intermittent energy machine and tends to make that the ruling principle for his own writing, his interest in the writings of others, his publishing activities. When the energy is surging he generates literary activity in himself and all around him, a kind of walking serial poem. When it stops surging he goes heavy, quiescent, as though banking up fires for the next time. Such persons have a tendency to transform themselves and others into localized mythic arrangements and during the seven years he has been in Vancouver Persky has taken on something of that character, a mythic figure of the place.

But Creeley, Duncan, Olson, Spicer and Blaser were not the full extent of the American influx, the possibilities opened up. Though several of them had absorbed lessons from European dada and surreal sources into themselves, particularly Spicer and Duncan, the main drift of what they had to tell goes somehow past that fact. This may trace to Pound's interests. Deeply concerned with older orders of speech and song, he knows but simply slides by Zurich and Paris. The almost complete absence of reference in *The Letters of Ezra Pound* to the dozen or so major figures of the dada-surreal revolution in language, beginning with the

Cabaret Voltaire, is somewhat shared by Olson, Duncan, Creeley, Spicer and Blaser. There was a difference when Allen Ginsberg came to town in summer 1963 to join with Margaret Avison, Denise Levertov, Olson, Creeley, Duncan and Philip Whalen in a month-long poetry klatch. Ginsberg brought in a number of language possibilities: Whitman's open, free-flowing, catch-all line; the even more spontaneous improvised prosody he had learned from Jack Kerouac's 1951 *Visions of Cody*, and, riding in the midst of these, his own peculiarly North American dada approach to language. Subjected through childhood and youth to the most disturbing environment of all, for many years more full of such disturbances than any of the others, he turned to releases into mind-goofing language play ranging from the quiescence of "Transcription Of Organ Music" to the comedy of "America" to the built-up, ecstatic destructions of "Howl" and "Kaddish," that tormented selves be reborn. Carrying his Blake vision with him, as he always does, he places less emphasis upon messages from the spirit world, more on looking at the world around him from the heavenly point of view, the vast, sad, absurd tragi-comedy he sees on every face on every street. This provides him with a more simplified language concept than the other poets shared that summer: "Mind is shapely, art is shapely." Which opens the possibility for language explosions shut away from the other Modernists with their profoundly indwelling sense of language. If you move deeply into the interstices of words, as Zukofsky, Olson, Creeley, Duncan, Spicer and Blaser do, you are not likely to take the kind of free-wheeling, mad-rush word-flights for which Ginsberg is famous. As in the case of Whitman, such flights depend for their validity on strength of back, wing and claw. If you are to be a bird of paradise on this continent you can't sit twittering in some pear tree. Ginsberg's personal strength is of course legendary.

But beyond Ginsberg an equally profound language revolutionary arrived in Vancouver for a 1964 February Festival reading and in 1966 for an important week-long visit, Michael McClure. In the early 1950's he was a very young student in a San Francisco poetry workshop conducted by Duncan. But even earlier, perhaps always, he has possessed and been possessed by an exceptionally alive and hyper-sensitive physical organism. One thinks of Whitman's "I have instant conductors all over me." When Duncan, Olson and Creeley discover in themselves those surroundings to which they have been subjected, their sensibilities are such that they need less to revolutionize language than to re-interpret it, as mentioned, with Self as subject, Writing as verb, Living as object. Ginsberg presses nearer to a revolutionary North American dada, but he too stays somewhere on the near side of customary language. McClure comes closer to needing *an entirely new language* simply because his physical organism is subjected to such intensities from surrounding experience. There is that in him which is drawn to the roaring of lions, the roaring of motorcycles and the more distant roar in his ears of some once-known, now modified Anglo-Saxon sounds. If ghosts could talk, the dead, animals, plants, McClure would be the first to want a language for conversation with such ones. And this impulse presses curiously close to what begins to happen in Vancouver in 1966, the year of the McClure visit, when bill bissett moves into word-mergings, soundings, chantings, yelps and repetitious croonings, as though some strange soul of the place were struggling toward articulation. Of bissett, more in place.

Jackson Maclow, the last of the important American Modernists to visit Vancouver during the 1960's arrived for a week in February 1968. As with many of the other poets I have mentioned, Maclow was less a revelation, more nearly a confirmation by this time of certain language possibilities. Heavily influenced by John Cage's music, committed to group readings based on the chance operation of words, Maclow introduced language dramas. Shuffled card packs of words were read at specified time intervals by a cast of mostly Vancouver poets — Frank Davey, Gerry Gilbert, Colin Stuart, Gladys Hindmarch — rituals in which the shaping spirit of language was intended to pervade the auditorium as the participants, strolling the aisles, read individually on impulse; and in unison on the stage, as visual images flashed onto screens and toy music instruments were produced from Maclow's magic suitcase, handed around at random, and played likewise. Formidable production problems turned the performance into an impromptu, a demonstration. But the language lessons were evident, though in my opinion his full influence, like McClure's is yet to come. But it was clear that by 1969 the American story of Modernist writing had been pretty much told through in Vancouver. Most of the Vancouver poets were by this time out from under the American influence into a Modernism of their own devising. Interest in the American writers continued but the intensity began to fade as the energy centre shifted to what was happening in their own home town.*

2 The Humanists Were Going

It will doubtless seem strange to some that I have farmed in so many Americans as a starting point for Modernist poetry in the Canadian west. But during the formative 1960's the issue was not national but continental, and finally not continental but world-wide. Modernism has crossed all borders — or at least has tried. Because self becomes the subject of most Modernist writings, nationalism gives way to a personal localism, not the *place* where you are, but the place where *you* are, each poet his or her own city state. Such localism can look past national identities to North American realities. Modernism caught on in the Canadian west because it was right for the west, where the environment is so open and undefined that the self stays open and undefined, child-like perhaps, easily given over to a sense of inner wonder, The proprioceptive eye solves a major dilemma of modern times. Moving to "sensibility within the organism" it can discover those marvels within the self which can transform the growing viciousness everywhere evident in the surrounding environment. Rather than concentrate on the viciousness the Vancouver poets began to concentrate on the wonder that came bubbling up from within, and upon possible languages which would permit it to bubble on out

* If I neglect to mention several other American Modernists who visited Vancouver during the 1960's, Lawrence Ferlinghetti, Ed Dorn, Lew Welch, Gary Snyder, it is because their interests coincide with those of the others discussed.

into living sentences, life come alive again, day by day. Which explains why they were so little influenced by the Canadian east during this period. As early as the late 1940's Irving Layton, Louis Dudek and Raymond Souster had established active contact with the very American Modernists who would later show up in Vancouver. The truest of these three poets, Souster, with an authentic and active northern eye, happens also to be the least given to pronouncements, having a down-in-the-mouth reluctance to talk poetics except via poems. But when he edited the important 1966 anthology *New Wave Canada* he did briefly establish the starting point of what might have been, *but wasn't*, an earlier eastern counterpart to the activity which emerged in the west during the 1960's:

> To start at the beginning: the most important fact for Canadian poetry has been that Canada is situated on the northern border of the United States of America. But until the early 1940's, no one would have been remotely aware of this given the poetry written before that time. In that decade two or three Canadians poets began to read and be influenced by the work of certain modern American poets,   most notably Ezra Pound and William Carlos Williams, ... and several others to a lesser degree.

When Souster says there was no awareness of Pound and Williams in Canada until the early 1940's he is falling inadvertently into the trap of implying that national differences over-ride continental similarities. There are ways in which they do, but the reaction to Pound and Williams isn't one of them since he could have pointed to a similar ignorance in the United States. It wasn't until the mid 1940's that Pound and Williams became influential for a small group of U.S. poets, Olson, Duncan, Ginsberg, Creeley, the very group who found their way north to Vancouver in the early 1960's. Until New Directions Press began to relay the news, literary United States ignored, ridiculed or patronized not only Pound and Williams but Gertrude Stein, H.D., Hart Crane, Louis Zukofsky — that is the entire Modernist movement in American writing, one which begins a lot closer to 1900 than to 1950 and which also happens to stem much more decisively from European and Oriental sources than from any particular American influence, exceptions, one Walter Whitman and one Emily Dickinson.

Crossing back into Canada to Souster's "two or three poets who began to be influenced by Pound and Williams" it's clear he has himself, Dudek and Layton in mind. But the connections are less close than might seem except in his own case. For their emphasis on the whole is more nearly upon a man-in-the-street Humanism than it is upon Modernist writing, self as subject, writing as verb, living as object and the reader as correspondent. Layton, the most spectacular of the three, has been the least involved. The first number of *Origin* magazine is spring, 1951, and the first number of Creeley's *Black Mountain Review* is summer 1954. In these magazines, crucial for U.S. Modernism, Williams, Olson, Duncan, Zukofsky, Creeley, Dorn, Levertov, Ginsberg, and Kerouac provided in form of letters, notes, reviews, stories and poems direct extensions of what Pound, Williams, Crane, Stein and H.D. had pioneered. Discovered early on by Williams, featured in *Origin 14*, and listed as a contributing editor to *Black Mountain Review*, Layton seems likeliest to have assimilated the new possibilities into himself. However, it's clear that from *Here And Now, 1944*, on through to the present, he has concentrated upon himself as object and scarcely at all upon the language innovations necessary in order to enter Modernist writing.

In North America there is a diminishing tribe of persons, and Layton is one, who respond to the alien feel of the place and people by an early and conclusive clutching to themselves of their individuality, making that the fulcrum on which all else swings. Dwelling so close to home they seem to dwell outside the going social scheme, citizens of no metropolis save their own sweet selves. Williams loved such persons for all the ways in which they are intractable and unphasable, exclusively their own self. In his New Directions volume *The Farmer's Daughters* many of his best stories enact their psychopathology, hectic with original force, white but wild. Hence his admiration for Layton, brimfull of energy and billy-be-damned the others. All of which seems like the beginnings of a first-rate Modernist, self as subject. But wasn't. For Layton failed to move from perception, which fixes on the surrounding world, to proprioception, "sensibility within the organism." And so he turned to Humanism, that ultimately most obvious of virtuous complaints against the ultimately most obvious of local, national and international facts, man's vicious inhumanity to man. And as he turned outward to such commonplaces (page one, any newspaper) he relied not on proprioceptive activity — inner stars in their hidden courses — but upon an increasingly embattled ego. Because proprioceptive writing poses self as the subject of the sentence it cannot pose self as the object — me-me-me. The person who does is likely to become, in D.H. Lawrence's fine phrase, "fixed on the hub of the ego" and go "on and on without wandering." Dwelling always with the self as object, mirror, mirror on the wall, such persons often stay strangely youthful even in age, Huckleberry forever. But they repeat themselves. And even those who admire them most, often end by flinching. Souster conveys the feeling in his fine 1958 "Salvo For Irving Layton":

>if I'd never met you
>if this was the first time
>
>just the way you startle
>the Sunday night calm
>of this over-scrubbed coffee shop
>
>quick-striding in and up
>to the table, one hand busy
>loosening the tie around your neck
>the other pumping our hands
>with a wrestler's tight grab
>
>if I'd never met you
>if I'd never read one line
>
>how could I ever mistake you
>for anything but a poet

> you with the wild hair
> and battler's chin
> you with the ten crazy wheels of living
> churning within you; mad torrent
> welling up bursting over flooding
> our pansy cemetery world!

Anyone who has met Layton even casually can appreciate how effectively his presence is established, not descriptively but actively via a language that captures his qualities into the poem, the man himself. Souster's ear is close here, the syllables cat-footed as with off-rhymes, natural speech intervals, the suspense created by the "ifs," and the suspension in time created by the repetition of "you," he builds a rhythm of the whole. When articulation is so distinct the mind is clear, here in terms of careful word choices that blend a sense of Layton's energy with a sense of his aggressiveness. In line 10 a lazier attention might have settled for a "wrestler's tight grip" rather than the much more telling "grab" — very sincere, and you'd better believe it! Souster is effective then because his quickened responses to Layton are active in the language. And, of course, there's more. "If," he says, "if I'd never met you . . . if this was the first time . . . if I'd never read one line," *then* I would know beyond all mistake that you are a poet, striding, loosening, pumping, grabbing, wild, battling, crazy torrent of a man. But comes, of course, the unspoken dawn: I have met you before. This isn't the first time. I've read plenty of your lines. And have been forced time after time to accept you as anything but a poet. By riddling his reservations into if-land Souster can enact his admiration yet remain equally true to the reservations, guns booming for Layton — strike up the band — but leveled directly at him — kid me not, Irving. A barbed Salvo then because Souster remembers to keep track of the meeting within those interstices of himself and of his language where it is taking place. One imagines that his hand in Layton's was firmly a little less than firm.

Reading "Salvo," noting Souster's care with language, one is reminded how disastrously Layton has long since forgotten. When the self turns to proprioceptive knowledge within the organism it can dream as many dreams as dreaming itself will let surface into the endless permutations of language. But when it stalls too exclusively with itself as object no amount of energy can prevent the poetry from stopping there too. Layton has boasted a fine ear and there are strong if conventional strains of beauty in his earlier poems, as in the conclusion of his well-known "The Birth of Tragedy":

> A quiet madman, never far from tears,
>   I lie like a slain thing
>   under the green air the trees
> inhabit, or rest upon a chair
>   toward which the inflammable air
> tumbles on many robin's wings;
>   noting how seasonably
>   leaf and blossom uncurl
> and living things arrange their death
> while someone from afar off
> blows birthday candles for the world.

The feel for words is evident, making it extremely difficult to understand how Layton could have avoided responding to Pound's, Williams', Olson's, Duncan's, Zukofsky's and Creeley's preoccupation with what happens in the language, the field of action, as the poem is being written. Or why none of Williams' life-long concern for measure rubbed off, particularly during the 1950's when Williams breaks through to such a beautiful oneness with his surrounding environment — wife, children, friends — as in "Of Asphodel, That Greeny Flower," "To Daphne and Virginia," and "For Eleanor and Bill Monahan," an old man young by way of subjecting himself so completely to his environment after those humbling strokes, and so completely to the life sentence his writing had become. By sacrificing the potential of language to his far less than proprioceptive self, Layton cuts the potential of that language down to the dimensions of his embattled Humanist stance. Which is perhaps why on of his earliest admirers, Dudek, confessed in *Delta* magazine, 1959, inability "for the past three or four years" to "read anything by Irving Layton" because he "seems to me too much the ego builder."

However, fair is fair, and if it is necesary to chronicle those tendencies of Layton's poetry which made him of little or no direct use to west coast Modernists, it would be a mistake to forget that the very persistence with which he kept up an assertive, confessional, often outrageous, sometimes puerile, swinging around of his increasingly embattled ego has had impact for poetry in Canada. In a place with a strong penchant for staying complacently "good" — that tattle-tale grey visitors sometimes notice — Layton has managed to stay spectacularly BAD. More, even more admirable, he has raw courage in his makeup, not afraid to reveal the badness of his badness, the inner imbecilities and cruelties that gnaw and fester those times the self turns savage under the whips and knives of the times. Most of us cooler customers haven't nearly his nerve for letting the crudity show even though it can be the very ore in which vital energies are locked. Which is only a way of saying that at a time a Calibanish man was needed to break the hold over poetry in Canada of genteel ersatz English versification, along came Layton. And did more than anyone else to take poetry down into the streets, the gutters, even lower. In view of this achievement the fact that he nailed his ego to the mast (and his ear with it) is at least understandable. And from his influence a line of Humanist poets have followed, early Leonard Cohen, Alfred Purdy, Milton Acorn, Alden Nowlan, and from the west coast John Newlove, Pat Lane, and a number of others. But Humanist poetry of their variety is a little bit like Mother. Who can resist a heart worn on a ravelled sleeve as it cries, take care, take care? Modernist poets can, not because they are opposed to mother or caring for others but because their deeper allegiance is to Mother Tongue and caring for others-in-themselves.

On the face of it the second of Souster's candidates for a Modernist emphasis, Dudek, seems much more effectively involved with those permutations in the language needed to establish the life sentence the Modernist writer seeks. He notes that his own serious reading of Pound begins in 1948, but trying to follow Dudek's tracks from then to now is an assignment that would cause even the most dedicated Mountie to leave the force. A seemingly explicit guide is in his 1957 *Delta 4* "Note on Metrics" in which he joins in with the break from closed-form, jog trot stress, metre and rhyme in English." And he approximates Pound's belief in "an absolute rhythm" that "corresponds exactly to the emotion or shade of emotion" when he argues that "each poem is an original piece of music, a form that cannot be borrowed or counterfeited." The music is "that of your sounds as they fit the content of your poetry," leading to "unique form." As ablest practitioners of "unique form" Dudek cites Williams, H.D., Wallace Stevens, e e cummings, and Pound. A curiously mixed assortment, particularly Stevens, whose tremendous visual imagination often moves in conjunction with a very conventional ear.

Moreover, Dudek rejects Pound's claim that "poetry separated too far from actual music tends to decay" and rejects as "the same primitivist error" the crucial Modernist insistence that poetry is an oral art, a form of speech or song. He even implies a certain contempt for voicing when he adds that "the inner ear in all poetry since 1650 appreciates a more subtle music or at any rate a different music from the noise made by the vocal chords." Noise, indeed. Attempts to unite actual and vocal music are even more suspect, as for instance the "audience and platform seeking of the jazz poetry combinations of San Francisco." Take away audience voicing, audible music and sit down to sessions of sweet silent what? In *Delta 8* "Functional Poetry: a Proposal," Dudek tells us — "thought . . . thought itself," and goes on to reject Williams who "simply did not have a lot (enough) to say," and Pound for "believing, alas, to the end in music (pure) and in the aesthetic vacuum." To Pound's vacuity and Williams' meagreness he adds "the dullness of most recent poetry even the best." Prose he tells us is the villain who may yet be the redeemer. Villain because it stole the thinking function from poetry some several centuries ago, though Dudek neglects telling us how prose managed this theft. Redeemer because the prose emphasis upon "thought itself" is poetry's best chance for a renewed life.

How crassly reactionary these views of Modernist art are, unsympathetic to the very poetry with which Dudek had claimed affinity, comes clear in Renald Shoofler's 1960 *Delta 11* review of Donald Allen's *The New American Poetry, 1945-1960*. Olson's work is dismissed as moving in a "stratospheric vacuum," as irritatingly pointless a remark as Dudek's earlier claim that Pound moved in "an aesthetic vacuum." Duncan's poems earn him a place as "the same old murky visionary." And Creeley's, the most ludicrous connection of all, too tin-eared to be believed, are "a lot like Roethke." Shoofler's opinions are directed at some of the finest achievements of mid-century Modernism, including Olson's magnificent "As the Dead Prey Upon Us," Duncan's astonishingly orchestrated "Poem Beginning With A Line By Pindar" and Creeley's "The Door," "The Awakening" and "The Innocence," poems that were part and parcel of the singing school the young poets of Vancouver were attending. Assuming that editors share responsibility for the reviews they print one can only conclude that Dudek's attention must have been elsewhere the day that one came in.

The mystery of what he does approve clarifies inadvertently in "Groundhog Among The Stars," his 1964 homage to Souster's work. The writing is concentrated, testifying to his high regard for the poet with whom he has been so closely associated since the long-ago 1940's. But as the observations of an adept the essay is disappointing, little more than a careful rundown of recurrent attitudes in Souster's poetry: ambivalence toward women; a tendency toward brown-study depressions intermitted by increasingly infrequent outbursts of joy; modesty yet pride in knowledge that he is a poet. Fair enough, yet nothing one mightn't have guessed of almost any sensitive modern poet without reference to his poems. When the world becomes a bad place poets are likely to feel the strain. The difficulty is that Dudek forgets to bring his own previously articulated poetics to bear on Souster's work. Whether Souster has or hasn't moved in a functional prose realm of "thought itself" Dudek doesn't say. If the sounding of the poem fits in with Dudek's crucial insistence on "unique form" this too goes unmentioned. In fact, any of the means, music, methods by which Souster individualizes his attempts receives no attention whatsoever. Dudek's focus is exclusively on content without reference to forms, and, lo, perhaps the Mountie has his man. All that criss-cross of explanation, definition and opinion scattered through *Delta* magazine as signposts to Modernist poetry is abandoned. The homage to Souster, careful as it is, and full of care, could nonetheless have been written by any number of persons with no interest in his Modernism.

What Dudek overlooks in "Groundhog Among The Stars" is discerned by Eli Mandel in his incisive 1963 review of Souster's *A Local Pride*. Mandel, one of the half-dozen or so brilliant Eclectics who form the middle ground of poetry in Canada, stays with the occasions of Souster's poetry only long enough to mention "the curious fact that as the volume of his work grows, his vision itself remains static" still caught up "as in the earlier volumes" with "cripples, drunks, whores, beggars, lovers in corners, shining nudes, sinister insects, and beaten animals." Mandel sees Souster moving through this mostly derelict menagerie as "plain dealer, malcontent, proletarian, melancholic, ecstatic, sensualist, rogue and saint." The list is enough to convince anyone that Toronto must be on the same parallel as Dostoevski's Moscow. But Mandel looks *and listens* past these traits to an inner resonance proceeding from "an unusual formalism," patterns "as stiffly stylized as the figures in an oriental scroll." Seen thus, via his language, Souster's most characteristic poems become "icons or idiograms so that the appropriate form is the pun, riddle, or puzzle, or a curious version of imagism which defies precise description." Probing more deeply still, Mandel senses, inside the icons Souster creates, "a kind of 'purity'," which will "prove tougher than any enduring joy or ill" he encounters.

In brief, Mandel goes to the language in order to discern what form his surroundings have assumed within the man. "Icons" impress me as apt since a Siberia seems to inhabit Souster, a region where speech falters toward silence because vision falters as his northern eye lifts toward endpoints where the vistas go bleak. He has the habit of ending his poems with limping phrases and lines as though appalled by the space that extends beyond the outposts his vision reaches. Persons with a northern feel in their bones do put in time wondering if the world was made for humans and the feel often shows in Souster's speech and in his humour. Are we really here at all? And if so, why? Which may be why he responded with such tumultuous enthusiasm when he greeted the poems in *New Wave Canada* as "the most exciting germinative poetry written by young Canadians in the last hundred years of this country's literary history. Of the 17 poets he includes seven are from the west coast; another, b p nichol, was born and lived in Vancouver until age 16; and another five, bissett, Bowering, Davey, Kearns and Newlove, were doubtless omitted only because their work had already reached national attention and needed no introduction.

My argument runs, then, that American Modernism had far more impact upon Vancouver poets than Laytonian Humanism. It is a revealing irony of the literary life in Canada that the Humanists, who began closest to the Modernists, (Layton, Dudek, early Cohen, Purdy and Acorn, to mention the most prominent) have been more hostile to Modernism than have the Eclectics, of whom I mention Eli Mandel as an outstanding example. There are others, (Margaret Avison, Earle Birney, Dorothy Livesay, Margaret Atwood, Phyllis Webb, D.G. Jones, Midiam Waddington and Dennis Lee) who also draw on all sources for their poems and poetics. It seems accurate to see them forming a middle-ground since such eclecticism points to that open catholicity of mind which is the most conspicuous and appealing trait of intelligence in Canada. In a country that has grown up surrounded by an English, a French and an American fact, many of its best minds become capable of handling multiplicity sympathetically without the need to choose up sides and start yelling. Multiple-city. *But there is a tide or undertow throughout the modern world which makes the eclectic position more and more difficult to maintain.* Birney, who taught creative writing at the University of British Columbia through the 1950's and well into the 1960's, experienced some of the difficulties. As students, many of the west coast Modernists were in his classes. All have testified to his openness and generosity in responding to a Modernism he as poet happened not to prefer. He allowed them maximum freedom in class, write what and as you want. And he used his influence as one of Canada's leading poets to help them obtain assistance, grants, publication, the varieties of encouragement young poets need, praise not in departure, but at the outset. A notoriously touchy man when it comes to critics, academic enemies, and others who may oppose him, ruled by a temper that can blow the lid off fahrenheit, he nonetheless has a remarkably democratic loyalty to the tribe of poets — all of them.

But in the late 1950's, when he was instrumental in forming a creative writing department at UBC, his eclecticism entered in as he, the least academic of men, let it be formed in the image of the academic world. He should have started yelling. The study schedule for young poets was the same as the study and requirement schedule for all other students at the university. Inevitably, the teachers of such courses were more involved with the university (and with the larger community of creative writing departments at other universities around the continent) than they were with the energetic community of poets in Vancouver. It may have been in part his dissatisfaction with the academic pall that began to settle in which caused Birney to give up his teaching post at UBC.

There is another, personal, factor that enters into Birney's relations with the west coast Modernists, indeed with the world at large. I mentioned his touchiness, which stems from a deeply-experienced supersensitivity, the source doubtless of his art. Generous, democratic, open-handed to other poets he certainly is, traits of the eclectic man. But he is also the isolato, the loner, and for this reason the wanderer. Able to draw on a wide range of influences, he is not inclined to join in, and much of his poetry which takes Canada as its occasion testifies how alien he feels in his own country. It is when Birney is on the road, in Mexico, China, India, where he *is an alien*, recognized as such, that he seems to relax into his finest delicate-eared, quick-eyed poems. His "Canadian" poems reveal not only the pain but the writing strain of the alienation he feels. Modernist art, in which the self is subject and the ultimate object to live all you can, calls not simply for approval from the correspondent, the other, whether he be teacher, writer or reader. But for a joining in. Because Birney is not a joiner, few of the poets were able to experience a Birney-in-themselves. Aware as they were of his benevolence, few of them were able to take him as a source for their poetry. Conversely, they were unable to keep Duncan, Creeley, Levertov, Olson, Ginsberg, McClure, Spicer and Blaser out. So the broad story runs that it was not Layton's Humanism or Birney's Eclecticism that moved into town and into their hearts, but the American Modernists. In these dicey times I can only hope to avoid misunderstanding by repeating that the issue during the formative 1960's was not national but continental, and finally not even continental but world-wide. One can test the political climate of any country by noting the reaction the Modernists receive from the state. There are nations in the world who do not like their artists to take *self* as subject. It challenges the state since its fundamental proposition is, as mentioned, L'etat, c'est Moi. As I dream, awake!

3 "Wonderful, Wonderful, Wonderful"
Charles Olson, in conversation.

I have been arguing that Modernist writing has shifted emphasis from the perceptive view in which attention focuses on the surrounding world to a proprioceptive view in which *self*, having subjected itself to its surroundings, becomes the *subject* of a new writing which it is easiest to define as a *life sentence*. Self is the subject, writing is verb and the object is life, to be as fully alive as one can manage by way of sight, hearing, thinking, feeling, speaking — that is, writing. The reader becomes the respondent, hopefully the correspondent, one reason that Olson named so many of his poems "letters." And I have been arguing that North America, with its essentially unformed, misformed, or misinformed environment, is a natural stamping ground for the Modernist spirit, like buffalo come back again. I would also argue that western people are more conscious than easterners of the unformed spirit of the North American place.

From ten miles north of Vancouver on out to the north pole is 99 and 44/100 percent pure wilderness. Heading east, the towns come few, small and ramshackle, huddled near heavy-shouldered mountains with heavier, higher mountains back of them, and back of them more mountains, heavier, higher still. The waterways are such that all boats are little boats, and from the west the greatest of all oceans still rolls schools of whales toward Indian villages on the western beaches of the Vancouver Island. Beyond these villages only Chief Crazy Foot could walk the footless hills. The environment itself, the manifest reaches of humanly untouched space, creates in Western children an aching spirit as of an emptiness, wanting to be filled. When some such children grow up and turn to poetry they are likely to set up shop as wonder-merchants. Poetry for them is less a "literary" activity than, as Duncan had demonstrated when he arrived in town with his enchanted mind, a marvel.

So back to the Sunday afternoon in August 1961, last day of Duncan's visitation, and George Bowering, Frank Davey, David Dawson, Lionel Kearns, James Reid, and Fred Wah decided to start *Tish* magazine. Kearns declined to be an editor but, as it turned out, for all practical purposes was. *Tish 1* appeared in September 1961, and the next 18 numbers appeared on schedule, a phenomenal 19 consecutive months through April 1963 when Bowering, Davey and Kearns finished their MA exams at UBC and began to do what young men so situated do: get married, think about travel, jobs . . . get-out-of-town. In the seventh number the subtitle changed from "a magazine of Vancouver poetry" to "a newsletter of Vancouver poetry." But in a deeper sense it was neither magazine nor newsletter but a meeting place for their lives. When the proprioceptive poet subjects himself to his environment in order to become the subject of his sentence, he is likely to move into contact with his and the environment's vital energies. Inside yourself you may stumble onto well-heads. And phenomenal shared energy was the most obvious fact of the *Tish Place* they had created. Poems written one week went the rounds the next, were argued and selected or rejected the next, and printed, folded, addressed, stamped and mailed the next. Not waiting for subscribers the editors compiled their own mailing list, paid postage from their own always almost empty pockets, and distribution was free. Poems and letters received were responded to within the day, the week. Everything that was feeding into their lives was being fed directly into a flood of poems: the city, their day-to-day activities, their love affairs, quarrels over poetics, their differences with Layton, Purdy, Acorn, Gwen MacEwen — one another.

A seventh, unnamed "editor," Gladys Hindmarch, was near the centre of their energy vortex. At that time she was writing nursery rime variations in prose rhythms derived from Jack Kerouac and from high-school-age experiences playing tenor sax in a Vancouver Island dance combo. Because the magazine was devoted to poetry, her "fiction" didn't appear. She was evidently born proprioceptive, so sensitized to her environment, so quick to internalize it, making it her own, that she lived in a state in which she had almost no public identity other than that created by the person or persons she was with. On still spring evenings, not a whisper of wind, when she walked out through the door the leaves on nearby trees would flutter into a welcoming dance. Possessing such marked extra-sensory powers, working entirely by intuition, she provided endless hours of direct personal response to the lives and poems of the other editors. Because her being was so volatile at that time, she became for all of the others whatever image of the feminine they happened to need: mother, sister, muse, lover, consolation, inspiration, sounding-board, scold, conscience, mover of leaves on poet's trees. Unable to categorize, classify, or indeed even to speak until speech was *given*, when she said "no" to a poem, or went silent, the other editors tended to put that poem aside. She was a living metaphor for the numenousness around, the most distinct single human form of the wonder of the place.

Two related groups were drawn into the vortex of energy swirling in the *Tish* place, one willingly, the other with a certain interested reluctance. The willing ones were a number of fractionally younger writers, Robert Hogg, Daphne Buckle (Marlatt), Dan McLeod, David Cull. The more reluctant but interested ones lived "downtown," Gerry Gilbert, Judy Copithorne, Maxine Gadd, bill bissett, Roy Kiyooka, John Newlove. Already oriented toward Modernist art, music and film, and interested in the American poets *Tish* was emphasizing, they distrusted what seemed a heavily academic orientation — that all the *Tish* editors were students at UBC. But energy and a sense of the wonderful is a difficult combination to resist, so the downtown poets became, if not fully convinced, definitely interested and sympathetic. There were exchanges, an uneasy alliance, wry eyes watching wry eyes, the kind of friendships that are active and warm but have blank spaces. What *Tish* did not have for the downtowners didn't come clear in decisive ways until the original energy began to wobble in spring, 1963. *Tish* continued that summer and then, intermittently through to 1968. But almost as if energy were being transferred from one centre to another, in October 1963 bill bissett stepped in with *Blew Ointment Press* and a poetics that had not been in the *Tish* vortex began to come alive. bissett, himself and energy vortex and wonder-merchant, became the new centre for the energy that *Tish* had generated. As *Tish* continued on a still important but wobbling pivot, *Blew Ointment Press*, a house for the houseless bissett, began to push the Modernism into new dimensions.*

Within close distance of the *Tish* place and bissett's *Blew Ointment* house, like various balconies and porches, or right next door, or just across the street, are more magazines and presses than I can discuss, *Talonbooks, Intermedia, Circular Causation, Very Stone House* and *Vancouver Coomunity Press*, the cluster of which brings into presence the work of Maxine Gadd, Judy Copithorne, Gerry Gilbert, Roy Kiyooka, Jim Brown, Ken Belford, John Newlove, Scott Lawrence, jorj Heyman, Pierre Coupey, Seymour Mayne, Pat and Red Lane, Stan Persky, Barry McKinnon and Brad Robinson. The most consistent and dedicated of these

---

*I must note here that both *Tish* and *Blew Ointment* helped to waken the energies in Toronto of a closely related complex: *Coach House Press, Weed-Flower Press, Island, Is, Ganglia,* and *Gronk Press,* with Victor Coleman, Nelson Ball, Michael Ondaatje, b p nichol, and Steve McCaffery as leading spirits. Much of the most intelligent new news of this continent flows from their activities.

presses, *Talonbooks*, edited by David Robinson and Gordon Fidler, is significant for all the ways in which the publishers as artists enter into league with the writers as artists, a correspondence, as though the hands and eyes of the press were sensitive to the writers they publish, resulting in books that are in themselves works of art.*

The third defining force to enter Vancouver during the 1960's, **Iron** magazine, stems directly from the influence of Spicer's 1965 lectures and from Blaser's presence in Vancouver since 1966. In *Iron* the serial poem begins to emerge as a major possibility, particularly in the work of Brian Fawcett; and a romantic poetry of the beautiful in the work of Colin Stuart. Although it is an oversimplification, one can see *Tish*, *Blew Ointment* and *Iron* providing a broad spectrum for Vancouver Modernism during the 1960's. What happens in these three publications to a considerable extent charts the activity that was going on in all the others. Which carries attention to so many poets that I can sketch, and only sketch, a few of the more representative names and tendencies.

John Newlove stands at the end of the spectrum nearest to the Humanists. While in Vancouver in the 1960's he was as attentive as any to language subtleties. But he is less oriented toward himself as the subject of his environment and sentences than as object, victim of the environment. It is only when the artist makes himself the subject that his writing can transform otherwise grim surroundings. Newlove tends to see only the grimness and so writes sorrow songs as grey shades toward black and the sense of alienation from the environment increases. The great, almost sacrificial, strength in his poetry is the appalling tenacity with which he repeatedly confronts the alienation. Something like the boxer's, axiomatic, stay on your feet, at all costs stay on your feet. Most boxers can manage this only as long as they have some hope of winning. Newlove does it

* Because the discussion is confined to a poetry that emerges during the 1960's, I am avoiding reference to more recent developments, *The Poem Company* and *Pulp Press*, and to poets, some of them very important indeed in present-day Vancouver: George Stanley, Dwight Gardiner, Roy Stone, Jon Furberg, Rosemary Hollingshead, Leslie Keyworth.

without any particular hope, which testifies to the depth of his humanity. Yet however much one can admire such gestures on behalf of us all, it needs to be recognized that he is in a stalled position, just as Layton, Purdy and Acorn are stalled. He is much more the purist than they but their dilemma is also his. Cry "Wolf" enough times and readers will come to realize that there is indeed a wolf at the door. But continue crying it and the words will blunt under the repetition. So . . . there's another wolf at the door . . . so? The Modernist poet's transforming task is to realize that wolf packs in the night are singing. In this parable it is when the poet lets the wolf into the house that the transformation can occur and the songs take over from the snarling. Down goes Newlove again. And back up on his feet. And down again. And back up. Weary work, as the wolves close in.

George Bowering's *Autobiology* is at an opposite proprioceptive end of the west coast spectrum. Rather than tell the *story* of his life (which is what the Humanist poet tends to do) Bowering tells the story of his *life*, the life that is in him. Breaking through psychological, social, political levels of consciousness, he explores direct physical consciousness, a biography of his physiology as insight into himself as writing instrument. Using a repetitive, divining, almost incantatory style as a way of reaching physical levels of consciousness, Bowering is able to regress to stories his body remembers, zero-at-the-bone moments which spell into the fact that a sensitive Bowering in the B.C. garden grew. The writing becomes a kind of life-line along which he strings out moments from childhood and youth as waystations in the education of his life. Although the writing is different from Gertrude Stein's or D.H. Lawrence's, the incantatory method resembles theirs, the way Stein can all but baby-talk her way back to a rich childhood and Lawrence, through repetition of highly charged words and phrases, can reach levels below his educated consciousness. Bowering concentrates on a long series of physical injuries to himself and others, breaks, bumps, cuts, bruises, batterings (accident prone) and another series of mindless accords and discords with the very stuff of nature and man; animals, machines, implements, trees, relatives. This is not a Humanist locating himself as an object in the environment. It is a person counting over the education of his aliveness in light of the fact that the aliveness is specific need of his poetry. One writes by way of alivenesses. Our deadnesses don't write.

However, Bowering is many-leveled and by conscious choice carries on an active literary life which includes teaching, editing and publishing *Imago* magazine and *Beaver Cosmos Folios* while writing criticism as well as poems, stories, a novel. *Autobiology* itself provides clues to the restlessness and recklessness that cause Bowering to push out into all forms of literary activity as though they might become containers for a fullness of the life that is in him. This same recklessness gives him over to impulsive statements the succession of which tends to confirm Whitman's view of contradictions. Bowering isn't afraid to go opposite to himself in order to see where it might lead. He has claimed closer affinity with Newlove than with his former *Tish* compatriots. Yet he has a much closer affinity across temperamental differences with Frank Davey, another of the British Columbia sensitive plants.

Davey also teaches, edits *Open Letter* magazine, one of the present meeting places for Modernist writing in Canada, writes extensive criticism, prolific poetry, is restless, reckless. It may or may not be coincidental that both have written recent works in which Tarot cards figure prominently as occasions for the poems. Both have a penchant for social personas as front men for their sensitivity, in Bowering's case an "us-fellers" mannerism, which has begun to fade, and in Davey's a play of supercilious wit. In some other age they would have enjoyed playing dandies back of whose assumed mannerisms a deadly seriousness sits in form of the nerve to use all their energies. Were it not for the personal largeness with which they have advocated Modernism it would have far weaker footing in Canada, both west and east, than it now does. Casually as they may seem to do so, Bowering and Davey have for over a decade kept steady pressure on their poet friends for more work, more life, more work. As the truly proprioceptive man must. With himself as subject, the friend is in himself, and when the work falls away the self is diminished.

Just as Bowering and Davey have been the two most active public apologists for west coast Modernism, both have in their recent poetry revealed strong affinities with the poetics that Spicer and Blaser introduced. Bowering's *Autobiology* is in effect a serial poem as is Davey's *Weeds*. The surrounding environment to which Davey has always been most susceptible is female, the woman with whom he is in or out of love, the relationship that goes on in either instance, and with women's possibilities for men generally: lover, wife, mistress, adultress, muse, dear friend, deadly enemy. So caught by the feminine, Davey is perhaps the most passionate of the Modernists, a Romantic who passes from outright adoration to painful disturbances as though he, she, the bed, the house, or the cosmos were coming unhinged. Following from the Middle Ages magic Duncan, Spicer and Blaser introduced, Davey's vision is full of spells, magic, charms, conjuring, their wonder worked upon by a contrary terror, pity, cruelty, disillusionment. Because the serial poem has that reflexive mobility which permits the poet to stay where the energy is, *Weeds* is based on a garden image returned to again and again. He goes in and in and in and each time it is the same place, but each time different. Until it comes to rest. If it does.

The third most "public" *Tish* advocate of west coast Modernism, Fred Wah, is somehow not public at all. He also teaches (by example) at Selkirk College in the B.C. Kootenay country, where he grew up, 450 miles east of Vancouver, just above where Idaho and Washington State join. After leaving Vancouver in 1964 he made literary journeys to New Mexico, where he studied with Creeley, and helped edit *Sum* magazine, and to Buffalo where he studied with Olson and Creeley and helped edit *The Magazine of Further Studies*; at Selkirk he has been closely involved with *Scree* magazine, another meeting place for the Modernist community in North America. But Wah doesn't write criticism and concentrates less on the general literary world than Bowering and Davey do, more on *his* literary world, those writers he knows in direct ways. When he returned west from his literary wanderings south and east he was asked to lecture at Simon Fraser University — a kind of where-are-you-these-days-

Fred? report. Significantly, Wah read a clutch of letters from poet friends, poems of theirs he had printed in *Sum* and *The Magazine of Further Studies*, told anecdotes concerning the poets, letters and poems, and then read a few of his own poems. That is where he was, and conversely, one of the places they were — in himself as subject.

Wah is also more concentrated in a geographical sense than the other west coast Modernists, the Kootenay region being for him in many ways what Gloucester was for Olson. A sentinel-like circle of peaceful-seeming mountains protect the long lake from which the area takes its name. Several valleys, several towns, and several rivers are so distributed as to make it one of the most hauntingly beautiful of all regions in western Canada, a balance point between man and nature. At certain hours of most days it turns mysterious, a kind of Shangri-la. From his father's side Wah inherited a half-strain of Chinese blood which may help account in him, as the Spanish in Williams, for a certain "otherness" in attitude, perception and proprioception, a more direct awareness of where he is than his more exclusively North American fellow poets can quite command. Many Europeans and Orientals speak English far more vividly than those of us for whom it is Mother Tongue. Which shows in Wah's poetry, much less prolific than Bowering's or Davey's, but more concentrated on the occasions which move him to write. Recently his separate volumes *Lardeau*, (a mountain of the region), *Mountain*, and *Tree* were collected into *Among*. Among himself.

Tree, one of the most beautiful poems to emerge from the east, is also one of the most consciously proprioceptive, celebrating a literal affinity with trees-in-himself in a speech so deeply musical that it sways tree thoughts, presences and impulses into the presence of the words. Wah was a music major when he first attended university and has mentioned his fear of the music in language, a counterpart to Duncan's love of those dissonances which will prevent words from slipping into strains of a merely sentimental education. But the potential "easiness" into which the music-footed poet can slide is braced in Wah's instance by a strictness which has helped him to create a number of those poems Pound had in mind when he indicated that a single poem in a career can make the poet of more importance than another who may have written a thousand. Lady Language has her own house, and wherever it is, it's likely that some of Wah's poems are in one or another of the many rooms. An effective way to experience the difference between a fine-eared Humanist and a fine-eared Modernist is to set several of Newlove's poems alongside several of Wah's.

The "otherness" that brough Daphne Marlatt into poetry is of a different order than Wah's. Born in Australia she grew up on the Malay Peninsula in one of the last of the British Colonial families. When the exodus began she found herself in a strange Vancouver, age 10, an old house where the Empire ways went on but surrounded in schools by a new empire which must have impressed her parents as a very wild west indeed, children who mocked her speech, her manners, her social assumptions. But Marlatt had, as the colonials might say, "advantages," the kind of inner strength the British acquired during their long sojourns in alien places. And the impulse to write. By the time she reached university she possessed perhaps the greatest "natural" ability of all the west-coast poets, wildly unformed, all over the place, but the words must have been whispering "magic" to one another, "magician."

At that time and ever since her handwriting was minute, the letters like strings of tiny beads, close together, both an artistic and a psychological trait. The same minuteness shows in the exceptional closeness of her attention to the movement of language: syllables, words, images, sounds, silences, phrases, lines, sentences. Duncan once paid her the compliment of observing that she remembered writing lessons he had all but forgotten. Put it another way, lessons no one else has learned. Her exceptional sensitivity to language makes her writing dense, so closely woven that the patterns can seem baffling. Think of a Penelope so entranced with each evening's weaving that she forgets all about the suitors, and Ulysses too, because enchanted with the design. Enchantment does enter in since words have divining powers for Marlatt. In poems she has given names to Vancouver places and discerned conditions which were confirmed to her only *afterwards*. In a group she once read Whitman's "Dirge For Two Veterans" in ways that made it clear to some of those present that either they were with Whitman at the funeral scene more than a hundred years ago or that he was in presence via her speech. It is such powers perhaps that prompt her interest in the older Vancouver of dark corners, rickety buildings, obscure stairways, down at the heel (hell) pubs, and odd or ancient men and women, as though the origins of the place were on the invisible prowl among all of these. Drawn to places where the city is caught up in an almost brooding dream of itself, she dreams back awake in poems that bear closer resemblance to the brothers Grimm than to Hans Christian Andersen. As he emerges from her inner spaces, the Ancient of Vancouver Days has a hooded, an almost spectral eye. In the deep reality of things, she is probably the foremost historian of this city. When the true history of Modernist writing on this continent one day gets written her "strange powers of speech" are certain to figure as important.

Although he too is "other" there is nothing strange in David Bromige's powers of speech. His progress goes from England, where he was born, to Vancouver in the late 1950's and early 1960's to California where he now lives and teaches. Like Davey, the environment he most readily takes into himself as subject is the feminine, his intense interest in women being the inner space he most characteristically brings into the writing place. But where Davey's interest is Romantic, having to do with the spells women cast, Bromige's is more domestic, household misunderstandings, visits by friends, minor incidents which move him like a Hamlet or a Yeats into thought. Perhaps old England is influential here, a magnet that pulls him toward the philosophical. Over a long and difficult "period" Bromige learned the hard way to deal with the diabetes he during that period didn't know afflicted him. But even beyond the period of severe physiological disturbances, storms in the organism, his intense reactions to the minute particulars in his relationships has continued. Bowering, Davey, Wah and Marlatt all turn, as by natural impulse to the wonder that comes up. Bromige turns to the somewhat different wonder

— again a Hamlet — of his inner honesty. Having experienced deep physiological griefs he seems able to suffer corresponding griefs of thought. At the personal surface he is one of the most appealingly human of the west coast poets, perfectly willing to reconcile himself to whatever comes along on a given day, hence enjoy this moment, that moment, no questions asked, no answers needed. But his poetry is informed by something inside that doesn't flinch and won't budge, I cannot bear to tell a lie. Pound's "man standing by his word."

Disturbances of a different order than Bromige's stand back of the poetry Robert Hogg writes. As is often the case with those who come to poetry exceptionally early (age 15) he begins with severe isolation. The inner spaces are occupied by scarcely anyone other than the sole self and are ruled by inner laws because he is scarcely aware of those that operate outside, in the environment. Such persons often show vivid, mobile and obliging faces to surroundings that are inaccessible and are as good candidates for turning to disastrous crimes as to the salvation of language, the channel that lets the inner self out into the world and the world into the self. Such a condition can create extreme intelligence just as the man on the tight-rope achieves exceptional balance. I'm not suggesting that Hogg led a youthful life of crime, but that his poems concentrate on word-intelligence, the words telling him what he knows or needs to know. The language becomes vividly that part of the poet's anatomy through which he thinks, feels, hears, sees. As indeed it is. Speech is of the body. A density comes into writing as though it were flesh. Incarnation. Hogg has studied linguistics extensively almost as though it *were* anatomy, a vocabulary for defining a word-being. His characteristic poems are instances of his being's thought. It's somewhat as though Hogg could get up and walk away from the table leaving the word-self to continue writing the poem. Because intelligence is the ruling spirit, his word-self is exceptionally quick to need and "get" the connections between persons, objects and events in the surrounding world. Put Hogg in a room with a number of other persons where things are being suggested and he will be likely to grasp what is going on more or less instantaneously. If it involves himself he will flash into adjustments. The quickest mind from the west.

Like Bromige and Hogg, Lionel Kearns is a third whose poetry reflects inner disturbances. But his are more readily intelligible than theirs based on an inner capacity for joy constantly thwarted by the human environment which surrounds him, but constantly renewed. When the Humanist poet attempts to affirm himself perceptively, as object, in relation to the environment, he is creating a dragon-world out ahead, the danger that he will come to hate self and environment, hate others. Kearns' inner joy stays alive in form of wit poems, less satirical than humorous, comic. His are very different from the poems Victor Coleman writes in Toronto in which the wit if proliferated as a pressure which will disturb the reader or listener so that he will come to realize and share the disturbances Coleman feels. Kearns is laughing at the woe, wanting to transform it. If a series of recent poems on time themes are a sign, Kearns may be in the process of deepening his consciousness below levels of suffering to the region where the joy wells up. There are many hints of this in his early poems and now it is as though he is passing through barriers formed by his songs of comic circumstance. And has reached areas in which, peacefully, the wonder of the world becomes manifest. Since this is very near to what Modernist art is all about — each poet his own living paradise — it is an important move.

When one turns to bissett the humour goes away and is replaced by a steady fever or fervour for a place that doesn't yet exist, call it Amerindia — the name Lawrence liked. As early as October 1963 bissett announced his affinity with the spirit world, somewhat ruefully, on the first page of the first number of *Blew Ointment* magazine. There is a preacher in the man, or a shaman, or a witch-doctor, and the spiritual intent of his poetry corresponds to the same intent in Whalen, Kerouac, Ginsberg, Snyder, Lew Welch and McClure. For these poets eternity is where writing begins, self partakes of that eternity in a ruined world, and the writing becomes messages from the eternal twined in the tangled ruins we call cities. bissett is an exceptionally independent artist and moved into a similar drift more by affinity than by direct influence. Because the artist in him has equal standing with the poet the printed word has strong visual implications. In 1966 co-incident with a visit by McClure, bissett began adding sound as yet another dimension of his overall poetic, chanting, keening, wailing. Also, he is very fond of collage art, pop-art, paste ups. So an accurate compositeof a typical bissett poem would need to include all the above means: a drawing, the impression of which creates echoes ranging from an Egyptian to a west coast Indian world; print in which one line often blurs closely into the next creating a moving veil in the reader's eyes; words considered as pictures (concrete) yet intended to be chanted, sung, spoken. bissett's way into adeptness in all these areas is reminiscent of Kerouac's: to proliferate each activity and in the process of proliferation gradually intuit those methods and effects which provide the truest register of his consciousness. Draw a hundred lines in order to locate the true one. It's a little like creating a city ten times as large as you need in order to locate gradually where and amid what objects you truly want to live.

For bissett there are a number of places, the foremost being art, the difficult task of letting the art create not simply works of art but a life style, a life. Just as his interests cover a wide range of activities his life styles have undergone a series of shifts since 1963. Beginning as a downtown bohemian Modernist, he shifted later to a wild west self and has since shifted beyond that into an Indian self. Thus recent chantings, based on strict breath control, have moved into realms of sound potential that are not of the English language, a transformation. These evolving selves are nothing so simple as choosing a new role in order to see what will happen. They come from within via language possibilities which carry him to new life possibilities. At the present stage of his career a legendary elusiveness is involved. He can always be contacted via his *Blew Ointment Press* address. Yet no one ever knows quite where he is living, is he in town? somewhere up north? who saw him last? One view might be that he lives in the *Blew Ointment* house, that is, *in* art, that his art has led him, perhaps temporarily, into a country of which he is the sole citizen. And that his infrequent readings, unexpected telephone calls, poems, mailed gifts to others, are tokens of his life in that country. Call it, as mentioned, Amerindia, population one, beckoning to others. As such, he is a kind of ghost, haunting the place.

Jim Brown, Scott Lawrence, jorj Heyman, Maxine Gadd, Judy Copithorne and Gerry Gilbert are nearer in their language experiments to *Blew Ointment* Modernism than to *Tish* Modernism. Not that their work resembles bissett's or one another's since individuality is one essence of Modernist art. For Copithorne words have increasingly come into location on the page or in the voice in relationship to a larger context, often indicated by drawings, in which they are located alongside other objects in life, corresponding closely to clothes, or furniture, the kitchen, warmth for herself and her cat. Her strength is to strive for a deliberate simplicity in order to resolve complicated inner reactions. By transforming the complications into the simplicities she arrives at a life style which brings a needed clarity into her values and relationships. Gerry Gilbert is something like an opposite twin, another side of a similar coin. Inwardly he is perhaps the "simplest" of all west coast poets, a simple soul who takes great delight in what is happening on almost every occasion, day by day — on a bus ride, making telephone calls, eating in a cheap restaurant, shades of William Carlos Williams. But in his writing these inner simplicities are transformed into an exceptionally rich language play, often based on chance operation of words. There is an affinity with Jackson Maclow, but not direct since Gilbert was into word play even before Maclow's 1968 visit and is far less "serious" than Maclow, puckish, full of delight, in love with the unusual. When you let chance rule the words you are into intuitions and one suspects that Gilbert is most pleased when poems come unexpectedly alive underhand, the ability to enter some new world and enjoy it without the need to categorize or define it. I write as I please. Great inner freedom is implied.

Before turning to writing in the 1960's Roy Kiyooka had already been for many years one of Canada's leading Modernist artists and teachers, an endlessly restless experimenter whose word compositions bear close resemblances to his paintings, collages, assemblages and photography. Something in him cannot resist crafting almost any material that comes into his hands, plastic, gloves, wood, crowds of people, metal — words. All the surfaces of his intelligence derive from North America, the prairies where he grew up, Vancouver where he has mostly lived. But as with Wah's partly Chinese ancestry, Kiyooka's Japanese origins, some inner eye for the fineness in things, may account for the strict formalizing impulse with which he lets words come into place. If Kiyooka sees an object in an unusual or grotesque position he has no impulse to interfere. But he will see through to the formalized possibilities of that arrangement. An old glove, fingers all awry, will occur in his eyes as an ideogram. Similarly with words in a poem. He feels no rigid impulse to untangle them but sees the formalized syntax in the midst of the tangle. In brief, a penetrating eye. Looking at a word cluster he can see the skeleton beneath, an underlying syntax. It is perhaps his respect for all arrangements in his environment that causes him to let the arrangements be and yet see through to their inwardness. Which is what his writing then arranges.

No Vancouver poet seems farther from bissett than Robin Blaser, the former's proliferating language techniques giving way to the meticulousness in all things the latter attempts. Yet they are curiously complementary poets. The ultimate implication of proprioceptive art in which self is the subject is that having turned the art into a life activity one turns his or her life into a work of art, day by day, which is what bissett in his expansive way and Blaser in his meticulous way both do. The house in which Blaser lives, one of the most impressive on the Pacific Coast, is itself a work of art, partly because it contains one of the few substantial collections of San Francisco Romantic paintings, including a number of early masterpieces by Jess Collins. Likewise the garden which surrounds it, in which every plant is known and placed with an instinct for interesting relationships. Likewise his cooking in which he will expend endless shopping efforts to bring the necessary ingredients into arrangement in the pot. Likewise his writings. Outstandingly the most knowledgeable poet in Vancouver, an omniverous reader and researcher, he lifts the level of poetry to an art of transformations in which his deepest inner experiences, often of suffering, are carried over into a meticulous and highly specific work of the beautiful. One has the feeling that he would think nothing of driving 40 miles to obtain the specific word needed in order to properly furnish a particular poem.

"Transformations" is perhaps the key word. An adept at Tarot reading, his special skill is to see through the card arrangements visions of the changes to come in the lives of others. Similarly, when he goes on journeys, as recently to Greece, he is not there to see the sights but to discover possible transformations in his own life. His poems occur in relationship to all the other equally important activities of his life. The gourmet cook wouldn't dream of giving a dinner every night or even every week or month. Only when the time is right. Nor would Blaser dream of writing a poem until all the ingredients for that poem gather and begin to simmer. He is very much the occasion poet, perfectly willing to wait out many weeks, even months, of living until a particular occasion comes unexpectedly along in which he can enact himself as work of art. His "Image-Nation" poems are in their various forms so many instances of himself, a different kind of art collection in which the deep-down struggle is to come clear of Blake's realms of night in order to dwell in those "realms of day" that "a human form display." Probably the most profound of all the Vancouver Modernists, his influence on his fellow poets is pervasive. And surely the implication, that the life shall be art in order that the art shall be life, is near the heart of Modernist writing.

I trust it is evident that the various sketches are intended less to portray individual poets than to provide an overall impression. Oversimplified as each sketch patently is, hopefully the aggregate forms into a picture from the west. It would be nice if the critic could have a large studio or alchemist's shop with all the poets scattered around, on chairs, shelves, tables, benches, on the floor, leaning in corners, so they could be disassembled and re-assembled as *the poet*. At first the assemblage would resemble a three-sided vase, human height. Press bissett and Blaser together and put them in place as one facet; then press Bowering, Davey and Wah together as a second; and Hindmarch and Marlatt as the third. While they are growing accustomed to this arrangement, over a warm fire, a large kettle, into which, sorry Scott Lawrence, I need your direct, blue-gazing eyes; excuse me Maxine Gadd while I squeeze several Indian yelps from you; hold still Lionel Kearns while I draw off a beaker-full of inner joy and mix it with an equal portion of Gerry Gilbert's free delight. From you, David Bromige, a large scoop of gut-honesty to go with a scoop of Robert Hogg's intelligence, it's beginning to bubble now and will bubble even more when I mix in several dashes of Stan Persky's ardour, and, for aroma, Colin Stuart's sense of beauty. Lest the concoction go entirely out of hand, a liberal sprinkling of Judy Copithorne's simplicity, just right.

No hurry now, a whole decade for the elixir to brew, begin to pour in the powers, numenous power, feminine power, mountain power, sea surges, and from all directions the ache of as much humanly empty space as the kettle can bear. Rouse Indians from their long pub slumbers and toss them in with old artifacts, fish, totem poles, potlatches, and whaling canoes pouring from their eyes. In one of Marlatt's closely woven nets catch city ghosts and blend carefully with Bowering's, David Dawson's and Davey's legends of Spaniards, Englishmen, Americanos — all the little boats. You, Chief Crazy Foot, down from the hills, lift it in your winged and feathered hands and pour it into the waiting vase. Now Roy Kiyooka, come on out from under that corner bench and get busy with your haiku fingers as it undergoes transformation into human form. I name it Wonder Merchant, a new Frankenstein monster from the west. And begins to stumble on elated feet eastward to Toronto where Victor Coleman, Michael Ondaatje and b p nichol keep a curious travel agency, which way to Amerindia? b p begins to answer in purest Alphabet as Ondaatje holds the word-camera steady and Coleman, cursing in total wit, clears the pathway. At one side Raymond Souster begins to laugh. Begins to weep. Begins to laugh. As Margaret Avison smiles her warm smile.

Something like that, these days, up north, out west.

The Genealogy of *Tish*

Beverley Mitchell, S.S.A.

(This article is part of a longer work, "A Critical Study of the *Tish* Group—1961-63," financed by Bell Canada Centennial Fellowships—ed.)

The "movement" to which the *Tish* poets aligned themselves was the "movement" which had its origin in the Imagist theories of the early 1900's, was modified and expanded by the developing theories of William Carlos Williams, and culminated—for the *Tish* poets at least—in the theories of the Black Mountain writers. In order to understand the *Tish* "movement", it is necessary to have at least a rudimentary knowledge of the theories propounded by their progenitors. Although much has been written to explain the Imagist theories, the theories of Williams are not so widely known. Even less is known of the theories of the Black Mountain writers. Before examining either the poetics or the poetry of the *Tish* writers, then, at least a cursory view of the poetic theories which influences them is essential if one is to come to terms with this "West coast movement".

The Imagists—Ezra Pound, Amy Lowell, H.D., and Richard Aldington—sought a poetry with "hard light, clear edges",[1] one which would satisfy their desire for clarity and disci-

[1] John Press, *A Map of Modern English Verse* (Oxford, 1969), p. 34.

pline. They defined poetry as

> the presentation of a visual situation in the fewest possible concrete words, lightened of the burdens of conventional adjectival padding and unhampered by general ideas or philosophical or moral speculations.[2]

As the name "Imagist" suggests, and as the phrase "visual situation" specifies, these writers were concerned with producing a poetry whose effect was primarily visual but which presented "an intellectual and emotional complex in an instant of time."[3] The Imagist poetics also emphasized a concern for auditory effect, for "new rhythms" composed in the "sequence of the musical phrase, not the sequence of the metronome."[4] They were striving to establish a 'free-verse' based on natural speech rhythm, to replace the blank-verse, or iambic pentameter, line that had been in English poetry since the Elizabethan period.[5]

In the principles of the Imagist Manifesto demanding direct treatment, economy of words, and the sequence of the musical phrases, as well as in the points listed in the Preface to *Some Imagist Poets, 1915,* one finds the nucleus of the theories which were to be developed by Williams and the Black Mountain group and incorporated by the *Tish* writers. As an examination of their poetry will prove, the *Tish* writers took to heart Pound's injunction that

> The neophyte know assonance and alliteration, rhyme immediate and delayed, simple and polyphonic, as a musician would expect to know harmony and counterpoint and all the minutiae of his craft.[6]

Furthermore, *Tish* poetry will also reveal the similarity be-

---

[2] W. Moody & R. Lovett, Eds., *A History of English Literature* (New York, 1956), pp.465-466.
[3] Ezra Pound, "A Retrospect," *Modern Poetry: Essays in Criticism*, ed., John Hollander (New York, 1963), 4.
[4] Press, p.41..
[5] William Pratt, *The Imagist Poem* (New York, 1963), p.35.
[6] Hollander, p.5.

tween the beliefs Pound articulated in his "Credo" and those the *Tish* writers demonstrated; that is, belief in

> an 'absolute rhythm,' a rhythm, that is in poetry which corresponds exactly to the emotion or shade of emotion to be expressed . . .

and the belief that

> The proper and perfect symbol is the natural object, that if a man uses 'symbols' he must so use them that their symbolic function does not obtrude. . . .[7]

In the Preface to *Some Imagist Poets, 1916,* one finds the directive which is so frequently repeated in *Tish,* that "a cadenced poem is written to be read aloud, in this way only will its rhythm be felt."[8] Like the Imagists, the *Tish poets and* their predecessors, Williams and the Black Mountain group, believed that "poetry is a spoken and not a written art."[9]

As a "movement" Imagism was short-lived and "diminished to insignificance when Pound and Eliot decided that vers libre had gone far enough."[10] The influence of the Imagist movement was not short-lived, however, for the two principal features of Imagist poetics—that poetry be "uncluttered" with philosophical abstraction, and that it be expressed with a metric suited to its subject—formed the basis for William Carlos Williams' theories, which in turn were further expanded by the Black Mountain writers and the *Tish* poets.

Two themes were to dominate Williams' poetics. The first of these was Williams' insistence that the poem be a response to the locale and life of the poet; and the second, as corollary to the first, that it be expressed in the language and with a metric natural to that locale. The subject matter for Williams' writing, prose as well as poetry, was almost invariably the world with which he was familiar, that of

[7]Hollander, p.9.
[8]Press, p.44.
[9]*Ibid.*
[10]C.K. Stead, *The New Poetic* (London, 1964), p.111

Rutherford, N.J. Just as he was consistent in his choice of the "local" in practice, so was he consistent in his emphasis on the local as the necessary concern of the writer, in his prose statements on poetics. An examination of Williams' works will show that in the term "local" he included not only the physical objects of the poet's immediate surroundings but also the people, the past and the present, the culture—in short, all the facets of life and experience which are involved in giving a location unique and distinguishing characteristics. Writing in his "mythical history" *In the American Grain*, Williams said:

> But he who will grow ... must sink first ... He must have the feet of his understanding on the ground, his ground, *the* ground, the only ground that he knows, that which *is* under his feet.[11]

Williams' insistence that poetry be concerned with the local and particular stemmed from his realization of the false culture of the modern American society of his day, a realization which he shared with the Black Mountain writers. He was aware that not only writers but also the vast majority of his fellow countrymen experienced the

> virtual impossibility of lifting to the imagination those things which lie under the direct scrutiny of the senses, close to the nose.[12]

Williams' search, therefore, for a poetry which would enable him "to refine, to clarify, to intensify that eternal moment in which we alone live"[13] was prompted not only by a dissatisfaction with existing modes of poetry but also by a dissatisfaction with the way people perceived the life around them. Unlike the Imagists who apparently considered the poem restored to its former condition as "the beautiful stark bride

---

[11] Walter Scott Peterson, *An Approach to Paterson* (New Haven, 1967), p.4.

[12] Hollander, p.22.

[13] William Carlos Williams, "Spring and All," *The William Carlos Reader*, ed., M.L. Rosenthal (New York, 1966) 321.

of Blake"[14] an end in itself, Williams considered the poems as a means to an end, the end being an improvement in the quality of life. As a practising physician he was constantly in contact with "ordinary" people—thus it was personal observation which led him to the conclusion that

> ... the trouble with modern American culture was that the meaning of life [had] been obscured 'by a field of unrelated culture stuccoed upon it', obscured by what he called the 'aesthetic adhesions of the present day."[15]

For Williams, then, poetry was the means whereby one would be made aware of the "meaning of life" and would be led to see the possibilities for beauty inherent in even the most mundane aspects of one's locale. In other words, it was poetry—but a specific kind of poetry—which would effect a culture indigenous to the people and the place. Writing to Horace Gregory in 1944, Williams said:

> It is the poet who lives locally and whose senses are applied no way else than locally to particulars, who is the agent and maker of all culture.[16]

The fact that Williams—and the Black Mountain writers as well—saw poetry as the means to an end has often been overlooked by their critics. Consequently, the emphasis of these "movement" writers on a particular kind of poetry—in Williams' case a poetry concerned with the local and particular; in the Black Mountain writers, concern for "projective verse"—is misunderstood when seen only in terms of poetry as such. While it is true that these "movement" writers directed their efforts towards establishing a particular mode of poetry, they were motivated by what they considered would be the consequence of such a poetry for poet and reader alike. Thus there were philosophical implications to the "movement" to which the *Tish* writers were

[14] Press, p.42.
[15] Hollander, p.350.
[16] John C. Thirlwall, *The Selected Letters of William Carlos Williams* (New York, 1957), p.225.

aligned, and it is important, if one is to understand the "movement", that one know not only *how* the type of poetry which was sought would be realized, but also *why* such a "new" poetry was considered necessary.

As we have seen, Williams envisioned poetry rooted in the local and particular as the means of effecting an uniquely American culture, not, however, because his attitude towards his country was chauvinistic but because he realized the necessity of coming to grips with the "real", of recognizing the "impact of the bare soul upon the very twist of the fact which is our world about us."[17] Like the other "movement" writers, Williams expressed his poetic theories not only in prose statements but also in his poetry. Writing in "A Sort of Song", he says:

> Let the snake wait under
> his weed
> and the writing
> be of words, slow and quick, sharp
> to strike, quiet to wait,
> sleepless.
>
> —through metaphor to reconcile
> the people and the stones.
> Compose. (No ideas
> but in things) Invent!
> Saxifrage is my flower that splits
> the rocks.[18]

Williams thus influenced the *Tish* poets both by precept and by example. His familiar thesis "no ideas but in things" which also appeared in "Paterson", was repeated in the prose statements of the *Tish* writers and in their poetry. There can be little doubt that this was an idea which impressed the Vancouver writers. However, it was not only Williams' idea as such but also the poetic techniques by which he demonstrated this thesis which the *Tish* poets adopted.

[17] Hollander, p.350.
[18] William Carlos Williams, *Selected Poems* (New York, 1949), p.108.

Williams used as subject for his poetry "things"—natural objects, art, people, history and daily events, even poetic theories—and presented them as vividly as possible with an economy of words. He used these "things" in such a way that while they stood for themselves as images in the poem, they also had a metaphorical function expressive of some abstraction or "idea", a technique which was used by the *Tish* writers and which David Dawson attributed directly to Williams' influence.[19] Williams endeavoured to use the idiomatic speech of the people of his locale—that is, a speech free from poetic inversions, sprinkled frequently with colloquialisms and slang, and having the natural rhythms peculiar to a locale. So, too, did the *Tish* writers. In their choice of subject matter, in the poetic techniques which they employed, in their prose statements, and in their realization that poetry was the means to an end, the *Tish* writers gave evidence of the considerable influence Williams had on their poetry.

One might, with justification, claim these attributes of the *Tish* poets were equally due to the influence of the Black Mountain writers, for there were remarkable similarities between Williams and the latter group, both in theory and in practice. Clarity and precision, an avoidance of abstractions per se, and the recognition of the natural object as "proper and perfect symbol" characterizes the poetry of the Imagists, Williams, and the Black Mountain writers alike. The concern of the Imagists for a " 'free-verse' based on natural speech rhythms" was also the concern of Williams and the Black Mountain group. There were differences, however, and before examining the tenets of the Black Mountain writers, it may prove helpful in understanding the "movement" to determine the extent to which Williams succeeded in evolving a "new" prosody.

Williams' concern with prosody stemmed from the fact

[19]Information in a letter to the author from David Dawson, Seattle Community College, June 2, 1971. In this letter Dawson also cites Duncan's influence on this sense of metaphor; Pound's on image; Olson, Creeley, Williams and Zukofsky on rhythm; Duncan, Zukofsky, Pound, Trager and Smith, any linguist, the OED, "his own ear" on language "that in its form delights."

that while he considered traditional metrics failed to capture the rhythmic patterns of the American idiom, he also considered that "free" verse, which ignored a structured metric, lacked the necessary form and discipline he believed inherent in a work of art. As he saw it, the crux of the problem lay in the inflexible structure of the traditional foot, and its solution in what he termed the "variable foot".

Williams was provided with his concept of the "variable foot" by the following lines from "Paterson II":

> The descent beckons
>   as the ascent beckoned
>   Memory is a kind
> of accomplishment
>   a sort of renewal
>   even
> an initiation, since the spaces it opens are new
> places
>   inhabited by hordes
>   heretofore unrealized,
> of new kinds—
>   since their movements
>   are towards new objectives
> (even though formerly they were abandoned).[20]

Describing this innovation which Williams believed provided the form and discipline "free verse" had been wanting, he said:

> The grammar of the term, variable foot, is simply what it describes itself to be: a poetic foot that is not fixed but varies with the demands of the language, keeping the measured emphasis as it may occur in the line. Its characteristic, where it differs from the fixed foot with which we are familiar, is that it ignores the counting of syllables in the line, which is the mark of usual scansion, for a measure of the ear, a more sensory counting....[21]

[20] William Carlos Williams, *Paterson* (New York, 1963), p.96.
[21] Roy Harvey Pearce, *The Continuity of American Poetry* (Princeton, 1965), p.343.

Since "variable foot" is apparently a contradiction in terms —"variable" denoting a capacity for change, "foot", at least in traditional metrics, denoting a fixed unit of measure—it lacks the precision and clarity requisite for a proper definition. Furthermore, an examination of the lines in question reveals that Williams has used a variety of traditional feet— for example, anapest and trochee in the first line, pyrrhic, iambus, and trochee in the second—and if one listens to Williams reading the lines in question,[22] one discovers that he stresses those syllables which would be stressed according to the rules of conventional scansion. However, in a letter to Richard Eberhart written in 1954,[23] Williams explains that to each line in the triadic stanzas from "Paterson II" he (mentally) prefixes a numeral:

(1) The descent beckons
  (2) as the ascent beckoned
    (3) Memory . . .
      (etc.)

and each numeral receives a single beat. In effect then, Williams' "single beat to each numeral"[24] becomes a single beat to each line. Since both scansion and the poet's reading reveal that each line receives two stresses, one must conclude that a single beat rhythm is not an integral part of the line itself, but is external to it and must be imposed. This can be recognized if one beats slowly and rhythmically or uses a metronome, for as George Bowering states:

Williams senses that measure in poetry (and American speech) is comparable to measure in music, with quantitative time units whose duration is determined by a measurable number of beats.[25]

---

[22] Listen, for example, to Williams' reading of these lines in "William Carlos Williams Reading His Poems," Caedmon TC1047.

[23] Thirlwall, p.326.

[24] Thirlwall, p.327.

[25] George Bowering, "The New American Prosody," *Kulchur* 15 (1964), 10.

Although it is doubtful if Williams' concept of the "variable foot" as such had much influence on the other "movement" writers, it is significant in that it indicates the concern of these writers for a "new" approach to the problem of measure in poetry; it also has much in common with Lionel Kearns' experimentation with "stacked verse." Williams did, however, make contributions towards the establishment of a "new" prosody, for he succeeded in realizing a metre which approximated the rhythms of the speaking voice. Furthermore, he also succeeded in breaking away from traditional verse patterns with his unconventional use of margins and with the inclusion in his poetry of prose passages which were not patterned at all. Insofar as the *Tish* writers were concerned, he contributed as much by example as by precept, and, as an examination of *Tish* poetry reveals, showed them:

>   The instant
> trivial as it is
>   is all we have
>   unless—unless
> things the imagination feeds upon,
>   the scent of the rose,
>   Startle us anew.[26]

As was noted earlier, Williams had much in common with the Black Mountain writers both in theory and in practice. Both Williams and the latter group considered traditional poetry inadequate for coming to terms with the "real" world of their day; both were concerned with evolving a "new" poetry and were preoccupied with the question of language and form; and both saw poetry as a "tool" for discovering something beyond the poem itself.

The theories of the Black Mountain group were introduced to the *Tish* writers by Robert Duncan during his visit to Vancouver in the summer of 1961; their influence on *Tish* was thus much more immediate than those of either the Imagists or Williams. Although the Black Mountain poetics are a continuing development of the theories propounded by

[26] William Carlos Williams, *Paterson*, p.26.

the Imagists and Williams, they are fraught with difficulties for the novice. The "group" here will be limited to Robert Duncan, Charles Olson, and Robert Creeley, since both Duncan and Creeley were known personally by the *Tish* writers, while Olson's essay "Projective Verse" was the Black Mountain theoretical document which most inspired them.[27]

There are various reasons for the difficulty the "uninitiated" experience in coming to terms with the poetics of the Black Mountain writers. Although all were published, they were not particularly concerned with publication and their prose works were not written for the general reading public.[28] Furthermore, their poetry was intended to be read aloud by the poet himself. These factors, combined with the following, militate against an understanding of the Black Mountain writers: the peculiar telegraphic style of the prose which they used in their communications with each other is even at best mildly baffling and at worst totally obscure; the esoteric nature of their scholarly pursuits—for example, Olson's concern with Mayan civilization—makes many of their allusions incomprehensible to the uninitiated; and, finally, the profundity of thought contained in the poorly expressed and often incomplete statements will elude the reader, simply because it *is* poorly expressed and often incomplete. The most complete statement of the poetic theories of these writers is contained in Charles Olson's essay on "projective verse". Even this essay is characterized by the faults which mar the other writings of the three for the ordinary reader: it, too, is poorly expressed and incomplete.[29]

---

[27]There were others classified as "Black Mountain" writers—for example, Edward Dorn or Louis Zukofsky—but because their contact with the *Tish* poets was not so immediate as that of Olson, Duncan, and Creeley, they will not be discussed here. The term "Black Mountain" comes from Black Mountain College, N.C., where Charles Olson served as rector from 1951-1956.

[28]Donald Davie, "The Black Mountain Poets," *The Survival of Poetry* ed., Martin Dodsworth (London, 1970), 217.

[29]*Tish 5*, p.5. Here Frank Davey states: "This work[i.e, "Projective Verse"] appears to me (as Warren Tallman has repeatedly suggested) as a series of notes and suggestions on poetics, rather than a definitive study. . . . I suggest that the person who benefitted most

However, if one examines Olson's essay in the light of his other works and those of Duncan and Creeley, its meaning becomes clearer. Since an understanding of the Black Mountain theories is essential to an understanding of the *Tish* poetics, it is necessary at this point to take various statements from Olson's "projective verse", examine them in the light of other statements which he made, and illustrate them where possible with examples from the works of Duncan and Creeley.

First, let us consider Olson's declaration that a "poem is energy transferred from where the poet got it, by way of the poem itself, to the reader."[30] To understand his emphasis on the poem as "high-energy construct" or "energy discharge", it is helpful to know Olson's theories concerning the role of the ancient Greeks in the heritage of Western civilization. These are to be found in his essay "The Human Universe" and may be briefly paraphrased as follows: the simple act of experiencing (or "discovery", to use Olson's term) is inextricably involved in the human being with the act of defining this experience. The Greeks, with their fondness for speculation, elevated this "act of definition" to the point of making a "universe of discourse".[31] Thus logic, classification, and abstraction became more important to the Greeks than the act of experiencing itself, and in Olson's opinion, resulted in the partitioning of reality and a removal from the totality of experience by making a dichotomy between discovery and definition. In other words, Olson considered that the habit of thought—that is, the propensity for logic and classification—which Western civilization had inherited from the Greeks, interfered with man's ability to "stay in the human universe". Man was so concerned with his *thought* about experience that experience itself became a matter of minor importance. Thus its full implications were not

from Olson's "Projective Verse" was Olson; perhaps because it is more self-communicative than anything, that a hypothetical reader finds parts of it so nebulous."

[30] Charles Olson, "Projective Verse," *The New American Poetry*, ed., Donald M. Allen (New York, 1960), 387. Subsequent references to "Projective Verse" will be from this text hereafter cited as "P.V."

[31] Charles Olson, *The Human Universe* (New York, 1967), p.4.

realized. Lionel Kearns expressed this same idea in "Professor":

> Spring had always been mud and leaves and the grass burning. But noting the possible mythological extension: incense, the sacrificial offering, a ritual death before germination, he fitted it into his system

and forgot the smell. (*Tish 18*, p.13)

When this fondness for abstraction and classification was carried into the realm of poetry—and Olson saw that it was—the poem ceased to be an "energy-discharge" or "high-energy construct" and the poetic experience became instead thought about the poetic experience. The reader was thus removed from the reality which inspired the poem. Furthermore, the poet had removed himself from the totality of his experience by moving into the realm of abstraction, and in Olson's view this act had serious consequences. There are, as we shall see presently, philosophical implications in Olson's theories which involve an approach to life itself, but for the present we are concerned only with their application to poetry. It would appear, then, that what Olson is concerned with at this point is a poem in which the poetic experience is transferred to the reader with as much immediacy as the poet can summon—that is, with the experience itself rather than thought about the experience being communicated. Robert Creeley demonstrates this thesis in the following line from his "I keep to myself such measures":

> There is nothing
> but what thinking makes
> it less tangible. The mind,
> fast as it goes, loses
>
> pace, puts in place of it
> like rocks simple markers,
> for a way only to
> hopefully come back to

>   where it cannot. . . .³²

Similarly, in "A Place" Creeley reiterates Olson's idea that the totality of experience is lost when it is intellectualized, even if the act of intellectualization is not abstraction for the purpose of classification, but simply memory:

> The wetness of that street, the light,
> the way the clouds were heavy is
> not description. But in the memory I fear
>
> the distortion. I do not feel
> what it was I was feeling. . . .³³

It follows as a logical consequence that if the poetic experience is to be transferred with as much immediacy as possible to the reader, the poet "can go by no track other than the one the poem under hand declares for itself"³⁴ and that "form is never more than an extension of content".³⁵ To order one's poetic experience to fit a pre-conceived form would only result, in Olson's opinion, in a partitioning of reality—in the ascendence of thought about experience, by the very act of ordering, rather than a focus on the experience itself. William Carlos Williams expressed this idea more graphically when he said, "I was early in life sick to my very pit with order that cuts off the crab's feelers to make it fit into the box."³⁶ To say that "form is never more than an extension of content" is not, however, to imply that form is of little or no importance, for the poems of the Black Mountain writers — and of the *Tish* poets — are highly structured. This structure is not achieved by adherence to either traditional forms or metric patterns of conventional verse, for as Robert Duncan indicates in "Keeping the Rhyme":

---

³²Gary Geddes, ed., *20th Century Poetry & Poetics* (Toronto, 1969), p. 298.
³³Geddes, p. 299.
³⁴Olson, "P.V.," p.387.
³⁵*Ibid*.
³⁶Sherman Paul *The Music of Survival* (Chicago, 1968), p.79.

> By stress and syllable
> by change-rhyme and contour
> we let the long line pace even awkward to its period.
>
> the short line
> we refine
> and keep for candor.[37]

Just as the idea that form must be an extension of content followed logically from the idea of the poem as a "high-energy construct", so, too, does Olson's next point, that "one perception must immediately and directly lead to another perception."[38] If we can understand by Olson's use of "perception" that union of discovery and identification of which we spoke earlier, then we can see that if one perception did *not* lead immediately and directly to another, it would lead, because of our habits of thought, to intellectualization—to classification and abstraction which Olson felt must be avoided, because, as he states in "The Human Universe", the confuse confuse confound"[39] Thus Robert Duncan in "Poetry, A Natural Thing states:

> The poem
> feeds upon thought, feeling, impulse,
> to breed itself,
> a spiritual urgency at the dark ladders leaping..."[40]

using the blind impulse of the fish struggling up the falls as metaphor for a poetry in which "one perception must must must *move, instanter, on another*!"[41]

Robert Creeley summarizes Olson's "projective verse" to this point by demonstrating that what Olson has done, in effect, is provide a basis for structure in the poem in terms of its *kinetics*: "the poem itself must, at all points, be a high-energy construct and at all points, an energy discharge...";

---

[37]Robert Duncan, *The Opening of the Field* (New York, 1960), p.51.
[38]Olson, "P.V.," p.388.
[39]Olson, *The Human Universe*, p.17.
[40]Duncan, p.50.
[41]Olson, "P.V.," p.388.

the *principle* of its writing: "form is never more than an extension of content"; and the *process*: "one perception must immediately and directly lead to a further perception."[42] These are the characteristics of structure which distinguish "projective verse" or "composition by field" from what Olson considers to be "non-projective" verse, that is, traditional verse as we know it, having "inherited line, stanza, and overall form."[43]

Having provided the bases for structure of "projective verse", Olson next proceeds to emphasize the dual roles of syllable and breath in this poetry, stating "that verse will only do in which a poet manages to register both the acquisition of his ear *and* the pressures of his breath."[44] By the "acquisitions of his ear" Olson appears to mean the syllable, which he sees as the "king and pin of versification, what rules and holds together the lines, the larger forms of a poem."[45] There is nothing new about this observation, nor is Olson's statement that "it is by their syllables that words juxtapose in beauty, by these particles of sound as clearly as by the sense of the words which they compose"[46] particularly original. Furthermore, his declaration that "the line comes (I swear it) from the breath, from the breathing of the man who writes, at the time he writes..."[47] seems to be simply an extension and application of Williams' search for a "new measure consonant with our day"[48] which for Williams was satisfied, as we have seen, by his discovery of the variable foot. It would appear that here Olson is merely saying that the function formerly attributed to metre, rhyme, and syllable—that is, sound—is in "projective verse" solely determined by the syllable, and that whereas formerly the line was "fixed" by adherence to a traditional metric pattern, now that this traditional unit of measurement is not employed another must be found. For "projective verse", this measure is the

---

[42] Allen, pp.409-410.
[43] Olson, "P.V.," p.387.
[44] Olson, p.388.
[45] *Ibid.*
[46] *Ibid.*
[47] Olson, "P.V.," p.389.
[48] J. Laughlin, ed., *New Directions* 17 (Norfolk, 1961), p.253.

breath. This appears to be simply echoing Williams, who

> ... hears the spoken words naturally cohere in clusters that form the units of rhythm, and that these clusters are determined by the heartbeat, the breath, the felt syntactic emphasis, the instinctive pace. . . .[49]

There is nothing in Olson's essay to indicate that he means more by syllable and breath than this, save for the following rather enigmatic statements:

> In any given instance, because there is a choice of words, the choice, if a man is in there, will be, spontaneously, the obedience of his ear to the syllables. The fineness, and the practice, lie here, at the minimum and source of speech.[50]

Following another reference to the elements and minims of language, Olson says:

> I say the syllable, king, and that it is spontaneous, this way: the ear, the ear which has collected, which has listened, the ear, which is so close to the mind that it is the mind's, that it has the mind's speed . . .
>
> it is close, another way: the mind is brother to this sister and is, because it is so close, is the drying force, the incest, the sharpener . . .
>
> It is from the union of the mind and the ear that the syllable is born.[51]

However, Olson was concerned with syllable and breath far beyond the simple conclusions suggested. Indeed, all the Black Mountain poets—and their followers among the *Tish* group—had a keen interest in the "mystery" of language and the possibilities and implications of the phonetic alphabet. This particular area of their poetic theories is so complex only a lengthy study could do it justice. Suffice it to say here that

[49] Bowering, p.12.
[50] Olson, "P.V.," p.388.
[51] Olson, "P.V.," p.389.

they recognized two levels of language, one which was spontaneous and involved the primary levels of consciousness, and the other which was "learned". In "The Human Universe", Olson distinguished these as "language as the act of the instant" or "shout", and "language as the act of thought about the instant" or "logos". If one remembers that Olson saw "discovery" or experience as being inextricably involved with definition, and his theory that undue emphasis on the latter resulted in a partitioning of reality, one can understand his concern for a return to the "minims and elements" of language. In Olson's opinion, language—in this case "logos"—served to remove man from reality.

There were further ramifications to Olson's concern for language, however. When he speaks of the syllable as being "spontaneous", he implies that somehow there is a correlation between sound and experience. His insistence on listening:

> Listening for the syllables must be so constant and so scrupulous, the exaction must be so complete, that the assurance of the ear is purchased at the highest—40 hours a day—price...[52]

suggests that there *is* in fact a correlation between sound and experience, that there *are* words whose syllables respond in sound to the experience. Thus if the poem is to be an "energy-discharge" its language must appeal to the reader on the level of "shout". It must, in the opinion of Olson, be written on the level of "act of the instant". This is what Robert Duncan appears to imply in the following lines from "Keeping the Rhyme":

> This we remember:
> ember of the fire
> catches the word if we but hear
>   ("we must understand what is happening")
> and springs to desire,

[52]*Ibid.*

> a bird-right light
> sound.
>
> This is the Yule-log that warms December
> This is new grass that springs from the ground.[53]

When poems of the Black Mountain writers are read aloud, it is possible to hear that the "line comes from the breath, from the breathing of the man who writes" as Olson indicated. Because of the convenience of typewriter margins, one can also see how the poem is to be read. George Bowering states:

> Olson emphasizes the usefulness of the *typewriter* to record the sounds a man makes as controlled by his breath (and his other faculties). He compares the possibilities of typewriter notation with the bars and staves a musician can use bit by bit in the creative act of recording the imagination's stepping. Now there is no need to record vocalization by the number of syllables: the composer uses his typewritten page as (like musical) *score* to play from.[54]

However, it is this aspect of "projective verse" perhaps more than any other, which puzzles—and infuriates—some readers. In a review of J. Michael Yates' *Contemporary Poetry of British Columbia*, Ralph Gustafson states:

> ...but group feel-ins are absent, few creaks are heard, the rhythm is mostly under control (that hiccough "breathing" marking the *Tish* school is beautifully absent; perhaps they got frightened)....[55]

Gustafson's review serves to illustrate the point that "projective verse" must be examined on its own terms if it is to be examined at all. To apply traditional criteria to it is futile, for

[53] Duncan, p.51.
[54] Bowering, p.13.
[55] Ralph Gastafson, "Its Own Type of Flea," *Canadian Literature*, 47 (1971), 80.

what "conventional" criticism is concerned with in poetry is not necessarily to be found in "projective verse". Commenting on this, Robert Creeley said of the "non-projective" writers and critics:

> They argue the poem as a means to recognition, a signboard as it were, not in itself a structure of 'recognition' or—better—cognition itself. Some, then, would not only not hear what Olson was saying, but would even deny, I think, the relevance of his concerns. The great preoccupation with symbology and levels of image in poetry insisted upon by contemporary criticism has meant a further bias for this non-hearing, since Olson's emphasis is put upon prosody, not interpretation.[56]

Even when "projective verse" is examined on its own terms, the adverse criticism which it receives is frequently justified. As an examination of the *Tish* poems will reveal, there are certain weaknesses inherent in this "new" poetry: in an effort to make the poetic experience immediate, the poet does not always discriminate between those experiences which can be meaningful for his reader and those which are so personal they can be meaningful only for himself; although "form is never more than an extension of content", the content is often so insignificant that the poem appears to be merely an exercise in technique. There is considerable irony in the realization that although Olson intended "projective verse" to be the means whereby poetry would be brought back to "reality", it is frequently treated as an end in itself and has become, in fact, an obstacle to reality. This is observable not only in the *Tish* poetry but also in the works of the Black Mountain writers themselves. The exigencies of "projective verse" are such that often they will permit only a very limited reality.

The first part of Olson's essay concerns "what" projective verse is and "how" it is realized. The second part of his essay gives the partial explanation of "why" he considered it to be so important. Here, too, it is necessary to look at his other works for a fuller explanation of his theories, for without an

[56] Allen, p.408.

understanding of these basic ideas, Olson's emphasis on "projective verse" appears to be "much ado about nothing". The first reference to the fact that more is involved in "projective verse" than prosody, comes with Olson's statement:

> ... the projective involves a stance towards reality outside a poem as well as a new stance towards the reality of the poem itself.[57]

His discussion of "objectism" whch Olson defines as "the kind of relation of man to experience", serves as introduction to Olson's theories concerning a "stance to reality outside a poem". He states:

> Objectism is the getting rid of the lyrical interference of individual as ego, of the 'subject' and his soul, that peculiar presumption by which western man has interposed himself between what he is as a creature of nature (with certain instructions to carry out) and those other creations of nature which we may, with no derogation, call objects. For a man is himself an object, whatever he may take to be his advantages, the more likely to recognize himself as such the greater his advantages, particularly at that moment that he achieves an humilitas sufficient to make him of use.[58]

We have seen Olson's theories concerning the role of Greek thought in Western civilization, and his thesis that by attaching undue significance to logic and classification Western man has effected an artifical separation between "discovery" and "definition". The point of Olson's thesis seems to be that there is an interference on the part of what we have learned with what we are experiencing. In other words, when we do experience, we immediately begin classifying this experience in terms of what we know—and because our knowledge is limited, we fail to realize the full significance of our experience.

[57]Olson, "P.V.," p.394.
[58]Olson, "P.V.," p.395.

It is this propensity to select from experience only those elements which can be classified in terms of what is already known which, in Olson's opinion, makes not only writing unsatisfactory but also living unsatisfactory. As he says in "The Human Universe",

> It comes out a demonstration, a separating out, an act of classification, and so, a stopping, and all that I know is, it is not there, it has turned false. For any of us, at any instant, are juxtaposed to any experience, even an overwhelming single one, on several more planes than the arbitrary and discursive which we inherit can declare.[59]

Comparing Western civilization with that of the Mayans who have not had these artificial classifications introduced into their culture, Olson concludes that in contrast to the Mayan, Western man has ceased to be "natural". He states:

> The trouble with the inherited formulations which have helped to destroy him—i.e. Western man—(the notion of himself as the centre of phenomenon by fiat or of god as the center and man as god's chief reflection) is that both set aside nature as an unadmitted or suppressed third party....[60]

Thus Olson's belief that man's "stance towards reality" must involve his seeing himself as an "object"—that is, without the arbitrary distinctions inherent in Western civilization—if he is to experience full satisfaction in living. This belief is also implicit in the following:

> If he sprawl, he shall find little to sing but himself, and shall sing, nature has such paradoxical ways, by way of artificial forms outside himself. But if he stays inside himself, if he is contained within his nature as he is participant in the larger force, he will be able to listen, and his hearing through himself will give him secrets objects share.[61]

[59]Olson, *The Human Universe*, p.5.
[60]Olson, p.8.

Olson's use of the word 'sprawl" is somewhat confusing but it appears that he is using it in the sense of not being recollected in oneself, of not "listening and hearing". From what has been seen in his other writings, one can understand by "artificial forms outside himself" those arbitrary classifications and definitions inherent in Western civilization. What Olson appears to be implying is that man has constructed for himself a way of life which is so artificial and sterile that he has almost completely de-humanized and depersonalized his existence.

When examined apart from their application to poetics, Olson's theories thus appear to be primarily concerned with an approach to life itself. One can see that there are remarkable similarities here to the theories of Blake and Wordsworth—and Olson's conviction that man "if he is contained within his nature ... will be able to listen and his hearing through himself will give him secrets objects share" resembles Hopkins' declaration that "there lives the dearest freshness deep down things". These similarities did not go unnoticed by the *Tish* writers as Frank Davey's essay "One Man's Look At 'Projective Verse' " in *Tish 5* proves.

It is their attitude towards nature, both man's own human nature and that greater life force of which he is part, which makes the Black Mountain poets appear at times to be approaching mysticism. Common to the three with whom we have been concerned is a fresh sense of wonder about the mystery of life and concomitant mystery of man. Although their writings appear at times to be advocating an anti-intellectualism or at least denigrating the body of knowledge which is the common heritage of Western man, this is not necessarily so. What they were concerned with was a fresh approach to the mystery of life. It was their belief that man had stifled his sense of wonder—and that the artificial restrictions "learning" had placed on man's thinking prevented him from fully participating in the life around him. Poetry, specifically "projective verse" was the means they chose to bring man back to what they considered was his rightful place in the cosmos. It was for them, then, the means to an end, not an end in itself. In "Towards an Open

[61] Olson, "P.V.," p.395.

Universe", Robert Duncan states:

> Central to and defining the poetics I am trying to suggest here is the conviction that the order man may contrive or impose upon the things about him or upon his own language is trivial besides the divine order or natural order he may discover in them.[62]

As we have seen in the preceding pages, there has been a continuous development in poetry since the time of the Imagists, not only in terms of poetics but also in terms of the broader applications of poetry. Emphasis on clarity and precision, the "musical" phrase, and the avoidance of abstractions as such, begun by the Imagists was continued by William Carlos Williams. To these he added the ideal of a poetry in which "things" of a particular locale functioned metaphorically, the rhythmic contours of idiomatic speech, and the belief that such a poetry would create a culture indigenous to its locale. These ideas were further developed by the Black Mountain writers. With their concern for a poetry which would convey the poetic experience to the reader with as much immediacy as possible, they relied on the resources of the phonetic alphabet for sound, saw the "form" of the poem as an extension of its "content", and believed that through this "projective verse" one would come to realize, if not the "secrets of nature", at least the fact that such "secrets" did exist. This "movement" in poetry was thus as much an attempt to overcome the sterility inherent in modern life as it was an attempt to fashion a "new" prosody, and no examination of this "movement" can be complete unless these two aspects are recognized.

The University of Calgary, 1972

---

[62]Robert Duncan, "Towards an Open Universe," *Poets on Poetry*, ed., Howard Nemerov (New York, 1966), 139.

Before *Tish*,
from *Oral History of Vancouver*

Brad Robinson

Brad Robinson: Gladys, how did you come to live with Warren and Ellen Tallman?
Gladys Hindmarch: I had Warren as a freshman English teacher . . . I was extremely . . . I don't think depressed is the word for how a person feels . . . at university, if they're sort of below depression. If a person says 'I'm depressed', you're at a certain level of consciousness so you know what it is to be not depressed, and I think I was in a state where anyone who really recognized it would have sent me to a shrink. But because I was able to go through the line-ups in the cafeteria, went to classes, passed things, I suppose no one thought I should be sent.

The only person I met in the first year of university (U.B.C.) that I could really speak to was Warren, and I talked to him an awful lot and he turned me on to D.H. Lawrence. I was a non-reader, I didn't read for enjoyment, I still seldom do. Only in my last year have I read quite so much. It's my 'readingest' year.

The thing that turned me onto Lawrence was not the short stories which Warren gave me to read, but the *Studies in Classic American Literature*, which I bought in the Hudson's Bay Company in Victoria while waiting for my mother to do one of her typically mother things.

I began to keep a notebook, which was essentially an argument against many of Lawrence's sketches that I didn't like—mainly lines and phrases—and in the process of this, I learned a lot of things and because, not because of the notebook, but because of Warren, he talked me into getting back into university by having me signed up in Creative Writing without having submitted anything. He also managed to get me into second year English with Elliott Gose, and wrote me a note saying come to my class. Until all this, I had thought of joining the armed forces—just like I've got to do something with my life, not my entire life, just my immediate life . . .

Robinson: This would be around . . .

Gladys: It was the end of my freshman year, which was the end of 1958. I was going into my second year, and I met Frank Davey in the writing course I just mentioned—the teacher was Jake Zilber.

Frank Davey was a red-headed kid from Abbotsford, or Chilliwack—I think it was Abbotsford—I always get the two mixed, probably heard it wrong the first time. Very much a country boy, such as I was a country girl, but Frank had grown up inside the town . . . cars the main thing, and cruising after girls, but never very successful . . . the beautiful fuck-ups of kids that age . . . trying very hard, blushing . . . not blushing, you know how it is . . . and Frank and I used to sit together in this very large class. I think Jake had twenty-five or thirty people in the class, which is too much for a writing class, just too much really for any type of class where a lot of individual thought and perception is supposed to be going on, because you don't want to block it off. It's pretty hard with that number of people especially if you're used to talking, like Jake was. He would lecture for an hour, and then he'd maybe discuss some of the stuff we had written, and he would try and structure it, but even so, it was a pretty successful class.

It was a lot of fun and was certainly a focal point of that year for me—those Friday afternoons were, on the whole, so visible.

I was hurt a fair amount in that class—I don't think I should go into why I felt hurt by Jake, but like one of the things would be Frank, who would write parodies. I would get pretty good marks, and I was sort of mark-oriented, in a sense, at that time, not that I'd be pleased when I got good marks, and not pleased when I didn't, etc. . . . but, in a sense, underneath, I really was, but I wouldn't admit it. Frank also got good marks, but he at one point wrote a parody of something I had written that was put in the *Ubyssey*. Frank got five per cent more for his parody than I got for my original. Then another parody appeared in the class and I said, sort of jokingly, to Jake that I should get extra marks everytime someone writes a parody on something I had written . . . sort of like added on to whatever my total thing is.

I've never really liked satire or parody and I don't think I ever will. Partially, I don't really understand it, but my experience I had with it sort of hurt. . . .

Robinson: I can recall that you had once written a story an it was published in *Mademoiselle* . . . some sort of contest?

Gladys: The setup of the course was such that it called for an essay or a description. At that time Warren was writing something on Kerouac, which later became 'Kerouac's Sound'.

A girl that I knew from high school who happened to be in Victoria wrote me a letter on the same day that Warren had talked to me about jazz, and she wrote quick, quick, I've got a new boyfriend and I'm acting like I know more than I do, so sort of tell me something, and I thought: 'What a ridiculous question, like what's jazz, how can you answer that?' Also, I hadn't done any writing for Jake for a week, and so I sat down and started writing this essay that was quite rhythmical and very, oh, I don't know if I should describe the essay, but various impressions of various types, as I say, you can't just lump it all together, three types in words, even though these divisions aren't . . . just my own . . . I don't have any deep impression of jazz . . . I used to play sax in a dance band and I have a definite sense of improvisation . . . just what it's like to fool around and have fun on an instrument. And Jake really liked this piece and I sort of put it away—you were supposed to hand in revisions after a certain length of time and I just wasn't interested in revising what I had written.

There was a fellow in the English Department who was going to give a lecture on jazz and literature, and so Jake said to me: 'Hand this back.'

And so, on the day that I was to hand my piece back, or the night before the day, as I was looking through this sort of folder that I have of all sorts of things in, I came across, in front of the jazz thing, this sheet from *Mademoiselle* which Jake had handed out to all the women in the class. So I typed my piece up, gave Jake a carbon, and sent the original of the new thing, with a sort of half of the other thing that I had written, off to *Mademoiselle* magazine. And, a couple of months later, I heard that I had come in second out of all the people who had sent in things, which meant that I had a relatively strong chance of going to New York if I wanted to.

Also Jake and I—this was sort of getting toward Christmas vacation and we were not getting along, from my point of view, I don't think he felt that—but he really didn't like the nursery rhyme things that I was doing, meaning really, that he gave me 70-75%, and I thought this meant that he didn't like me. This is where I don't think they should mark something like creative writing. I don't think you should be marked in English either. It's just so stupid. And because of the contest, I was this sort of smiley girl and I got A marks.

Robinson: The terms had changed.

Gladys: Yeah, right.

Robinson: At this time, had the second issue of *Evergreen Review* appeared?

Gladys: Gee, I don't know. I was never very aware of *Evergreen*.

Robinson: I asked because that was the number that sort of classically defined the writing scene of the time. I believe Warren's 'Kerouac's Sound' was also printed in that issue.

Gladys: Oh no, that would be much later. He'd just done 'Kerouac's Sound' in November of '58 and that came out in February of '59. I know he showed me the *Evergreen Review*, and as with all other things, I just wasn't interested. I found the things hard to read, and I was feeling pretty low. And I was reading Beckett and that made me feel even lower—not lower, but it just didn't make me feel warm to find someone who was in despair. Yet I would read writers like Hardy who made me feel better.

Robinson: So at the end of that summer you had established

links with Warren and Frank Davey?
Gladys: I'd come back from New York and went to sit in on one of Jake's summer classes. There was this large teddy-bear kind of figure, a guy with really curly sandy hair and gentle quick smile, who turned around and said: 'You don't know me, but I know you.' And it was Lionel Kearns. We only talked for about three minutes. But I'd heard from Warren that this guy was a *poet*, like a great writer, and we really had nothing to say to each other at that point. I was really a pretty plump girl then—160 pounds or something like that. Not much chit-chat or razzimatazz.

Moving to the fall of that year, I met George Bowering—I had started going to Writer's Workshop . . .
Robinson: Where was that?
Gladys: Tony Friedsen, who then became a member of the Writing Department, had a writer's workshop that ran for three pretty solid years. Actually, I had met George Bowering in my first year . . . I had read something of his in *Raven*, the UBC literary magazine. I really liked everything in the magazine, there were things of Barry Hale—but I walked up to George and introduced myself on a rainy day. I remember we didn't have much to say, but I recall sitting there for about ten minutes feeling very warm, and picking up a couple of stones on the parking lot when I went back to the dorms. It was one of those 'good' days.

And when I went to this writer's workshop, it was quite crowded. It was down on 4th Avenue or 6th—somewhere in the Kitsilano area. It's hard to tell when you don't drive—I had no sense of the city at that time, other than I didn't like it. I've had senses of Vancouver in earlier times, like when I used to sneak into the PNE under the fence.

At any rate, I sat on a couch next to George Bowering, and we met. So it was pretty rapid, once we hit that sort of time in terms of when you meet people, not sort of what starts happening. We're now into my third year of university. I took a course from Warren which they called English 406: An Introduction to Poetry. In that class was Frank Davey, Barry Hale — who later became a writer for the Toronto *Star* and is now an art writer, and Lionel Kearns. Even though I'd met Lionel that summer, it wasn't until after Christmas exams that he came back from the middle of the room. I always tend to sit in the very last row, or second last row, preferably close to the door or window. Anyway, Lionel came down and said: 'Can I read your paper?' And I said: 'Can I read yours?' And he said: 'Well, I don't really want you to see mine.' I said: 'Why? I'm so shy and I'm showing you mine?' And so we read each other's papers. This was getting into the spring of '60 . . .

Robinson: What was Warren teaching?

Gladys: Warren's idea was that university students have to read *so* much, and they don't really absorb all the reading, they don't ever have a course that is relatively light—not light-hearted, but that the reading load is light and has focus.

So I think his idea was that you only teach nine or ten poems in the entire year—for instance, a month on 'The Ecstasy' by Donne and a month on 'The Garden' by Marvell—and by that spring we got into Hopkins and Lionel and Frank and I yakked all through the class. Mainly me yakking and them having to listen. But they did sort of talk.

We just didn't pay attention, in a sense, to the rest of the class. It's then that we really got interested in each other.

I really don't know how Warren stands all those twirps in the back of the room, draining all this energy, but he does, and that's one of his great advantages as a teacher. He lets all sorts of things just simply happen.

Robinson: By this time you were living at the Tallmans'?

Gladys: Right. Third year was when I moved out of the dorms and moved into the Tallman house. In the spring of the second year I used to visit there quite a bit. They had a washing machine there and it used to cost fifteen cents to wash your clothes at a laundromat, so I said: 'Well, can I use your washing machine and babysit the kids in return?' And I thought this was just great. And then I would stay for supper, which was always better than the dorm food.

So I sort of had this social life centering around food—suppertime— it got so I was always eating there. And the day I won the *Mademoiselle* contest, I mentioned it in the car to Warren—we were driving *out* to supper. Warren had this '48 Chev or something like that, and he steered it off the road.

Robinson: He drove it off the road?

Gladys: Yeah—he couldn't believe it—a little freshman girl going off to the big city!

Robinson: Well, during the time you lived there, that would be '59, early '60, right? Were the younger people starting to come around to Warren's place at that time?

Gladys: I'm not sure. But I do remember Frank Davey, after he had written a new poem, getting so out of his head with excitement, and driving over to Warren's and sitting down. We'd always sit down and read it . . .

Robinson: Out loud?

Gladys: . . . always out loud, even previous to our Black Mountain influence—before the *New American Poetry* anthology came out. This is before any of us got into that.

So I haven't got a clear sense of numbers of people dropping over at that time, 'cause mainly the people I was talking to were quite a bit older than myself and were the people I was meeting through the Tallmans.

Robinson: You said after Frank came over, there wouldn't be much to talk about. Was that because the poem was bad?

Gladys: No. Warren would say it was great or something like that, but, in one sense, we had no aesthetic to talk about. And by that I don't mean any definite aesthetic, I just mean any aesthetic other than 'the perception is good, the images are strong'. No language sense in terms of sound and rhythm that could be of any worth in terms of criticizing or helping— even on lines.

Ellen Tallman's complaint at the time would be like: 'This guy's just come in, and you've spent hours together, and you don't say anything, and nothing's happened.' So I guess we just talked about our courses, problems, little jokes Frank had written about Pope and what not.

When we got into Hopkins that spring, that's where Lionel and I start to argue out a sense of writing. We go around shouting 'Holy Moses!', getting drunk with Lionel, George and Kenny (Tallman) in the car and yelling 'Holy Moses!' What an escape!

But the real pickup isn't until we have to skip an entire year—that's when *New American Poetry* comes in.

Robinson: This is 1961?[1]

Gladys: Yeah. And after the spring term. Fred Wah and

[1]*The New American Poetry* was published in 1960, & came to

Pauline Butling, who later becomes Pauline Wah, were members of Warren's next poetry class. The *New American Poetry* anthology came out and they looked at it. Pauline wrote a piece on Duncan and Fred wrote something on Williams that I was really impressed by—my first meeting with him was over an essay that he wrote.

Warren then arranged a thing where everyone got together on Sundays (this was after the term's over) and we decided to sit down with the *New American* and try to read through it. Well, he just decided to start with Charles Olson, and we had four meetings and we didn't get through the first section of the first poem—there was no sense, we got into big arguments about what 'sprawl' was and what not.

I should say that the origins of *Tish* began when Lionel and Fred decided to start a magazine called *Cock* or something like that, and Warren says: 'Start a magazine? You don't write enough, you don't know enough to start a magazine.'

And so this group got together, it was quite large—about 20-30 people . . .

Robinson: All discussing *New American* writers?

Gladys: Yeah. *New American* poetry. We'd all read 'Projective Verse' and were not getting anywhere. It was sort of like out of 'Songs of Maximus to Himself': 'words, words, words all over everything'.

'What does this really *mean*?'—we kept doing that sort of thing—'What does this really mean?' Warren comes from the New Criticism school and later, after he reads *New American*, he switches. But as a sort of in, we kept getting hung up on content in the sense of the meaning of it. And we eventually had Robert Duncan up—we all had to pay five dollars—and Robert Duncan came up . . .

Robinson: How was it that you became aware that Duncan had force . . .

Gladys: We'll have to flip back a year. Ellen's father has a heart attack, Ellen flies to San Francisco, and who does she run into but Duncan, who she knew back in 1945-46 when she went to Berkeley. And he said: 'You know, I'd like to come up to Vancouver and read.' And they arranged a reading in

general attention (probably thru Warren Tallman & Miss Hindmarch) in Vancouver in the fall of that year. — ed.

the Tallman's basement in December.[2] This was just previous to the *New American* anthology coming out, and he was just fantastic, but 'Strawberries Under The Snow' would be the only poem you could make any sense of, and his sense of understanding, it was just this guy doing this huge dance with words, and nothing like anyone had ever heard—sort of a foreign language, but you know it's English.

People like Bobby Hogg came in from Chilliwack or Abbotsford, whichever one it is. Frank brought his old high school teacher, Alan Dawe. Bobby Hogg was still in Grade Twelve at that time.

So now let's flip back to the summer. We were going to get Duncan up here to tell us a little bit about Creeley and Olson. But all Dunky talks about is Robert Duncan... he has such an expansive mind though, just so total in encouraging you to write your way through life. He just lives in the world of life and writing. You get all sorts of charges going, even if we didn't get that far on Charles, we kept hearing about this *huge* man.

And Duncan arranged a reading at the end of that, which, for some reason or other, I didn't go to—I don't think I was asked to—it was just that he asked poets—and David Dawson wrote 'Fart In The Snow' for that, and Fred had three poems, and after that reading it was decided they would start *Tish*.

Warren sort of objected to it, and Duncan encouraged it. I think it was sort of a manoeuver on Warren's part—to object—so that they had to have a certain strength, to pull together and do it—which they did.

from Oral History of Vancouver

[2] Possibly December 1959.

Stan Persky's Section
from *Oral History of Vancouver*

Brad Robinson

Brad Robinson: Okay, you came up here in 66. Prior to that time, you must have heard of Vancouver, & what sense did you have of what you were coming to?

Stan Persky: My first strong notion that there was a place called Vancouver had to do with *Tish* & George Bowering. About 1961-62, I was involved with the publicity for Jack Spicer's book, *The Heads of the Town up to the Ether*, & it was a typical San Francisco comic opera that was taking place, in which Spicer wanted certain kinds of advertising, he immediately hated the publisher about one day after it came out, it looked like an army manual rather than a book of poems. I sent a copy of the book up to Bowering, to this guy George Bowering. I didn't know Bowering from borscht at this point, & Bowering wrote a review of it . . .

Robinson: He didn't like surrealism . . .

Persky: . . . & he was just in a complete fog, but it was a guy who read a book & wrote a review of it, & there weren't any other reviews of it, there weren't many others, & that was a review. *Tish* at least was oriented enough to what was going on to write a review of it. He said he didn't like surrealism. He obviously didn't understand what Spicer meant by "surrealism," so I wrote Bowering back one of my typical vicious postcards at that time, & Bowering said, "Why don't I just publish your postcard?" & I said, "Why don't you just read the book again?" It was one of those typical literary impasses. All this wouldn't be too important except that Spicer comes to play a rather curious role in Vancouver within about three years. Then there's another incident that takes place in 1964. In 1964 I was editing *Open Space* magazine in San Francisco, & one of the things that did come across my field of vision was this absolutely horrible piece of writing by someone named Carol Berge, which was titled *The Vancouver Report*, an account of this conference that took place in Vancouver, so I knew that something was going on there. She had a horrible passage about Robert Duncan, & we reprinted this passage from *The Vancouver Report* in *Open Space* as a satire of how stupid a description of anything can be. All thru this there was some kind of idea that there was something going on.

Robinson: Were you aware of the conference up here?

Persky: Not really at all. Spicer came up to Vancouver, I think, in early 1965, so Warren Tallman must have been aware of Spicer's work at that time. He may have become aware of it thru Duncan or something. I'm trying to figure out how it was that I met Vancouverians from the first moment, & at this moment the first thing that occurs to me is that Spicer is back in San Francisco, & we're doing our absolutely epically typical thing sitting in Gino & Carlo's Bar, & it's the Berkeley Poetry Conference of July, 1965. Now I was up in Vancouver once before with Spicer & Blaser in a bus. We read at the New Design Gallery there, & we stayed at Tallman's house. The gallery was run by Gerry Geisler at this time, which was later turned into the Adrienne Campbell Fashion School—this house was painted a wild, heliotrope color, & now that entire block, which is right over Burrard Bridge, is completely wiped out. We're sitting in this bar. Now another thing flashes in on me. My first impression of Vancouver is of being lost in Vancouver; that is, it's night time, it's dark, we're coming over a bridge, & I can never figure out which way we're going during those first two days. I know where the Tallmans' house is, & I don't know where anything else is located, no sense of map. Now I do remember a sense of coming over a bridge—it may have been the Oak Street bridge. I have a vague memory of some huge billboards: "Shell welcomes you to British Columbia," so that would be the Oak Street bridge, rather than coming over Burrard or Lion's Gate . . . that confusion. We're sitting in Gino & Carlo's Bar, & Harold Dull is there, I am there, & all of a sudden these people who have heard Jack Spicer read . . . I guess he read in February of 1965 at the Arts Festival in Vancouver . . . two birds came in. The way they sort of zoomed into the bar, right to Spicer, was like the way two seagulls come across the horizon, & Harold Dull, who's a gull man . . . it was really comic the way these people just homed in on Spicer. It was Rick Byrne & Dennis Wheeler. It took me thirty seconds to decide I was in love with Rick Byrne. I think it took Jack Spicer about thirty seconds to have gotten interested in Dennis Wheeler as a person. They had heard Spicer, so at this point I must have already met Gladys Hindmarch. It was also my first kind of contact. She came down to Berkeley. Neap Hoover was down there. I remember reading in the New Design Gallery looking at the room, & you know how you look at people you don't know. I remember looking at a guy . . . there's no word between "man" & "boy" in our language, a guy with blond hair & incredibly intense eyes, & it took me thirty seconds to fall in love with that person without knowing him. That must have been Neap Hoover at that time.

So those were flashes, rumors down the coast that there was another city on the coast, which was curious, because Seattle & Portland which are two obvious cities where poets ought to be & there ought to be scenes, don't have any poets & don't have any scenes. & of course I had a contemptuous view of Vancouver poets, having looked at some *Tishes*, & oh yeah, Robert Duncan is writing some essay called "The Novitiates of Vancouver," & we figure, yeah, that's Duncan doing his typical thing of getting interested in local people, making sure that he'll get invited back, & at that point I was under the influence of Spicer, who was conducting a great war against Duncan. I had what seemed a jaundiced, unserious view, it seemed like imitative poetry, though at this point I would have no objection to imitation. It would seem to be the road to the road. Eventually, I get here. Blaser & I are living together in San Francisco, & Robin is finally sick of working in libraries, & finally gets a job thru Warren, & then thru Warren he meets Ralph Maud, & between them all they wrangle Robin a job teaching at Simon Fraser. We were due to come up to Vancouver in July of '66, Robin's due to come a month later, & at that point I'm living with Robin. Right now it's just not possible to say what the state of our relationship is. I don't seem to have enough distance . . . a love affair that was so intense, & so thoroughly confused in my own mind, & for my life in Vancouver, our relationship as lovers lasted until May of 1968, but all thru that period it was a complete entanglement. It is particularly entangling because my normal pattern of falling in love is to find this beautiful young person & then fall in love with that person, & see if that person's a person. & with Robin, it was completely the other way around. He was this absolute master of poetry. He was one of the three immortals of San Francisco, & I'd fallen in love with that person, who also happened to be very physically beautiful, like Cocteau being beautiful. But my own confusion about my sexuality in terms of our relationship, I'm still too close to sort it out. But in coming here, from that point I was completely tied up with Rick Byrne, in a love affair with Rick, & Rick was the image of a young poet . . . this was a guy who might turn out to become a poet . . . we didn't know if he would be a poet. I may have also been in love simultaneously with Neap at that time, Neap Hoover, who was also a young poet, a guy who had come from Vernon. If I've got the story straight, Neap Hoover & his wife Leni — & Leni is Glady's sister — all of these things are neatly tied together . . . Neap Hoover, & Leni, whom I disliked intensely over her advantages, were living in Arrowhead for the winter. They were teaching school in this small town, Arrowhead. Now I remember better. Spicer came back from his third trip to British Columbia, which was in June of 1965. The poetry conference was in July of 1965, & that's when we see Dennis Wheeler, Rick Byrne, & Gladys Hindmarch, but Spicer has made his real connection in June of '65, in which he gave three small lectures here which are now known as the Vancouver Lectures, which were Spicer's first statement of his own poetics. When he came back from Vancouver, he looked incredibly healthy. There was an image of radiant Jack. & while he was in Vancouver, he had clearly something that corresponds to poetic vision, & at that time he was writing his last book, *Book of Magazine Verse*, & a section of that book is for the Vancouver festival, & in those seven poems there's a vision of a city located in the mountains. He had gone up with Ellen Tallman to North Vancouver, up in Capilano Canyon, & he had some kind of vision of the Runciple Mountains, imaginary mountains in which a city made of diamonds was located, & this played on Spicer's own pun & fascination with baseball diamonds as a metaphor, & so there was a real vision of that thing. Spicer came back & participated in the Berkeley conference in July of 1965 & died in August of 1965. So I was already in communication with Gladys, & somehow, since I was responsible for Spicer in some personal way over the last two years of his life, I was also responsible for communicating the death news & telling about that. Gladys recently showed me the letter I had written about Jack, about the last meetings with Spicer, & at that time I had made some kind of arrangement that I should write to Neap in this desolate Arrowhead as a kind of contact, & wrote him a series of love letters over the winter. So maybe I was still in love with Neap, but upon arriving here, that relationship became more real, i.e., it dissolved. Leni really broke thru to me, so that I could see that their relationship was a real relationship, not half the secret fantasy of my relationship with Neap, & so Rick Byrne was clearly the focus of my interest during that time.

Robinson: I can recall the first time meeting you was in the cafeteria up at UBC, about some rock & roll, no, blues show, that you were associated with, or something like that. & it had the white rabbit insignia. But I do remember that very early on, when you started getting involved with politics, the public life . . .

Persky: Yeah, so the issue here is personal, if we're trying to deal with the issue of how does a poet live & what does a poet do. For me at that time, that period was very difficult as a writer. I was unclear about myself as a writer. I had written in 1959, a kind of early brilliance among San Francisco poets. & by 1965 I was absolutely puzzled as a writer. I wrote very few poems. I'd been given Spicer's world . . . that is, when you're that age, in your early twenties, what you're looking for is a world that you can believe in & work within. So every time I wrote a poem I thought it had to be in Spicer's world. I had to say to myself, is this poem really being dictated from the source that dictates poetry? Is this really a line of poetry? & I was hooked into the imitation of it. Now, at this point, I see myself on the other side of that, & see that Spicer's theory of poetics is a great theory, but not necessarily one that I have to make my world — that's clear. When I got here in 1966, the first things that happened to me had not so much to do with writing, since I seemed to be displaced as a writer. I didn't know what I was doing at all. The first things were political, that is, I went to a meeting . . . I had signed up at UBC. I had heard a rumor that there wasn't adequate housing for students, & a meeting was being held at somebody's house. At that point I was very non-political. My political concerns were accidental. That is, I'd had one experience in Berkeley in 1965, going with Allen Ginsberg to a meeting of the Vietnam Steering Committee & marching in Berkeley in a parade over Vietnam without knowing very much about it. So my own political sense . . . I sort of followed politics the way people follow hockey or baseball, but I didn't see that politics had to do with me in any way. & I came to find out that politics had to do with me by accident. I went to this meeting of these people who were political, & they proposed that they would set up some tents in the main mall at UBC to demonstrate the inadequacy of housing. There was a tent-in, & I participated in this tent-in. Rick Byrne & I went & slept in a tent, another place to sleep with Rick Byrne at that point. Also hard to know what to do with that love—that was a powerful kind of love. I became more involved, increasingly involved, with politics.

Robinson: At this time you're still living with Robin who was . . .

Persky: Yeah, I was very concerned with Robin as a poet at that time. With his writing. I was having a long correspondence with George Stanley, which seemed to consist largely of letters about why I can't write & why I'm not a writer. I went thru a kind of dead phase. I looked through some old materials about a month ago & saw a page out of 1966-67, in which I said I'm paralyzed as a writer. I had thought ever since I was 13 that I was a writer. I even thought first I was a journalist, & then I discovered that you could think you were a writer. At age 12 or 13 I edited an imaginary newspaper in my own room, I had secret fantasies of writing. But ever since I was 16, I learned I was a writer. I learned in San Francisco when I was 18 & 19 that I was a writer. I got stuck with the identification in my own mind, & suddenly about age 25 I had to think, well, maybe you're not a writer. Maybe writing isn't the only road to salvation, the only way that a person becomes a person. Maybe you become a person, period. Which I later learned from Gestalt therapy. But in any case, you do have to do something, like the question what to do with yourself was a question for me; & then at that point I thought I would be an anthropologist. Right now that strikes me as one of the most incredible notions in the world, that I was so lost that I thought I could be an anthropologist. It's very clear that one of my dangers is diffusion of my own power thru editing. As it turns out, I'm a lovely editor. I have a care & a talent & an instinct for showing other people's work to its best advantage, & that's a trap as well as a gift. That is, you can become interested in printing other people's work & not write.

Robinson: To what extent were you involved with the early development of *Iron*? Were you in that at all?

Persky: No. My interest in terms of magazines, was *Tish*. My secret plot was to capture control of *Tish*, & it seems like right now we've still got this problem of Canadian-American; that certainly weighs on my mind now in some ways since we have this cultural nationalism. That's something we have to face these days. But at that time I wasn't thinking that. I was thinking, well, *Tish* is the magazine in town, so *Tish* is the magazine you're supposed to be, & I didn't really get involved with *Tish* until around '68. *Tish* at that time was going thru a very desultory existence. McLeod was sort of haphazardly editing it, & in 1967 he started the *Georgia Straight*.

Robinson: There was well over a year between *Tish* 40 & 41.

Persky: & then you & Dan . . .

Robinson: Colin & Neap were supposed to be in on that.

Persky: . . . got together, & I had some notion of publishing another *Tish*. That is, I'd keep the title & publish another magazine called *Tish Local*, so there'd be this wierd circumstance, ironic circumstance, which I'm attracted to . . .

Robinson: I remember during that period one of your concerns was to set up a *Vancouver Review of Books*.

Persky: Yeah, I tried to do that with . . .

Robinson: The Niagara . . . the Quadra . . .

Persky: The Quadra Foundation, named for Vancouver y Quadra Islands. One of the first things I did in coming up here was I went to the Public Library in San Francisco & got my hands on every journal I could find that had to do with how men first came to this particular place—Vancouver. I read a lovely edition by Shepherd, of Alexander MacKenzie's journals, a really beautiful edition by Shepherd, published by the University of California. I read the absolutely dull journals of Simon Fraser. I read a lot of stuff on David Thompson, a lot of books around it, the De Boto materials, for example. & that was like my first way of coming to this place, & seeing this town from Granville Bridge, that is looking out over that industrial pit & seeing the dirty dinge of Vancouver, the thirtyish quality of it, & yet I finally did have a direction at that point. Somebody very quickly told me you could never get lost in Vancouver, because if you could see mountains, you were looking north, & that was a lovely piece of information, because then you always knew where you were. That was the most helpful thing that I got.

I almost published an issue of *Tish* while I was in San Francisco in 1965. Spicer, who was up here at the time, was supposed to send down some poems from young poets that he found, & his own poems for *Tish*. He did three poems for *Tish* which never got published at that time in *Tish*. They later did. He was going to send this down & I was going to mimeograph off an issue of *Tish* & zoom it back up to Spicer. It's that demand for the imaginative that characterizes the politics of poetry that I knew that immediately attracted my attention. Only after breaking up with Robin in May of 1968 did I come back to being a writer, clearly engaged as a writer. It was at that time I was actually able to think about *Tish* & getting involved with *Tish* & eventually ending up with *Tish* in my hands.

Robinson: Doing it for one issue or two?

Persky: I did it for about three or four issues until I really came to the conclusion that it shouldn't exist, that it was false for it to exist. I was never very interested in *Talon* or *blew ointment*, that is Jim Brown's or Bill Bissett's concerns which are also long-standing here. '68 . . . coming back . . . I must have something here which will get me back to where I am. Yeah. All the time I was up here I began to develop a migratory pattern of going up & down the coast. That's one thing very strong in me now, that migratory quality of my life. There's still people in San Francisco & Bolinas that I stay close to, & so it's going down thru Washington, Oregon, California, back up thru California, Oregon, Washington across the Nicomeld & Serpentine, back to this place . . . that kind of pattern stays in mind. In August 1967 I wrote a poem of that title. It was really very clear between Robin & me that this wasn't going to go on very much longer. It was really too painful & too complicated. I'd written about that in *The Day*—about three men in a triangular pattern, what kind of shape does that make. It has that kind of quality. In August 1967 I went down & visited George Stanley, who becomes really my closest friend in a deep strange way, & at that point I'm saying . . . I'm trying to locate where I am in relation to these two places, & I say something like "I have come from in the north," not my country, because Canada clearly wasn't my country at this point. But I've come from the north, down the coast, not believing the rain on my window, or the scattered cities or the network of stars. My search at that point is that I'm looking for the source of feeling is what that poem talks about, & in the north I'm a gyroscope, radio transmitter, reflecting body, so I must have an image of myself as a kind of disembodied energy, floating—the image of a gyroscope in there. & that was the first hint that I was coming back to a kind of writing, & then in December '67 or early '68 I was in love with Russ Precious. At this time again, it was clear that we were going our separate ways in terms of love & I wrote a thing called *Spanish Banks Poem*, which is the first place which clearly located me only in this place, in only this love. I'm fascinated by a field down by Belmont & Discovery St. There's a sunken field, & so most of the year during the rainy season, that field is flooded, & there are stands of trees growing out of the water. In the winter it freezes over & there's trees growing out of an ice pond, & then that's where I located myself. & saying the word "Discovery," having read the journals & history, I knew the Discovery was Captain Vancouver's ship for charting these waters & these coasts in 1792. So it's at that point that I'm located here, & it's in that poem I locate myself along that Spanish Banks beach, & so a poem says, what are the boundaries of your world, the boundaries of the world as it exists in the act of that writing, & at that moment, the boundaries of my world extended from the Jericho military barracks to the tower at Wreck Beach. Ironically enough, both of the boundaries of my world in literal-political terms, there's kind of a nice irony, have both exploded, like the edges of the world have exploded—the Jericho thing exploding as a youth hostel situation & demonstration last summer, & the same thing at Wreck Beach when people finally take off their clothes & get arrested for being naked. That makes up these Spanish Banks of that time.

& also some sense of Musqueam people . . . the land around that area is Musqueam reservation at the edge of the University of British Columbia. Musqueam still fish for shad down in those waters, so that's my literal world, & my emotional world is the sense of feeling lowdown on all fours, what they say is worshipping someone, & realizing that this is the story of myself taking place in this landscape. At the time we were living in that house. These were like the first waking up poems from a sleep. At this moment, like talking to you now, I don't know literally if I'm a poet. I feel such doubt, I must be back into that doubt that I'm remembering. That doubt has such deep pain & fearfulness, that it reappears in my body at this moment of talking about it & looking at these particular poems. But these are the first poems — like "You're writing again. Yeah, your entire life consists of about six or seven poems & maybe a short story that you've written in the last year." That's what this is saying. & each one of these poems I notice now is very local, that is . . . a poem called "Meeting Her," where an old woman carrying plants, lettuce that she's planted in the public forests, on the

University Endowment Lands, comes out of the fringe to the Blanca Street bus terminal, & I have a wierd moment with her when I recognize I'm meeting some figure that gives us extensions beyond our recognitions of the human boundaries, & that moment taking place for me....

Robinson: A lot of those early pieces, I remember the word around the community that Stan is writing again. It seemed to be founded on very fortuitous occasions, like sudden jerks back into remembering who you are. Like there's a certain reawakening.

Persky: I almost want to deny the loss. I wanted to deny that I was lost, so at this moment I want to say, Oh no... I want to give you some other image. Like, I was writing all along & it just looked like I wasn't writing. Now I accept that I was not writing, that I thought I was not going to be a poet, that I had to give up poetry, that I could not be a poet. Why is it so important? Why do you have to be a poet? That's a nice thing, though. I'm sure that people rarely hear that from poets, that that's one activity that exists... Right now I very clearly treat writing as one of many human activities. It's an activity that I most dearly know. Creeley has that phrase that "writing is the activity that gives me the most open condition of possibility of the world. In poems I've borne testament to my life in ways that no other possibilities could afford." I guess I have that sense that it's an activity. Of course my political sense tells me that it's an activity. I am sort of attracted by the theory of what a man is as a worker, how he works, & I come up to this room that we're sitting in now, this study, & I do my work—I work early in the morning. I get up early and write...

Robinson: What kind of role did you play in *Pacific Nation*?

Persky: Robin wanted to edit the magazine. Again, we enter the moments of comic opera. I'm absolutely fascinated by how silly poets are. "Silly" is also a word that used to mean "blessed" or something like that, as Jack Spicer once remarked. Just the silliness of us in a struggle. Robin wanted to edit the magazine. Jack Spicer, who was, strangely enough, a very political kind of man, he was deeply engaged in politics as you can see in his letters to Graham McIntosh which have been published in *Caterpillar*, that he really was a kind of Lewis Carroll type anarchist, very connected in that way with other poets who have been surrealists & political, & Spicer proposed that this really was the Pacific Nation, that's what our geography must be, outside of the actual practical problems we have politically, that is, the fact that Canada is a colony of the United States economically. But there was a thing that poets could identify with, their boundary was Pacific Nation, this strip of land down the Pacific coast, from Northern California thru British Columbia, & extending a little eastward, so we wanted to maintain that image of the Pacific Nation, & Robin wanted to edit a magazine, or I wanted Robin to edit a magazine, I guess, I can't quite tell. We published... when did we publish the first issue then? '67 maybe? Yeah, June of '67. It took months & months to get together, because Robin had such high standards of eloquence. The best summation of *Pacific Nation*, which lasted for two issues, though Robin continues to fantasize about it, was Robert Duncan's remark: "Well, yes, Robin, it's very nice that you've promised to edit the magazine for a period of five years, but you didn't tell us there'd only be two issues in five years." *Pacific Nation* as a concept never became clear at all.

Robinson: & yet the one appearance was very pivotal. You'd get a lot of local poets rubbing shoulders with the big stars, or whatever.

Persky: I think the second issue came out early in 1969. At that point the situation is kind of changed. In terms of my actual relations with writers here, there's a different story to tell. When you're in love with someone who wants to be a writer, you try to be helpful, & usually you're not helpful. I sound just like Jack Spicer saying that. One person I was helpful to was Gladys. Gladys was a completely puzzled writer & she had indicated something as simple as she wanted to write about her experiences working on boats along the British Columbia coast as a cook & a mess girl, & I said, Okay, Gladys, you go into your room (in this green building at 1607 Yew Street, a wooden green building which is now being torn down. She was living there in this apartment, & she was just starting to live there with Cliff Andstein), & I said, You go into your room & you write for one hour a day, & it started out in just as simple a way as that, &

then I'd come over the next day & she'd read to me what she'd written, & so I used to drive her. I was like the whip, & this is part of that editing talent, that thing of getting a person to do what she wanted to do all along anyway. I was really helpful to her. & she began, sat down to write on a regular basis. & pretty soon she was writing the kind of writing that we haven't seen here at all, a quality of writing that hadn't existed here at all. The quality of this book that she's now been writing for a period of four years or more, a series of boat stories, has its predecessor in Ed Dorn's *Rites of Passage*, the closest relative as a piece of writing, & suddenly all the properties of her mind have become revealed in her ability to work. Not only is the boat book going, but a whole kind of other writing is now available for her. & she is very clear as a writer in a way that's very interesting, because in some way we have to talk about George Bowering & Fred Wah, Frank Davey & Jamie Reid & David Dawson, & what's happening to them as writers. I still have harsh judgements about them, & it's painful to make harsh judgements. Fred Wah stands for me as a very real, clear, distinct, isolate man, who's clearly a poet. I was brought up short in August of 1969 by Warren Tallman. We were at his house. (This is a real turning point.) This was just before I thought about the first *Writing Supplement*, which came out in October 1969. I had done a few issues of *Tish* & Warren was encouraging me; Jim Brown had come out with this anthology called *West Coast Seen*, in which he used the concept of a Pacific Nation ironically enough, & George Stanley & I were putting it down & we were saying we'd have something called the *Vancouver Herd,* & Warren suddenly lashed out, that slow, northwest coast kind of anger, & it seemed to be at George, but it was really at me. Not to make an extravagant soap opera out of it, the message was, You aren't taking seriously the writers who are the writers of this place. Pay attention.

& that certainly has led me, did lead me back immediately to read *Tish* from its inception, from the authentic first nineteen issues edited by Frank Davey, to try & understand what that is, even where I'm not sympathetic, to try to understand that this constitutes the writing . . . poetry that this city actually has for ten years, eleven years, twelve years, right now, that kind of thing where you can say this is the beginning of poetry in this particular place. Suddenly the city has an imagination. It didn't have one before, a collectivity. Suddenly people are writing as Vancouver poets. Not only did it drive me back to have to face that, it also started me writing a book called *The Day*, & so I ended up describing being in Warren Tallman's house, which for me is the center of the city (I don't mean this in descriptive terms, but as a purely personal focus of energy). This is where the city is located, this is the ark. How many times have how many people been sweating, dancing, drinking, shouting, screaming, cuddling up to each other within these walls of this house. How many times has Warren pulled out another case of Carling Black Label beer? That's the image, & that's what allows me to say it starts with this, which is like the first statement of the day, it starts with this, being in that house, & then having that, being faced with Warren, who I was trying to shuck off as this fuzzy-headed sympathetic guy who gets on to right things, but really doesn't know the difference between good poetry & any kind of poetry. So that's a big start for me, in that it really starts me writing a book here which I wrote all thru 1969, 1970, called *The Day*, & I'm still working on the revision which turns out to be the simplification of that piece of work.

Beaver Kosmos Folio 5

Black Days on Black Mountain

Frank Davey

In the last few years it seems to have become fashionable, for a few Canadian 'critics' at least, to blame what they variously call the 'Black Mountain group', or the 'Pound and Williams school', or the 'Olson-Jones school', for much of what they see wrong with new Canadian poetry. What this school or group has done to earn its position of chief whipping-boy, or from what its allegedly pernicious effect actually stems, is seldom clear. For these 'critics', the very invocation of the words 'Black Mountain', 'Pound', or 'William Carlos Williams' seems sufficient to call up all the evils that can befall poetry, and they therefore scorn to add any arguments or evidence to support their innuendo.

Examples of this new fashion in literary slander are not difficult to find. In *Canadian Literature* 21 Marya Fiamengo thought it sufficient to say that George Bowering 'believes in Charles Olson, something called "locus" and a general attitude that might be defined as "the poet as a semi-literate garage mechanic" ' to explain the source of all his alleged shortcomings. Robin Skelton in the same issue says of Bowering, Lionel Kearns, and others that they 'have been affected to their disadvantage by the work of William Carlos Williams, and some of the Black Mountain poets.' Neither writer seeks to define what this being 'affected to their disadvantage' might consist of, how a 'Black Mountain' influence can be harmful, or even what 'Black Mountain' theories are. Skelton is silly enough to conclude his review by suggesting that Canadian poets 'throw away their copies of Layton, Souster, and Donald Allen's Anthology' again without offering one hint as to why he thinks these harmful, or even without showing any evidence that he might have read one or two of them. In each case the reviewer acts as if the harmfulness of 'Black Mountain' ideas were an established fact, as if there were no more need of proof of this than of the evilness of Satan.

Most bigotry being the result of ignorance, I suggest that this deliberate snubbing of 'Black Mountain' is from the same cause. Miss Fiamengo displays her ignorance openly, her 'something called "locus" ' being a stupidly non-comprehending comment about one of the more accessible parts of 'Black Mountain' theorizing. And though Mr Skelton does not give himself away quite as badly, his failure to point directly at one weakness in 'Black Mountain' writing, or to suggest one link between 'Black Mountain' failures and the alleged effects to disadvantage, leads one to suspect strongly that he is unable to do so. For to impugn something you know well without giving one's reasons is to disqualify oneself as a critic, and although such disqualification might not be too unhappy an event for criticism in Mr Skelton's case, I am sure he would not wish it to happen. One can only believe, then, that he impugned something of which he knew little, which leaves him still a critic, but a slovenly one.

Miss Fiamengo and Mr Skelton are certainly not alone in their lack of knowledge, however. Across Canada, suspicion of 'Black Mountain' theories is eclipsed only by total ignorance. Most of the reviews of Ryerson's *Poésie/Poetry 64*, in which the work of at least four of the English-language poets falls under the American influence, shows a conspicuous unawareness of 'Black Mountain's' existence, and the few that mention it at all do so only with sneers at the derivative.

For the good of Canadian poetry, both the ignorance and the suspicion of 'Black Mountain' should be dispelled quickly. Firstly, derivativeness is an irrelevant issue, all good poets being derivative in the sense that they all accept established techniques and theories that they feel to be useful. Actually, if Tom Farley's appraisal in the Winter 1964 *Canadian Author and Bookman*, of the history of Canadian poetry is at all correct, Canadian poets should be stampeding everywhere in a search for useful theories; by turning a blind eye to 'Black Mountain' and all other foreign influences they will merely restrict the boundaries of literary possibility unmercifully. Secondly, a large number of recent Canadian poets have already had considerable contact with 'Black Mountain', and whether critics like it or not, these probably constitute our major poetic tradition and Canada's best chance for an important poetry. Dudek, Layton, and Sutherland edited *First Statement* in the early 1940's under a definite American influence, particularly that of the 'Black Mountain' hero, William Carlos Williams. Dudek's moving to New York to attend Columbia University brought him into personal contact with two of the founders of the New American Poetry, Paul Blackburn and Cid Corman, and strongly under the influence of the poetry of Williams and Pound. His changing literary orientations were reflected at that time in the contents of *Contact*, edited in Toronto by his friend Raymond Souster, and later in the magazine begun by Dudek, Layton, and Souster together, *CIV/n*, to which Pound was to write, '*CIV/n* not a one man job.'

From *CIV/n*, the magazine modelled on the first 'Black Mountain' journal, Cid Corman's *Origin*, has evolved not only our country's most dependable publisher of poetry, Contact Press, but also the junior magazine *Cataract*, and Dudek's own ventures, *Delta* and the McGill Poetry Series. Whether Canada likes it or not, through this work of Dudek, Layton (who taught at Black Mountain College), and Souster, Black Mountain has come to influence the careers of Eli Mandel, Phyllis Webb, F.R. Scott, W.W.E. Ross, Daryl Hine, Milton Acorn, R.G. Everson, Eldon Grier, George Walton, Alden Nowlan, George Ellenbogen, Michael Malus, Leonard Cohen, D.G. Jones, Alfred Purdy, Peter Miller, David Solway, and Gwendolyn MacEwen. In fact the work of Layton, Souster, and Dudek preceded a direct 'Black Mountain' influence to the West Coast; Kearns, Bowering, and myself were being unwittingly prepared for Olson through *Delta* as early as 1957. Even *Tamarack Review* can claim relatives on Black Mountain. The recent undisguised 'Black Mountain' philosophy that emerged from Vancouver's *Tish*, however, caught everyone unaware of Canada's previous and widespread literary entanglement in the movement. Among those most deceived were, ironically, such poets as Henry Moscovitch and K.V. Hertz, Layton siblings who should have perhaps been most informed.

The fact is that even excluding such unashamedly pro-'Black Mountain' publications as *Island*, *Tish*, and *Image*, the recent literary history of Canada is affected to a greater degree by the 'Black Mountain' movement than that of the U.S. itself. Not only are the 'Black Mountain'-oriented poets, Layton and Souster, the best of their generation, but even the Reaney reaction and the Birney regeneration can be accorded to stimuli of 'Black Mountain' origin. And yet by and large both the second-generation poets of the Layton-Dudek orbits and Canadian critics in general remain convinced that the 'Black Mountain' movement, the headwater of most recent Canadian poetry, had been safely dyked in by the International Boundary until the breakthrough at Peace Arch Park. Surely it is time for a full-scale analysis of 'Black Mountain' history and theory so that all Canadians interested in poetry can know precisely what tradition lies behind the literary renaisance that their country has experienced since 1951 and *CIV/n*.

It seems astounding that this tradition is so little known, especially when one realizes that the antecedents of the 'Black Mountain' movement are clear and that its beliefs are spelled out in various little magazines in both poetry and prose. Admittedly, the collecting and reading of the relevant materials take some effort, but when one considers the effort other critics have expended in life-long textual scholarship in the work of early writers, the effort of research required to excavate Black Mountain seems little less than insignificant. 'Black Mountain' writers have not been reluctant to express their views on poetry, and have openly acknowledged their indebtedness to Pound and William Carlos Williams, both of whose critical writings are easily obtainable.

However, lacking the space for a thorough presentation, I shall try to indicate here the location of some 'Black Mountain' material and to summarize the more important ideas. First, I should perhaps attempt to discourage the use of the rather 'cute' 'Black Mountain' tag, for beside inviting glibness, it suggests a uniformity of style that is not verified by comparison of the writers' works. Writers herded into the critics' Black Mountain corral do share certain antecedents, certain ideas about the language of poetry, and a general respect for the concepts of man and life projected by Charles Olson, but definitely use various and conflicting approaches in writing, and frequently do not agree personally with Olson's philosophies. If these writers must be classified (and one must remember that classification is one of Olson's most frequent targets), it would be better to unite them under a tag that at least suggests their points of agreement, a tag that perhaps suggests their preoccupation with precision and directness of language, rather than to leave them grouped under one that tends to imply total cohesion and derivativeness. I use the old 'Black Mountain' tag here only because I wish my readers to recognize my subject and to get a little knowledge of the several principles shared by the people so unfortunately tied together.

Language and form are the two areas in which there is the most agreement among writers included in 'Black Mountain,' and are perhaps the only areas in which a group label could be fortuitously applied. The theories of language here had their infancy in the Imagists' rebellion against the verbiage of the Georgians. The three-point 'Imagist Manifesto' drawn up in 1912 by Pound, H.D., and Aldington has been enlarged by 'Black Mountain' writers but never repudiated.

1. Direct treatment of the 'thing' whether subjective or objective.

2. To use absolutely no word that does not contribute to the presentation.

3. As regarding rhythm: to compose in the sequence of the musical phrase, not in sequence of a metronome.

Here in points 1 and 2 is the basis of the 'Black Mountain' writers' suspicion of metaphor (the relating of something in indirect or alien terms) and of simile (the defining of something in terms of something else, thus detracting from its own uniqueness). 'Similie', says Charles Olson in a betraying metaphor, 'is only one bird who comes down, too easily.' It comes down simply because it diverts the writer's energy and the reader's attention from the central engagement. Stated baldly, simile at its worst is digression, and metaphor at its worst circumlocution—'at its worst' being when the shock of identification is not immediate and exact. Thus, contrary to Marya Fiamengo, Bowering's 'INDIAN SUMMER FOR GOD'S SAKE!' is more direct, precise, and effective than the circumlocutory 'Winter coming an injection/in the veins of September', which latter (I have tested this) takes even an experienced academic ten or more emotion-dulling seconds to unravel.

'Black Mountain' writing, then, and certainly the best of Layton and Souster, is austere in language for good reason. Pound quickly added to the manifesto the corollaries: 'use no superfluous word', 'go in fear of abstractions', 'don't be descriptive', and 'the proper and perfect symbol is the natural object'. His successors, aided by his continual proclaiming of himself in the *Cantos* as a nominalist hater of all abstractions and idealisms, his attempt to use words and word clusters as objects, as 'ideas in action' rather than as detested concepts, and by both his and William Carlos Williams' resulting use of clear unqualified images, have parlayed these into a tough, no-nonsense kind of verse. In fact the 'Black Mountain' writers' care for language, care to have the meanings of words based in the senses, such as Creeley's halting, haunting precision,

> I spent a night turning in bed,
> my love was a feather, a flat
>
> sleeping thing. She was
> very white
>
> and quiet, and above us on
> the roof, there was another woman I

122

also loved, . . .

has brought about in poetry the situation envisioned by Pound in 1911.

> As to Twentieth century poetry, and the poetry which I expect to see written during the next decade or so, it will, I think, move against poppy-cock, it will be harder and saner, it will be what Mr Hewlett calls 'nearer the bone'. It will be as much like granite as it can be, its force will lie in its truth, its interpretative power (of course, poetic force does always rest there); I mean it will not try to seem forcible by rhetorical aid, and luxurious riot. We will have fewer painted adjectives impeding the shock and stroke of it. At least for myself, I want it so, austere, direct, free from emotional slither.

The realization of this took longer than a decade. What Robert Duncan calls 'small-town protestantism' led by Tate, Ransom, and Auden at the *Kenyon Review* fought a passionless delaying action. Pound was locked in Purgatorio until Hugh Kenner and the 1950s, and the clean language of the new poetry did not emerge fully in the U.S. until 1960.

But it emerged, and startingly, in Canada with Layton, Dudek, and Souster more quickly than in the U.S., and accompanied by a revolution in form that also had its birth deep in the work of Ezra Pound. 'I have seen what I have seen', Acoetes tells Pentheus in *Canto II*, and Pound also in the *Cantos* has seen no more, can tell the reader no more. He would give the reader his eyes, if he could, for there is no other way to preserve the integrity of the things he wishes the reader to see but to make the reader follow him through the actual experience of direct sight. George Dekker has commented that Pound's method throughout the *Cantos* is based on 'his conviction that the things the poet sees in the sea of events are really there. They are not creations of his.' Thus Pound presents the masses of direct quotations which force the reader to duplicate the poet's experience. These experiences, the poet's materials, have a reality of their own, 'the god is inside the stone', and, as Dekker continues, 'the poet, like the sculptor, like the male, releases the form which is imminent in his materials; he does not impose a form on them. . . .'

From this nominalist respect for reality to the 'Black Mountain' theories of Charles Olson and Robert Creeley is hardly a step. If a man 'sprawl', says Olson, 'he shall find little to sing but himself. . . . But if he stays inside himself, if he is contained within his nature as he is participant in the larger force, he will be able to listen, and his hearing through himself will give him secrets objects share.' Which is precisely what Pound knew, when he preserved his materials in their original, objective form. In fact Olson says that 'Objectism is the getting rid of the lyrical interference of the individual as ego, of the "subject" and his soul', and is merely 'objectism' that Pound uses to preserve the integrity of actual experience. Further, Olson quotes Creeley as suggesting that 'FORM IS NEVER MORE THAN AN EXTENSION OF CONTENT', which is really only a more concise way of phrasing Dekker's 'the poet . . . releases the form which is immanent in his materials; he does not impose a form on them. . . .'

Again, then, 'Black Mountain' theories are not very new and not very mysterious. And I believe it would be exceedingly difficult to prove them either useless or harmful, as long as they are applied properly, especially since they are built on sound philosophical foundations. The 'philosophy' normally attributed to 'Black Mountain', the 'philosophy' of Charles Olson, seems at times no more than a working out of the implications of Pound's respect for his materials. Respect for one's materials is hardly a useful thing in a civilization built on the ruthless exploitation of nature. Few lumbermen can look at a tree and see more than a few hundred thousand board feet of timber. Rarely in the century except in the writings of the existentialist philosophers is there any suggestion that man might be little more than a working partner with his fellow man and fellow members of the universe. Rarely except in Pound or the existentialists is there any hint that a writer should not force his materials in the direction that his ego desires, or that a man should not treat his fellow men as either keys or blocks to the gratification of his own ego. Olson's importance as a philosopher rests chiefly on his making clear that the nominalist's respect Pound felt for his god inside the stone was the same as the existentialist's respect for the god inside every created thing, whether animate or inanimate. The 'philosophy' of 'Black Mountain' is nothing less than a personal and literary existentialism.

However, 'Black Mountain philosophy', like existentialism, extends back much further than this century. Abelard began a lot of it when he initiated the realist-nominalist controversy. Wordsworth began it in another way, suggesting that man drop his Aristotelian and utilitarian view of nature in favour of an awed and humble one. Heidegger mirrored Wordsworth's protest in this century when he proposed that man would be healthier to drop his traditional Aristotelian 'subject-object' relationship with nature where nature was an exploitable object to the individual man's ego, in favour of a 'subject-subject' relationship, where the fact that everything had an ego, wished to do its own doing, would be recognized by all men. Pound adopted this suggested humility in his attitude toward the materials of his poetry and in his approach to particulars, in which he made sure that they remained particular and did not become the food of abstraction. And Olson, finding that Heidegger's 'subject-subject' relationship still left the greedy ego unchained, went beyond Heidegger and Wordsworth by proposing an 'object-object' relationship, or 'objectism', where each man recognizes himself as an outgoing and dependent part of the greater field of nature and has all pride and isolation removed.

> Objectism is the getting rid of the lyrical interference of the individual as ego, of the 'subject' and his soul, that peculiar presumption by which western man has interposed himself between what he is as a creature of nature (with certain instructions to carry out) and those other creations of nature which we may, with no derogation, call objects. For a man is himself an object, whatever he may take to be his advantages, the more likely to recognize himself as such the greater his advantages, particulary at that moment that he achieves an humilitas sufficient to make him of use.

In another essay, 'Human Universe', Olson attacks Aristotle and the Greeks for being deluded into believing the world lifeless and thus knowable through abstraction and classification. There he praises the Mayas as an example of a people whose respect for the external world approaches animism. And he cites their Indian descendants as living examples of the total acceptance of the concrete world; for instance, they feel none of the white man's embarrassment at accidental body contact on a crowded bus.

This existentialist acceptance of one's flesh-and-bone reality and respect for all parts of one's environment, leads directly to the 'Black Mountain' term 'locus' that so perplexed Miss Fiamengo. 'Place' (cf. Souster's *A Place of Meeting, A Local Pride*) becomes important to a writer like Olson because, if a man exists in an 'object-object' relationship with external nature, and if he admits the integrity and right to particularity of all members of external nature, then the only way in which this man can approach and know nature is by participating in an established 'field' of objects, by acquainting himself with one place intimately. For the place must master the man, not man master the place. Or as Edward Dorn puts it, 'Place is brought forward fully in form conceived entirely by the activation of a man who is under its spell. . . .'

These explanations of 'Black Mountain' that I have given are only an outline of the work that could be done to give this group its true significance. And the tragic thing about such unread critics as Mr Skeleton, Miss Fiamengo, and others is not that they do not know this skeleton of explanations, but that they are so irresponsibly ready to join a considerable body of critics who wish to dismiss the whole Pound movement as an inconsequential and ephemeral flash. Pound has given the English-speaking world his life in order to cleanse its language of debilitating abstractions and its psychic patterns of the idealism that has nurtured corrupt social, economic, and political practices. Anyone can see these ills in our society; anyone can recognize our failure to fight for particularism anew. Pound dedicated himself to the renovation of his language and his society, not to be ignored as an eccentric, but to clear the way for a greater literature and a greater society. It is sad that the very kinds of writing that he proved to be rot and fungus are now finding acceptance throughout North America, that the purer kinds that he tried to foster must suffer on, either unrecognized, or condemned for lack of originality, and that many of the Canadian writers experimenting in Pound's techniques are even unaware of why he developed them. What I hope is not only that Pound and his students receive just recognition in our country, but that future writers everywhere will not be deterred by the ignorant from making attempts to discover and use the land that Pound and his workers have so ably cleared.

Tamarack Spring 1965

Lunchtime Reflections on Frank Davey's Defence of the Black Mountain Fort

Louis Dudek

Frank Davey's piece in the Spring issue of *The Tamarack Review* on the influence of the Black Mountain school on Canadian poetry will no doubt make some poets explode in guffaws, as I have just seen two Montreal poets do across the lunch table when I read them the list of twenty-one poets presumed to have come under the influence. (Both of these were included in the list, hence the guffaws.) However, Frank Davey really makes more sense than this reaction would indicate, and his article touches on some ideas which are central to our poetry. What it lacks is a few clear definitions and distinctions that would prevent confusion and misunderstanding in the future. I am willing to provide something toward this, since I was directly involved in the activity he describes, and I like very much the general tenor of his article.

I think Frank Davey deliberately lumps together 'the Black Mountain poets' and 'the influence stemming from Ezra Pound and William Carlos Williams' as though these were one and the same thing. Actually, he knows they are not. The twenty-one poets on his list can be validly related to Pound and Williams, but not to the Black Mountain poetry. It is only confusing to say that 'Black Mountain has come to influence' all our poets from F.R. Scott to Purdy. What is true is that something of which Black Mountain itself is a late development lies behind most of our modern poetry, and it is certainly useful to recognize this mainstream in the poetry of Olson and Creeley—and hence in Davey, Kearns, Bowering, et al. But the mainstream is not the Mountain branch.

One wants to distinguish between the nature of these two strains, the Pound-Williams and the Black Mountain poets. Also, one wants to distinguish between two separate elements in each: that is, Pound and Williams, and Olson and Creeley. A lot depends on these differences in trying to recognize the types of new poetry that turn up, whether in Vancouver or here in the east. We are all derived from a modern poetry which has several distinct strains, and the purity or mixture of these makes for the styles of the new poets in each generation.

I think Davey is right to talk about Imagism, particularly, and the free rhythm derived from Pound and Williams, in connection with our poetry of the 1930's and 40's. A.J.M. Smith's original Preface to *New Provinces* (1936), recently exhumed and published in *Canadian Literature*, is ample proof of the Imagist influence. This quality can be seen in W.W.E. Ross in the 1920's, and in both Smith and Scott in various short poems written in the 1930's. Later, the specific of both Pound and Williams is clearer in my own writing than either in Layton or Souster, or in any other of the 40's poets. Numerous book reviews and several articles, as well as the notebooks of my students for the past twenty years, will show that Pound and Williams are the two sources I have always insisted on, as the clearest and most profitable continuation of Modernism, even in preference to Eliot, Yeats, Auden, or Dylan Thomas, since each of these latter poets is, as I see it, in one way or another a distraction, a reaction, or a confusion of the main intent of the modern renewal. (My writing about Williams and Pound may in fact have led critics to assume that the Pound-Williams influence was deeper in some of the other poets than it actually was.) Thus, in general, Scott is more significant for us in Canada than Smith; Souster is more significant than Layton; Purdy more so than Reaney. These latter may be more gifted—even better poets—but the main line of continuing modern development runs through Scott, Souster, Purdy—and at present centres clearly in the activity in Vancouver.

One could argue that the Yeatsian aestheticism of Smith makes him something of a living anachronism—though a fine poet; that the rhetoric and the outdated metrical line in Layton—as well as the appalling confusion and barbarism of his language—makes him an astonishing sport, but not a key figure in this line of development; that the metrical experiments and jingling rhythms of Jay Macpherson and Reaney are really beside the point, however brilliant they may be—because the true-speaking line is carried on from Williams in Nowlan, Purdy, and the Vancouverites.

Vancouver, then, is the present continuation of the authentic modern tradition in Canada. But how does this differ from the main tradition, and what are the differences within the new poetry?

In the latest influences from the U.S. I think we should distinguish clearly between the style of Olson and that of Creeley. Olson is really Pound redivivus: in fact, he adds nothing valuable to Pound, and I do not think he is a poet who will hold a permanent place in poetry—he is Pound turned into a private business for profit. Creeley derives directly from Williams and he is a far more significant variation on the original, though again I doubt whether there is anything there that will last for more than a decade.

Now, about this 'thingy' business, the question of *particulars* that Frank Davey writes about, Pound used the concrete in the form of the ideogram: i.e., either as examples to illustrate an unstated general idea (a poor sort of concreteness), or as samples with which the reader would do his own thinking—an 'inspired mathematics' providing equations for the reader's private universe. Pound of course went into history and the entire heritage of art for his samples. This is the method that produces the abracadabra of Olson's Gloucester (the 'Maximus' stuff), the mazes of his Maya and other hobby-horses of the private imagination. (Olson is far more pretentious and eccentric than Pound, who was already a prize-winner in that respect.) Williams, on the other hand, stuck to the American grain: his particulars are humble backyard fences, red wheelbarrows, and old women munching plums. When he says 'No ideas but in things', he means that we should think about our real surroundings in terms of the objects that our senses reveal; that understanding should emerge through selection, empathy, and the aesthetic perception (eternity) of the ephemeral moving present. This preference for the contemporary 'thing', moreover, implies great honesty toward experience (such as we have in Creeley and in the Vancouver poets), also a will to purity in language, and integrity in the use of free organic forms.

There is no Canadian poet who has actually followed Pound (though Smith once called my long poem *Europe* 'Pound cake'), unless Marshall McLuhan is that poet. (I consider both McLuhan and Northrop Frye as really poets manqués, best appreciated when we read their speculations as imaginative constructs made out of their real materials, not as 'objective' or 'scientific' theorists at all.) 'The pie-plate is the cake' is more true for them than for the media they analyse. Williams, on the other hand, has a large unaccredited following in Canada.

Some influence of Pound, however, is there, especially as a kind of reinforcement of the Williams aesthetic. In D.G. Jones, for instance (who wrote his M.A. thesis on Ezra Pound, starting it at McGill), the Williams clarity and contemporaneity is the main characteristic, yet something of the astringent tone and austerity of Pound appears also. In my own poetry Pound is present mainly in the theoretical presuppositions which I derived from his poetry, not in the actual imagery, or language, or rhythm of the poetry (though reviewers have been misled by a few tags and quotations which I have sometimes thrown in as a kind of affectionate tribute to the old Pound). Layton has neither Pound nor Williams — he once said that he could write a dozen Williams' poems within half an hour — though he has a few specific poems in imitation of Williams, perhaps the remains of an effort to prove this boast. Nor could I ever get him to read the *Cantos*. Layton is rhetorical, in a fustian tradition that goes back to Klein and then to Marlowe rather than to any modern poet. It is really archaic stuff that will not pass technical analysis as twentieth-century poetry: Williams himself noted that this was the flaw in Layton's method — the metrics — and that he would eventually have to answer for it (or words to that effect). I suppose the letter exists somewhere. In other words, we have a lot of Williams in our make-up; a little of Pound; and a certain amount of irrelevant hangover type of poetry of one kind or another. There's a lot of the hangover (imitating this and that) in Smith, in Klein, in Jay Macpherson, and even in Nowlan and Acorn.

The same cannot be said for the new Vancouver poets, because their technique is the conscious part of their poetry, and their theories are in the main line of modern development — no matter how thin some of the results may be so far. They are derived, in their theory, directly from William Carlos Williams, as Frank Davey points out, with the Imagist doctrine of Ezra Pound as their ultimate source. But what is the difference between this Williams derivative, as represented by Corman and Creeley, and stemming from Creeley, Davey himself, or Lionel Kearns, and the original William Carlos Williams?

'Eureka!' I said to my friends over the lunch table as we were discussing this little point. 'I can explain it.' (Hence this little essay continuing Frank Davey's exposition.) Modern poetry is a great dissolution of the nineteenth-century forms and image contents of poetry. It is an anarchic transition where everything is possible and nothing is yet itself. Imagism was the reduction of contents to the mere particulars, precisely to shed poetry of its romantic meditations, its pantheism, its various philosophical and cosmic trappings. Free verse was the unstructured form that began with pure imagism and moved forward to speaking images, to ideas in things; possibly to new understandings and new forms. Williams in his late years wrote repeatedly of the New Measure, and hoped that out of the liberty of free modern rhythms there might emerge a new principle of order, a new measure, that would be the distinctive vehicle of true modern poetry. In Williams himself, the free three-line stanza he improvised in the late poems is the nearest he came to this measure. He was actually hankering after some kind of mathematical form, though he never yielded fully to this desire, and he was faithful of course to the principle of free verse.

The new school represented by Creeley, by Davey, and by Kearns (with his experiments in 'Stacked Verse') is really a hopeful continuation or would-be theoretical fulfilment of Williams' hope. These poets are concerned with theoretical questions of technique, with measure and the science of rhythm in speech. This is what makes them so different in appearance on the page from Scott, Souster, Nowlan, or Purdy. Of course, all this derives from Pound and Williams, but via the new theoretical distilling apparatus of Creeley and Company. So Olson's Gloucester is not the Idaho of Pound, and Creeley's New England is not Williams' Paterson. We may all trace our descent from Pennsylvania U., but not from Black Mountain College.

[Incidentally, corrections, Layton never did teach at Black Mountain College; and neither *CIV/n* nor *Contact* was 'modelled' on Corman's *Origin*; nor did Contact Press evolve from *Origin*. The extent to which *Origin* contributed to these magazines is correctly described in Wynne Francis' article in *Canadian Literature*, No. 22, Autumn 1964. (That article so far as I know contains no errors of fact, though it does contain, I hope, some errors of opinion.) Nor did 'Dudek, Layton and Souster' begin *CIV/n*. (Souster was hardly connected with it; and the magazine was edited and produced by Aileen Collins, Stanley Rozinski, and Wanda Staniszewska.) Oh yes, one more point further back: *First Statement* had no connection with William Carlos Williams, and no influence from that source can be found. At that time, no one in the group was much aware of Williams; in fact, John Sutherland received some poems from that poet — and rejected them! Also, a minor point: Pound did not write the phrase '*CIV/n* not a one man job' either about or to *CIV/n* magazine. The magazine was named because he had written this earlier, in a letter to someone else; *CIV/n* — i.e. civilization — is not a one man job; get together and do something — just as certain poets have been doing lately in Vancouver.]

Tamarack Review No. 36 Summer 1965

The Most Remarkable Thing About *Tish*

George Bowering

To me, the most remarkable thing about *Tish* has been that a newsletter created by a passel of young poets should emerge as something more responsible than a blurbing of self-indulgent romanticism. In fact, most of the adverse criticism has come from young romantics who feel that *Tish* poetry has been unemotional and academic, the two terms somehow thought of as interchangeable. Academic it has not been, except occasionally. George Hitchcock calls Olson, Creeley and Duncan academic poets, though, so at least among our correspondents the term washes out somewhat.

Let me explain what I mean by young romanticism. Nietzsche was asked about the poets, and replied, "The poets lie too much." This is my main objection against romanticism. The *Tish* poets have striven for accuracy and clarity, and have turned their attention upon the factual things that make up the world, men included among them. The young romantics (chiefly from Eastern Canada and in the U.S., New York and California) don't seem to have the desire to work for accuracy. Instead of communicating they fall back on some intensity of feeling, hoping to inundate the reader with expressions of their own superhuman soul, interpreted by themselves. They scoop a lot of slush into the space between themselves and natural phenomena. They think they have to *put* poetry into things; they don't have the sense and determination to find the poetry that is already there.

Often they think it isn't poetry unless they are wailing and screeching abut some injury done to themselves. They regard nature as a personal enemy or at least a personal insult. They want to reconstruct the great chain of being, with themselves at top.

Happily, over the past year and two-thirds, the *Tish* poets have resisted that kind of auto-advertisement. If they have too often proclaimed their Black Mountain forbears, that is more forgiveable than enshrining themselves as modern Rimbaud-type juvenile delinquents of the poesy game.

Frank Davey is moving to Victoria. Fred Wah is moving to New Mexico. James Reid promises to leave the continent. Lionel Kearns is going to lock himself in his writing room for a year. I'm moving to Calgary. That leaves Dave Dawson as the new editor of *Tish*, of which I approve heartily. He has a cordon of fresh working poets around him. That's what made *Tish* in the first place.

Tish, No. 20 August 1963

Anything But Reluctant

Frank Davey

Historically, little magazines have sprung up whenever new, animated, and serious writing cannot find a market. Thus these magazines are usually managed and edited by writers — writers who are anything but reluctant to publish their own works. The annoyance that gets such writers into the magazine business is, of course, that in any period both the commercial outlets — whether "literary" mags or publishing houses — and the glossy-paged scholarly quarterlies cater chiefly to established writers. A new group or school of writers cannot possibly get a sufficient quantity of its work published to make its presence felt. Some of the semi-professional literary quarterlies, such as Canada's *Tamarack Review*, tend to become coterie magazines, depending for almost fifty per cent of their material on a particular fixed circle of writers — again writers whose reputations the magazine knows are safe and established. Which is, of course, a sensible commercial policy, particularly in a country which has tended to be a graveyard for literary magazines.

Little magazines, on the other hand, never have to depend on "name" writers, their mimeo expenses being low enough to keep their losses at a minimum. But this is only a minor difference. The major one is still that little mags are published by *engaged* writers, not by semi-interested on-lookers. Whereas the commercial magazines or glossy-paged quarterly usually reflects one man's desire to be an editor, or a group's wish that their town, university, or whatever, have a "literary" mag, the little magazine nearly always reflects genuine writing activity and interest. While the editors of the *Tamaracks* and the *Prisms* seldom have any new work of their own to exhibit, seldom are engaged in creation with any excitement or persistence (but rather go altruistically or parasitically to those that are), the editors of little magazines are usually so absorbed in and dedicated to their own writing that they feel they *must* found a mag — in order that their work may receive at least some attention and criticism. Often, if not always, the little magazine reflects the presence of a group of writers of similar interests who are meeting, arguing, fighting, writing, almost every day — a group charged with literary energy that seems to keep continually overflowing into and out of their mimeographed pages.

One could take the founding of Vancouver's *Tish* as an example of the birth of a little magazine. All of its five editors had been writing for some time; George Bowering had been getting poems published in eastern Canada — though, he says, never the ones he wished to have published. With two visits from the U.S. poet Robert Duncan their bi-monthly meetings to discuss their own work became weekly meetings of intensive study of Charles Olson, Duncan, Creeley, Pound, and Williams. In no time literary theories and poems began filling the air, covering the desks, and some quick and dependable outlet for quantities of material had to be found. Even the established magazines willing to publish some of this work could not be relied on; they were too slow, and by the time one's poems were published one wished to disown them, ideas had changed so. Thus *Tish*, Vancouver's poetry newsletter, was born, and the energy, the intensive literary study and creation that began it show no sign of abating. If it did, of course, there would be no reason for *Tish* to continue, for, in order to be worthwhile, any little magazine must have this inspiring energy. Evidence of such energy is perhaps the prime criterion for judging its value.

Magazines with no energy whatsoever are, naturally, one of the other minor but important causes of the founding of little magazines. In Canada there are a large number of low-energy literary mags with no particular policy; for example, *Prism's* often nondescript collections, *Canadian Poetry Magazine's* usual dilettante sprawl, and *Fiddlehead's* custom of printing so nearly an equal number of bad poems to good ones that a writer begins to doubt the value of publication there.

All of which will tend to make the new little magazine editor angry and belligerent. He will be so proud of his strong direction and sense of development that he will often make a point of countering the petrified standards of the professional outlets with work initially as shocking as important. He will counter the nebulous — if even existent — editorial policies of the *Fiddleheads* and *Prisms* with an editorial line or bias strict enough to exclude almost all of the — to him — mysteriously-established establishment. It can almost be said that, to be true to the energy that has got him writing and publishing, the new little magazines editor must be of necessity rebellious — else have his magazine redundant.

Again historically, such ventures have often been successes. Writers such as Hemingway, W.C. Williams, Pound, and Aldington, to name a few, all began their careers in little magazines that have now either disappeared or evolved to unrecognizable forms. Since the last war little magazines such as Canada's *Combustion* and *Contact*, and the U.S.'s *Black Mountain Review, Origin, Migrant, Measure,* and *Yugen*, spawned most of the writers now finding recognition in Grove Press and New Directions publications and in professional magazines such as *The Outsider* and *The Evergreen Review*. At present in the States Robert Kelly's *Trobar*, Cid Corman's second series of *Origin*, and Le Roi Jones and Diane Di Prima's *The Floating Bear* are carrying on the fight for the acceptance of new writers the with undoubtedly the most vigour.

In Canada too we are witnessing a new crop of little magazines. In the last two years *Moment, Mountain, Evidence, Cataract, Tish* and *Motion* have all appeared. In Vancouver alone three new ones are projected: *Recall*, a new non-commercial mag of *Kenyon Review* tastes, *Spasm,* one probably in the "beat" tradition, and *Q*, "a quizzical monthly of satire and other social criticism." University magazines, such as Waterloo's *Chiaroscuro*, UBC's *Raven*, and Acadia's *Amethyst*, continue, but only as "student" publications — seldom with any attempt at absolute excellence.

Of the new and ambitious little magazines Toronto's *Evidence* is the only one to get above the usual mimeo format. Alan Bevan, the writer-editor, says that it "was born out of the conviction that there is a good deal of serious writing being done for which there is no adequate outlet in Canada." This is, of course, the best and only excuse for the founding of a little magazine, and so far Mr. Bevan has been able to find interesting writing. There have been frequent weaknesses, especially in the critical articles, but *Evidence* has still been superior to *Tamarack's* seemingly endless issues of unexcitement. Bevan's magazine can be lively — see No. 3's provocatively accurate article on marijuana — but, in order to counteract its cold, almost malicious reception by the Toronto establishment, should become even more boisterous and militant, and its editor should take a more prominent part in its revolutionary trends. *Evidence* does not seem to be the product of an active group; it looks like a one-man job, and, unless Bevan himself gets more lively, I forsee a dull future for his magazine.

Montreal's *Cataract* is certainly militant. Which is perhaps the best thing one can say about it. Militancy is fine when one has something to be militant about; *Cataract's* most obvious trouble is that its writer-editors seem to spend more time thumbing their noses than they do writing poetry. Irving Layton's "Open Letter to Louis Dudek" in No. 2 shows more concern for Layton's own waning reputation (see his defensive and high-schoolish "To a Lily" here too) than for Dudek's. But *Cataract* is the product of a group intensely active and outspoken in writing; it has a distinct direction. And it has had good poems (ignore Avi Boxer); Sydney Aster has had several lucky hits, and K.V. Hertz and Henry Moscovitch have consistently shown much talent and potentiality. *Cataract* is certainly not a pretentious magazine

— it even belabours its non-academic roots, and is definitely worth "bothering" with.

Moment is a Toronto mimeo poetry magazine at one time edited by poets Milton Acorn and Al Purdy, now edited by Acorn and his wife, Gwendolyn MacEwen. Like *Cataract* it is squarely in the little magazine tradition of being founded by cooperating poets to publish poetry that might not be accepted by the established markets. The poetry of Miss MacEwen is often "poetic" and esoteric, and at times beautiful and real; Acorn's is rougher, probably less poetic by anyone's standards. The outside poetry is diverse, both in quality and manner, and, with the lack of similarity between Acorn and MacEwen, the magazine thus appears to have little unity of policy. It is probably held together more by marriage than by literary interest. From what I have seen *Moment* is not dull and not lively, not consistently experimental and not quite reactionary, not sufficiently discriminating and not actually careless. It does have its triumphs, though — such as the Al Purdy poem in No. 6. A Toronto magazine.

David McFadden's *Mountain* from Hamilton is probably in one way the most ambitious and comprehensive little magazine in Canada. Its purpose seems to be not so much to announce something new, as to bring together and reannounce all of the new things that have happened recently in Canadian poetry. A sort of poor man's *Evergreen Review*, although one cannot call Padraig O Broin's poetry new, or John Robert Colombo's lines poetry. Still the first issue of *Mountain* marked the first time a Canadian reader could see together in one place most of his country's important new writers. With possibly only two exceptions, all of the writers were under twenty-seven years of age.

McFadden announced in No.1 that "*Mountain* has very definite and rigid editorial standards, but they change from day to day," and they must in such an eclectic mag. The only demands McFadden appears to have made of his writers are youth and quality, and even these he has very clearly lifted at times. In the next issues perhaps some direction will become apparent, maybe not from Hamilton activity but from McFadden's consciousness of the energies of young Canadian poets as a group. A long hope, but still even as merely "a lively review of current poetry," *Mountain* is indispensable.

Tish and *Motion* are two Vancouver mimeo "newsletters." *Tish*, the poetry newsletter, is now in its twelfth issue, and seems to have crystallized its determination to remake poetry a natural and spontaneous human occupation and rid it of the obscure and obviously "poetic" creations of would-be "artists." Man not art, and the universality of human experience, are two of its battle-cries, and battle-cries they are, for its editors seem to have made a fetish out of belligerency. A lot of their poetry seems weak and irrelevant, yet some of it is powerful and does show that their attempts at "natural" poetry have enabled them to write skilled and complex poems with the craft totally submerged and unobtrusive.

Motion, the prose newsletter, seems also to be working in favour of unpretentious style and subtelty of effect. However, with only two issues out the question is still whether *Motion* has work that should be published despite the rejections of established magazines, or merely would like to think it has. Either Canada or the U.S. I know of no magazine with which to compare *Motion*; the idea of a monthly prose newsletter seems to have been totally neglected, possibly because of the large amount of work necessary to provide sufficient material.

There is one other mimeo little magazine in Canada: another Toronto one, Padraig O Broin's rather harmless *Téangadoir*, now in its 39th issue. It claims to be a magazine of current Canadian poetry, and is, exactly, and is thus all over the map. O Broin himself will never pretend to be experimental, yet side by side with his own traditional lyrics he will publish even such uncontrolled ones as those by G.C. Miller. *Téangadoir* is an interesting little magazine, but not a vital one. There is obviously no group of fermenting young poets behind it; most likely it is a hobby to O Broin, who does not seem to have much difficulty getting his poetry published elsewhere.

These little magazines really comprise most of what is happening in Canadian poetry. The so-called "quality or mass magazines," the established glossy literary quarterlies, continue to grind on, but most of the changes that slowly but eventually occur in them are generated elsewhere between the rollers of someone's rusty Gestetner. Canada is fortunate to have such a large number of little magazines that the commercial literary outlets are never allowed the peace to become permanently stultified. What is sad is that most of these mags do not take sufficient advantage of their unique position — no one asks them to be responsible, and money is never available enough to be an objective — to further shake up the commercial world and speed the evolution of writing. As I said before, a little magazine must be either bold or redundant. *Cataract, Mountain,* and *Tish* are each in their own way somewhat brash, but *Evidence, Moment, Motion,* and especially *Téangadoir*, could all stand acquiring some reason for additional chips on their shoulders. An affable little magazine cannot help but be worthless.

Canadian Literature, No. 13, Summer 1962

The Vancouver Report

Carol Bergé

The following is an excerpt from New York City poet Carol Bergé's journal record of the Vancouver Poetry Conference, a conference held at the University of British Columbia in July, 1963, involving most of the *Tish* editors, and reuniting Olson, Duncan, and Creeley, the leading figures of the Black Mountain group. This conference occurs after the publication of *Tish* 19, the last issue to be edited by Frank Davey and the original group of editors, and immediately before the departure of Davey, Bowering, and Wah from Vancouver. Most of Bergé's report consists of notes made during the seminars and lectures of the conference. The passages reprinted here contain Bergé's general comments on the conference and on the contribution of the *Tish* writers toward it, plus her evaluation of several of the Vancouver poets.

Here, for a three-week Seminar in Poetry, are the following Big Names in Poetry Today: Robert Creeley, Robert Duncan, Charles Olson, Allen Ginsberg, Denise Levertov, and Margaret Avison. Also present, unofficially, the U.S. poets Philip Whalen, John Keys, Tom Jackrell, David Ready, Carol Bergé, & David Schaff. Creeley has been teaching a poetry course at this University for the previous year, will be returning to Albuquerque to continue teaching. Duncan has come up from his home in San Francisco; ditto, Whalen (tho late, that is, during the 2nd week of the Seminar.) Olson has come in from his Gloucester diggings. Ginsberg has been flown in from Japan, where he had been visiting Gary Snyder after the Indian sojourn. Levertov comes to us from her summer place in Temple, Maine northwoods. Avison comes from Toronto.

The students in the Seminar are from all over the U.S. and from the local B.C. area. The U.S. has sent such as David Schaff from Yale, George Palmer from Harvard, academically affiliated; and some less readily classifiable, such as Clark Coolidge and wife, from New England; some of the just-back-from-Mexico brigade; & the I'll-be-living-in-N.Y.-after-this brigade.

Perhaps the Black Mountain Spotted Virus is stoppable; if so, it will be despite the Canadian newspaper *Tish*, otherwise known as Virus Mary, and the formidable carrier *Origin*, which has weathered several years, gone into its second phase of virulence, and developed a strain of utter resistance to fresh air. Of the Vancouver poets closely associated with *Tish* and the Black Mountain way of seeing poetry, I would group (in order of susceptibility) Frederic Wah, David Bromige, David Cull, Dan McLeod, George Bowering, Peter Auxier, and Michael Matthews. James Reid, Robert Hogg, Sam Perry, and Frank Davey are in it all, but off to one side, influenced by other streams than the interpretation-of-Williams-via-Creeley.

Lionel Kearns is perhaps the only truly original thinker in the lot; he takes after no one and has even acquired a solitary convert. A Frederic Franklyn of Los Angeles, who produces his inaccurate version of Kearns' carefully-thought-through 'Stacked Verse.' Kearns, erudite in linguistics and deeply interested in the forms of communication, reminds me of Jackson Maclow in some ways, and of Rochelle Owens in some ways: both of whom are using the English-American language to make poetry of an exciting nature. He is the only Canadian poet I have read or met who seems comparable in any way to Charles Olson.

During one of the early Seminar sessions, one morning last week, Allen Ginsberg blithely and accurately and instantly tacked a label to the four poets leading the talks that morning: he himself is a 'beatnik,' Duncan as the 'nasty aesthetician,' Creeley as the 'maker of exquisite little poems,' and Olson as the 'father figure of us all.' Much delight and laughter at this assessment: so accurate, especially seen from the outside, as in the recent infamous and disgusting *Esquire* article and the various evil public distortions such as *Time*. But also much delight for its accuracy from the inside, much shifting of feet and egos among the poets themselves, those up front and those facing them. In the whole bunch of us, here, the only poet who stands four-square-to-the-wind on both feet, so to speak, is Charles Olson. Creeley and Ginsberg are going through a period of terrible doubt and negatively critical self-appraisal ('nothing I wrote before now is any damn good' or 'I'm not really sure about anything, I mean, not really; I mean...') and Duncan is in his usual warmly self-laudatory state of self-deprecation, wherein he describes his love of closed doors of self and poetics, and his fondness for archaism as opposed to progress or the modern. Ginsberg's stay in India has brought about a gnawing at the vitals of this poet's stance and way of being; he's always been a gentle and beautiful human, but these take the i form of self-effacement in the extreme, as when confronted with the direct attacks or snidely clever insinuations of the highly verbal Duncan. Nice Zen, but not much to cheer for....

I came to this Seminar convinced that nothing Robert Duncan has ever written is worth a damn, and that he is personally not merely a bore, but an offensively affected bore. I hate to be wrong and I hate even more to admit it: I *am* wrong. I still think he is not my dish of tea as a poet, but I say now that he is a vitally interesting lecturer and an unforgettable personality. He has a warmth of projection of personality which sweeps one along until one forgets to be annoyed. Somewhere along about mid-week, last week, I realized I compared Duncan to some of the professors I had in college: jolly, clever, unambitious, damn funny, a performer to the end. And then I visualized him in a jester's outfit (forgive the pun), which image has endured. Through a small insight like this, Duncan reached me. Once I realized that he is really not very important, not the poet or the person I consider Olson or Ginsberg to be, I could forgive him a great deal, and begin to enjoy him. His reading was full of roses, his appearance at the morning lecture sessions always stimulates the others; he is in white shirt and tie and suit and he wears an invisible jester's cap.

My dislike for Duncan rather took the edge off my original hosts' appetite for lion-hunts. The young Wahs, acting as Executive Assistants to Warren Tallman and wife Ellen in the arrangement and functioning of this Seminar, are, I found out just after I'd expressed my open opinion of Duncan, inveterate Duncanites: he 'adores' Robert and she is 'doing her Masters on him.' My reception was noticeably cooler, and I moved to hospitable quarters, with the Bowerings, after two days in the Wah home. I thought, for a while there, that I was (as those of you who know me and love me in spite of it will testify) paranoid as usual; but it turned out that the Wahs are noted in Vancouver for lion-hunting (I guess they thought I was not only a Duncanite but some sorta personage or other, when they invited me and my son Peter to be paying guests for the Seminar.) I admit I have difficulty adjusting myself to this image, and continued to wear my jeans, offer to wash the dishes, and say out my true opinions when asked. This way of being is offensive to certain kinds of people. Later, I established, by keeping my ear firmly pressed to the air, that the Wahs had roused the ire of many Vancouverites, by shifting things around so they were tops on the asskissing list re visiting celebrities and first in line for out-of-town assistantships, regardless of how they get them.

At this point, now that you see I am going to be most candid, disregarding your cries of 'sour grapes' and 'she is grinding some kind of axe' and 'yeah, Bergé thinks it so she thinks it's the word of God . . .' I might as well describe the setup at the University of B.C. and get away from personalities. First, to say that I find this part of Canada very beautiful: it resembles Monterey and, in general, California; esp. re climate. Hot, sunny, comfortable days, cool nights, like San Francisco but not foggy, smoggy or windy. An ideal climate. I hear there was a week of rain before our arrival, but there hasn't been a drop in two weeks; we are at one of the numerous beaches every day. Coming from the dank soot of the New York summer, this is heaven: a beach two blocks from anywhere! and no sharks, as off the Calif. coast, no swarms of noisy humanity as off the Long Island Coast. The second day here, Peter and I walked from the Wahs' apartment toward the beach, about a mile the way we went, through a fashionable and expensive suburb-type neighborhood; then down a steep wooded cliff, and to a beach which compares favorably with any on the Riviera, at Acapulco or Veracruz, or like that. It brought on a long and fairly (ugh) romantic poem, at the time, and we also got a sunburn.

So much for that. Also present are mountains and the Bay, as part of a view so classic as to seem one of those murals popular in the reception rooms of New York ad agencies, or little chichi restaurants, or lady chiropractors' offices. I mean, it looks good, from anyplace in the city. It's a low, sprawling city; takes a good hour to get from one end of the city to the other, and half-hour (with good bus connections, which happen almost never) to get from the University to downtown. There's a good bookstore, with Penguin editions of things you can't get in the States, etc.; they have one copy left out of either five or ten originally received, of the book FYLP, which you may be sure I looked for. Also have as hip a collection of everything except science fiction as Lawrence does at City Lights; plus the browsers' bench and table so sadly lacking at our own Eighth St. Emporium for Purveyance of Littacher.

The University's campus proper is nice: lots of lawns, green and crisp, and students walking on, studying on, just sitting on them (o god, is Washington Square for real??) and a beautifully executed Japanese garden, from the middle of which one can be another, if you know what I mean. Bamboo, yes; the stream, over rocks, a red Japanese Maple, a pool of waterlilies; a path with cross-sectioned logs for steps; rocks to sit on or touch; lichen, bees, a huge old willow; thickets of odd strong foliage and delicate groupings of slender reeds; much to delight. And this is right in the middle of a campus whose architecture is a sad hodgepodge of extreme glassy modern and pseudo-Gothic buildings; whose long malls are speckled with incredibly bad modern sculpture (one piece, a sort of inverted Henry Moore type, looks like a parody of a group of amputees, and the suturing wasn't too good, even so.)

Ed comment at this point: the students: poems, mimeo'd and passed around, contained gamut of quality. Work by the known poets, example Dave Bromige, of obviously higher quality. (His poem, 'At Last.' surely derivative of WCW-Creeley, yet sound in its own right.) Daphne Buckle, also Canadian, doing interesting things with form, but nothing much with content yet. (She, Dave Bromige, Geo. Bowering, Jamie Reid, John Keys, this writer, Bobby Hogg, and others had an evening reading midweek in the Seminar, which gave all an opportunity to get another dimension. There had been, earlier, an outdoor reading at Jamie Reid's pad, in the backyard: Jamie and I read amid the sounds of boats and planes of Vancouver Bay. There were a couple of other such readings, some impromptu, one also at Jamie's, toward the end of the Seminar, which I missed out on, regretfully.) — Judy Copithorne, doing wild stuff that with a better discipline might be Neruda; Helen Luster (the ladybird of the earlier-described agonies of AG, wherein he tried to free her a bit (scene: a party, the Tallmans' livingroom, this tall greying lady next to me on my left, AG and RC at my right, I ask her, how do you come to be here, my dear? she: well, I've raised my family, and since I have this great talent, I figured it's about time I *did* something with it!) Well, she does better than a million housewives who stayed home and complained about their arthritis while playing bridge. Tho the poems don't make it, they're a damn-sight better than some here. Fred Franklyn's pseudo-stacked-verse (to watch him try to define his work, stacked or au naturel, to a class containing at least three poets familiar with Kearns' work —) Karen Johnson's young-female version of Howl, in contrast to the sad formal speculations of a former missionary-woman or something... Kearns, which work I had put down firmly, and still quibble with, though it boils down to what I sd to him there: 'Such fine poems, Lionel; wish you'd get rid of

that line down the middle, it detracts from the reading....'
George Palmer's tight, dense work, tension visible in person and poems, promise of much. The incredible multicolored, multifaceted mind of Sam Perry, outgoing/outreaching into feeling/thinking and with this a weaving of senses, in the talk and the poems... his daughter is Karma, born in Tibet last year when he and Beth worked and taught there: their zest, the ability to make things happen! The sham-seeming but actually quite moving work of Fred Wah (it is *not* true that Pauline proofreads and edits every word the man writes; when he reads, you can feel his work and forget such stories and even the derivative forms he uses on the page.) Gentle, compassionate Peter Auxier, young like Jamie but, like Jamie, with a good sense of material and form (not from nowhere comes compassion or the ability to give/love, I say...) in contrast with the terribly skillful, almost masterful work of George Bowering, who, since he was mine host, revealed himself to be a man other than represented in the work, a disparity with which I carp, sharply: all well to be a good surgeon or cabinet-maker, in those crafts, but risk, as a strength of a poet must show in what he writes, or it will betray him eventually. Same can be sd for Denise, for many of the poets afflicted with Black Mt. Spotted fever earlier described: that eggshell between them and the material, and between them and reality.

George, Fred, Denise have learned too much from (or lean too much on) the work of such as Williams — consider the work of Olson or of Avison, only as to form; consider Diane di Prima, here in New York, as to both form and content; the feeling-through of Jackson Maclow and the unwillingness of some poets to rely on the form or method of those who preceded them. I resent a poem which looks like WCW wrote it; if WCW didn't.

Fuck Press, New York, 1963.

Introducing *Tish*

Frank Davey

1. Introduction to *Tish 1-19*

Tish, "a poetry newsletter — Vancouver," was conceived, planned, and first published during a seven-week period late in the summer of 1961. From the earliest deliberations the five editors had no intention of making *Tish* a shrewdly designed and polished magazine. Rather *Tish* was to be a record of on-going literary activity, a record that preserved every roughness, insight, and stupidity that this activity enclosed. The immediate models were two U.S. underground magazines, Cid Corman's *Origin* and LeRoy Jones' and Diane Di Prima's *The Floating Bear*. A more distant model was Louis Dudek's *Delta*, although to us even this magazine had a professional veneer which concealed whatever human contexts the writings had occurred in. Had we encountered copies of *Contact* or *Combustion* instead of *Delta*, they would have undoubtedly been more useful.

Origin, the most important of the various models, had been founded by Cid Corman in Boston in 1950. The architect of the magazine was Charles Olson, whose various letters to Corman at the time demanded that *Origin* be not the usual aesthetic object but a "field of force," that it be

a reenactment of,

the going reality of (approximate, shot at) *that
which is abreast of us:* now, here & now, ...

"*Aesthetics,*" he had exclaimed, "Pah bah shit (leave that to the already is-*all* mags now existent in Am And Eng, so far as I can see.")[1] These letters, of course, were not published until 1970, but their message could reach us thru the shape of *Origin* itself and also thru the implications of Olson's other writings — as in his admonition to "not be led to partition reality at any point, in any way."[2]

The impulse to create *Tish* had been sparked by Robert Duncan during three nights of lectures, July 23, 24, and 25, 1961, at the Vancouver home of Warren Tallman. Tallman, a professor of English at the University of British Columbia who had already influenced George Bowering, Fred Wah, and myself as students in his general poetry class, had begun in 1959 to make contact with the San Francisco poetry scene — partly at the suggestion of his wife who had known several of its poets during her college days. His efforts had brought Duncan to Vancouver to give readings in December 1959 and February, 1961. The first was held at Tallman's own expense in a hastily converted portion of his basement, the second as part of the 1961 UBC Festival of the Contemporary Arts. After the second reading Tallman encouraged various students, including Bowering, Wah, Jamie Reid, David Dawson, Gladys Hindmarch, and myself, to cooperate with him in financing a special lecture visit by Duncan for that July.

While Duncan was only the first of many avant-garde writers (including Creeley, Ginsberg, Levertov, Spicer, Olson, Blaser and Avison) that Tallman's energies would bring to Vancouver, his visit, which included more than nine hours of lectures, unquestionably had the greatest impact. As Tallman summarizes,

Duncan, a walking and talking university of verse lore,

[1] *Letters to origin,* (London: Cape Goliard, 1970), pp. 10-11.

[2] "Human Universe," *Human Universe* (San Francisco: Auerhahn, 1965), p.5, reprinted from *Evergreen Review* II:5 (Summer 1958).

filled the air with his most influential predecessors (Ezra Pound, William Carlos Williams, H.D.) and his closest contemporaries (Charles Olson, Robert Creeley, Larry Eigner, Denise Levertov). The gain for Davey and the others was not simply in the names but in the keys, clues and comments on the art of articulation. Tone leading, rhyme, sound resemblances and disresemblances, the musical phrase, composition by field and correspondence, as well as linguistic, musical, dramatic and choreographic analogies to writing — all these began to buzz about like bees. From which hive *Tish* was immediately born and for the next twenty months and issues kept up a steady hum.[3]

The dynamics of this birth were more complicated than Tallman indicates. All five of the founding editors had been writing for some years before this summer. Bowering, Dawson, Reid, and myself had taken courses within Earle Birney's creative writing program. Bowering was beginning to receive intermittent publication in eastern Canadian magazines. In May, 1961, the amount of writing produced by our unofficial circle had reached such proportions that Wah and Lionel Kearns were half-seriously proposing the founding of a little magazine to be named *Cock*. But the main push toward a magazine was Duncan's. His accounts of the histories of little mags such as *Origin, Black Mountain Review*, and *The Floating Bear* began to promise freedom from received standards and establishment bias should we venture to create a similar publication. By the Saturday following his final lecture the question was shifting from "should we" to "how." That night we arrived at the magazine's name. Our sense that too many of modern Canadian poems were synthetic, impersonally fashioned objects led our deliberations quickly to an idea raised in Duncan's initial lecture.

Almost every item of the holy has an expression in our common speech that means 'oh that's just nothing.' And

[3] "Poet in Progress: Notes on Frank Davey," *Canadian Literature* 24 (Spring, 1965), pp. 24-25.

every one of those 'that's just nothing's', every time we say them, well take "shit", which is extremely important in the whole of the magical operations, and we have only to think of agriculture, and that now we increasingly try to use chemical fertilizer, and not the actual shit. The actual shit we put into salt water where we hope it will do nothing . . And it's because the 'oh, shit' remark is entirely our disappointment that it has not yielded the experience. We know that people with aberrations . . . come into some kind of intense experience, eating shit, covering themselves with it, and so forth, and we do kind of know that as compost it works, I guess . . . But we are the first civilization that has thought the thing to do with it is to put it in a porcelain bowl and then quickly get it out of sight. And scientists, by the way, don't. Scientists at the present time — one of the wonderful ironies is that in the very period when we are triumphantly using plumbing, & yet the only time they did find out where the rice came from [here Duncan is referring to the research of Carl Sauer of the University of California into the origin of domesticated rice in the Amazon basin], by the way, and where the first wheat was grown, was because only five years ago did those archaeologists realize that people wanted to know what was in the turd, not what the bowls were like any longer. And suddenly they found a few fossilized — 'cause how did you know what the people were eating? You had no idea what the people were eating except in those few fossilized remains.[4]

After a few tentative and facetious suggestions we adopted the phonetic inversion suggested by Duncan himself.

Later that evening the politics of the magazine began with the need to select an editor and devise an editorial structure. None of us five wanted a strong "editor-in-chief" (not one of us, in fact, trusted the literary judgement of all of his colleagues). Having an editor with veto power seemed of little advantage over submitting our work to alien quarterlies. My election that night was, I am told, due to my

[4] Tape-recorded lecture at home of Warren Tallman, Vancouver, B.C., July 23, 1961.

appearing the least doctrinaire of the older editors (Bowering, Wah, and myself), and being thus least threatening to all. From the beginning, a majority vote among the editors was held necessary to admit material — including material by the editors. In practice, we usually attempted to dissuade fellow editors from publishing work we suspected, and, if failing to move him, accepted his judgement. The only exception I can recall concerned Bowering's second and succeeding "Meatgrinder" poems which were excluded by a painful and long-debated 4-1 vote.

Outside poets caused more controversy. Wah and I were originally in favor of excluding all except those of the Vancouver scene. Bowering disagreed, being anxious to publish well-known writers (Eigner, Blackburn, McClure) as a way of increasing both circulation and credibility. Our policy soon became to publish up to two pages of "outsiders" per issue as a means of defining our "tastes." In retrospect, this explanation was clearly a rationalization. "Taste," that affectatious word, was never a true part of the *Tish* vocabulary; as our beliefs about the kinds of writing which could be engaging, those were always more than evident.

In the months following the first issue, we gradually located *Tish*'s appropriate form and manner. By issue #4, the subtitle had become "a poetry newsletter — Vancouver" instead of the original "a magazine of Vancouver poetry." *Tish* was obviously a newsletter — a record of work-in-progress — rather than a magazine. Vancouver was the place of its poetry, not a kind of poem. In issue #12 an editorial announced a continuing "policy of publishing not just poetry of quality but also that of continual [?] originality and ambition." Again a *post hoc* recognition. By issue #13 my title had become "Managing Editor," a description much closer to my actual role of coordinating editorial opinions, answering correpondence, designing formats, typing stencils and licking stamps than was the original "Editor."

Throughout the nineteen issues which I edited, all five editors published many poems and statements which they would undoubtedly now wish to disclaim except as documents of their novitiates. Particularly embarrassing to me are the frivolity of the opening editorial, the pedantry of "The

Problem of Margins" (T3), the snobbery of my remarks on John Newlove's *Grave Sirs* (T7), and the wordiness of my attacks on Acorn (T11) and Layton (T12). Similarly, Dawson may well regret the glibness of his term "good poems" (T5) — a glibness which I see originated (T4) — and Bowering his intermittent name-dropping. The poems are a different matter; their failings were outside our power at the time, being mostly failings in knowledge and skill rather than judgement.

But the unrestrained and often unfocussed energy that contributed to the carelessness and hastiness which characterizes most of the issues did cause nineteen issues to be published and several careers to be launched. It caused writing to become during those two years the dominant concern of each of the five editors. It compressed and accelerated their development. My pretentious article on margins (T3) is quickly given a serious and usable dimension by Wah (T4). In T5 we see Bowering turn theory to metaphor and begin a substantial series of "meta-margin" poems. By T9 the late Red Lane joins the metaphor to begin a significant series of his own. Similarly, Bowering is able to feed quickly on a bridge image I propose as early as T1; David Cull can work with sequence forms and Amerind imagery established by Dawson; Bowering and I both follow Fred Wah's lead away from rhetoric and toward personal syntax and diction.

The highlights of *Tish* for me consist mostly of poems — Bowering's "Sunday Poem" (T2), Reid's "The Fear" (T1) and "The consolation of Violence" (T8), Eigner's untitled poem in T5, Bowering's "L.S." (T7), Dawson's "Tentative Coastlines" (T12). All of these in some way — sound, structure, point of view — moved poetry toward the kind of articulation of which we wanted to be capable. Reid's "The Fear," for example, was a tour de force of tone-leading on vowel sounds. Eigner's poem showed the phenomenologically-perceiving consciousness as convincingly as I have ever seen in poetry. "Tentative Coastlines" revealed Dawson as the first of us to work with the serial poem — an open-ended form already being explored in San Francisco but which Dawson, I believe, stumbled across accidentally as an extension of the mutli-section poem in progress. The unchallenged prose highlight of the newsletter is Warren Tallman's " 'When a New Music is Heard the Walls of the City Tremble' " (T3). This essay, in its supporting of Robert Duncan's insistence that poetry must reveal "the music at the heart of things," and in its decrying intellect for catch[ing] up those things that seem wrong in regions of experience by putting them right in realms of thought," declares the anti-humanism of *Tish* loudly and clearly. The essay is particularly important considering the confused thinking and execrable prose of most *Tish* editorial statements.

Tallman's essay also makes it clear that in the overall tradition of Canadian poetry *Tish* and its poets belong to the "universist" line of Lampman, Carman, W.W.E. Ross, Klein, Souster, Layton and Purdy, rather than to the humanist and rationalist one of Goldsmith, Sangster, Pratt, Smith, F.R. Scott, Finch, LePan, Reaney, Mandel and Gustafson. The distinction between these lines is not a firm one; poets like Acorn and Kearns seem able to participate in both at once, while Birney moves throughout his career from the humanistic line to its other. The differences lie primarily in worldview and concepts of form. The universist writers tend to see the universe as vast, divine, mysteriously structured, and essentially ungraspable by human reason. The humanists see it as finite, orderly, and mangeable by man. The universists regard form as active and alive; the humanists as a manipulated showplace for the human mind. To the universists the poem involves the poet in recognition and surprise, it leads him to more than he knew or planned. To the humanist it is a culture-object, moulded and chiseled to a shape preconceived by its author's intelligence and will —expressing *his* ideas, bearing the stamp of *his* style.

The universist line is by far the dominant one at the moment in Canadian poetry. Whether this dominance has been partly due to the influence of *Tish* is difficult to determine — certainly there have been many factors. The intellectual temper of our culture appears to have been shifting away from the humanist tradition of a man-dominated universe — as the recent importance of ecology, mysticism, dropping-out, anarchism, phenomenology, and hallucinogenics attests; even now this shift promises to bring man to a new and realistic view of his role in the immense plurality of cosmic phenomena. Whatever else may be said of *Tish*, it has participated in the changes which have been occurring on our cultural and literary consciousnesses. It has become, quite accidentally, an item of literary history, and is offered here in this collected edition for that reason alone.

Introduction to Tish 1 - 19.

2. *Tish,* B.C. and After

Tish, "a poetry newsletter—Vancouver" was first published in September of 1961. It had been conceived by myself and George Bowering, Fred Wah, James Reid, and David Dawson earlier that summer not as an eclectic publisher of known writers and predictable poetry, but as a record of on-going writing activity among ourselves and our acquaintances in Vancouver. Our models included Louis Dudek's *Delta*, which impressed us as a document of his personal engagements, LeRoi Jones' and Diane di Prima's *The Floating Bear*, a rough-and-ready mimeo newsletter of on-going writing in New York City, and *Origin*, a magazine formed partly in response to Charles Olson's admonitions to its editor, Cid Corman, that it should be not an aesthetic object but a "field of force",

> a *reenactment of*, the going reality of (approximate, shot at) *that which is abreast of us*: now, here & now, ...

What was abreast of us at that time was not only our own lives in a particular geography but also the lives of a number of remarkable men: Warren Tallman, a professor of English at UBC who had influenced all of us in his work as a student of contemporary poetry; Robert Duncan, the San Francisco poet whom Tallman had been instrumental in bringing to Vancouver to lecture to us for a week that July; and Charles Olson, William Carlos Williams, Ezra Pound, H.D., Jack Spicer, Robert Creeley, Larry Eigner, Denise Levertov, Louis Zukofsky—names that Duncan made large for us in his dramatic accounts and enactments of the inner life of 20th-century English language-poetry. *Tish* began as a documentation of the energy gained in a particular place from these various sources. The details of its genesis and evolution, which I have previously outlined in my introduction to the Talonbooks reprint *Tish 1-19*, are less important here than the fact of its documentary function. *Tish* measured itself not in terms of acceptability to any audience or reputation among critics, but only by the accuracy of its embodiment of the Vancouver 'field' its editors inhabited—a young and often madcap place. Its criteria were the local ones of person and place.

The stance of *Tish* was therefore decidedly anti-humanistic. In a general sense *Tish* belongs to the 'universist' line in Canadian poetry of Lampman, Carman, W.W.E. Ross, Klein, Souster, Layton, and Purdy, rather than to the humanistic and rationalist one of Goldsmith, Sangster, Pratt, Smith, F.R. Scott, Finch, LePan, Reaney, and Gustafson. As I wrote in the *Tish 1-19* introduction,

> The differences lie primarily in world-view and concepts of form. The universist writers tend to see the universe as vast, divine, mysteriously structured, and essentially ungraspable by human reason. The humanists see it as finite, orderly, and manageable by man. The universists regard form as active and alive; the humanists as a manipulated showplace for the human mind. To the universist the poem involves the poet in recognition and surprise, it leads him to more than he knew or planned. To the humanist it is a culture-object, moulded and chisled to a shape preconceived by its author's intelligence and will—expressing *his* ideas, bearing the stamp of *his* style.

I might have added that the universist seeks meaning in the local, personal, the multiple and idiosyncatic—the universal resides in the particular. The humanist is a cosmopolitan; he seeks meaning in the 'order' of generalization. Like A.J.M. Smith, he seeks centralization in the myth of cosmopolitan man, or like Atwood, in general themes of survival and alienation. For the universist, mythology is particularizing— myth forever springs alive in new circumstance; for the humanist mythology is generalizing—*plus ça change* and so on.

In my mind *Tish* marks the turning of British Columbia poetry away from the shadows of derived, humanistic, Toronto-focussed writing and toward the light of its own energies. Phototropic and decisive. Without an understanding of the nature and decisiveness of this turning, the subsequent history of poetry and poetry's politics in B.C. can appear, at best, mysterious and strange. Before *Tish*, B.C. poetry was a known and singular thing. Its poets wrote principally for an audience outside the province, usually an eastern-Canadian audience. They aimed for publication by eastern magazines—*The Canadian Forum, Tamarack Review, Queen's Quarterly, Fiddlehead, Delta*—and by the Toronto book publishers. Even when Alan Crawley published *Contemporary Verse* in the 40s and 50s, that magazine's directions were defined by the majority of eastern-Canadian writers whom it published. Most of the poets by which eastern Canada currently 'knows' British Columbia poetry—Susan Musgrave, Robin Skelton, Earle Birney, P.K. Page, Tom Wayman, Gary Geddes, the late Stanley Cooperman—still do write and publish for an extra-provincial audience.

It was partly in rejection of this audience's tastes that *Tish* was founded, partly in assertion of the need for a localism of both poetic and poetic concern. It was Charles Olson's insistence on the local, on particularism, on the "barbed wire" and "pemmican" of *A Bibliography on America*, on poetry specific to the breath and breathing-in-place of its poet, on which we pegged this assertion. The place would judge its own.

Since *Tish*, the poets by whom B.C. poetry is known extra-provincially have had increasingly less connection with the actual B.C. writing scene. *Tish* marked the beginning of a series of writers, magazines, and presses for whom local criteria and local response alone was relevant. For these writers recognition by eastern Canada was at most secondary, and certainly not to be earned by sacrifice of locally determined literary standards. For magazines like *Tish, Talon, Blew Ointment, Iron, The B.C. Monthly, Air, Scree, Pacific Nation*, or *NMFG*, the traditional forces which led *Contemporary Verse* and *Prism International* to gain eastern acceptance by publication of eastern-Canadian writers had no power; a local readership was the main goal. Similarly, for publishers like Talonbooks, Blew Ointment Press, Pulp, Intermedia, Raincoast Chronicles, Blackfish, provincial sales have been prime. With *Tish* began a localism of taste of considerable consequence—a tradition of B.C. poetry virtually unconnected with Toronto-based CanLit, with presses, magazines, and major writers mostly unknown east of the Rockies. At a Toronto book-launching party in 1974 I was asked by William French, bookpage editor of *The Globe & Mail*, then planning a short visit to B.C., for a list of B.C. presses and magazines. His acceptance was cheerful that B.C. was foreign literary territory—not his daily book-beat.

Today B.C. poets either write for eastern acceptance and become, deliberately, exiles in their own territory, or write to articulate the local and become mostly unknown outside their own province, except wherever in North America the local is valued. Colonialism vs. localism. The former can be found anywhere that cosmopolitan anonymity and its humanist counter-theme, alienation, are fashionable. The latter include among them many of the most significant writers of their generation—Marlatt, Bowering, Blaser, Gilbert, Bissett—writers who articulate universal process where it occurs in the ongoing weave of local and individual histories. In Gilbert's words, "AND AND AND AND AND...." Or Marlatt's,

> we'd house ouselves in, all this wind & rain. Confuse us. Driving lines that shift, the floor does, ground or under sea, to cast, at low tide what lies uncaught, uncovered traces only, of sun & the moon's pull.
> Unseen, how lines run from place to place, How driving from town she follows the water's push, the fields, drained by ditch to river to, the sea at, where she lives ...

The 'lines' of connection among these writers form not clique but community—Those who would believe that any two of Gilbert, Bowering, Marlatt, Blaser, and Bissett inhabit the same house, or could inhabit the same house, are perceiving them from an immense distance. Theirs are separate houses on a common ground of mountains, language, sea, and voice. It is this ground, on which writing is not a humanist tool but an act arising from the conjunction of one man and his familiars, on which writing can earn its value in the conjoining act of its own writing, which *Tish* first began to make clear and which now forms the base of a writing community from Steveston north to Prince George and Terrace and from Duncan east to Nelson, perhaps beyond.

In the fifteen years since *Tish*'s founding, this community of writers has constructed its own traditions and genealogies, again largely unknown outside the province. So that the current magazine of poetry news in B.C., *NMFG*, has roots in *Iron, Pacific Nation* and *The B.C. Monthly*, while *Iron* has roots in *Tish* and in San Francisco's *Open Space*, and *Scree* grows from both *Tish* and New Mexico's *Duende* and Buffalo's *Niagara Frontier Review*, and *Air* out of *Blew Ointment* in turn from *Up th Tube with One Eye Open*. And among the poets are other generations measured in decades, Blaser to Bowering and Kearns to Marlatt, Gilbert, and Bissett to Gardiner, Candas Dorsey, Scott Watson, Barry McKinnon, and (I'm guessing now) Rosemary Hollingshead and Watson looking back to Blaser, and Fawcett and Gardiner looking to Bowering and Blaser, and Candas Dorsey looking to Bissett, and Bowering looking many places including to Blaser. And some others aren't looking, they're second-guessing someone beyond the mountains. But now, after *Tish*, and after *Talon, Blew Ointment, Georgia Straight, Pacific Nation, Iron, Capilano Review, Air, NMFG,* Talonbooks, The Very Stone House, New Star Books, Blackfish Press, Caledonia Writing Series, Pulp Press, Intermedia, *and, and, and,* this isn't all that's happening.

from Western Windows, Vancouver, 1977

Poetics

Tish group at a party at Frank Davey's apartment in Jan. 1961. Far left is Daphne Buckle, Stan Persky (background) David Cull, Robert Hogg.

Rime, A Scholarly Piece
Frank Davey

Every schoolchild learns that "rhyme" involves the correspondence of terminal sounds of lines of poetry—"masculine rhyme," the correspondence of the sounds of final and accented syllables, and "feminine rhyme," the correspondence of the sounds of two syllables, the first heavily stressed and the second final and weakly stressed. Or that it denotes a poem which is built on metered lines bound by a pattern of corresponding terminal sounds—such as the quatrained "Rime of the Ancient Mariner."

Except for blank verse, almost all of English poetry up until the twentieth century has been based upon these definitions of rime. To many "men of letters" poetry almost *was* rime; especially adamant in asserting this have been the classically and traditionally educated who forgot both the extreme flexibility of Shakespeare's mature blank verse and the fact that little of classical Greek or Latin poetry was ever rimed. Even today these men who hold forts at Yale and at the offices of *Alphabet* and of *Canadian Poetry* will glance at a piece of poetry, note the absence of regular meter and of end rime, and toss it aside as "another bit of chopped prose."

What in many cases is offending these men, however, is not the absence of rime, but the absence of rime as they know it. Contemporary poets had come to the traditional resources of English poetry and found them arbitrary and unfruitful. Figures of speech, meter, assonance, alliteration, parallelism and end-rhyme had deteriorated to little more than embellishments through which any professorial greybeard could twist stale thoughts into complex "poetry." Although there were standard forms, such as the sonnet, there was no uniting theory of form or technique; worse, there was no theory joining form to content. End-rhyme itself had grown from possibly a mnemonic device in the middle ages, to a petterning device in Provençal, to a decadent toy in medieval French poetry (such as the "Chanson de Rolande"), to finally in English an arbitrary way of turning sentence patterns into poetry.

Clues existed even at the turn of the century that rime as the correspondence of terminal sounds of lines might not be an essential of poetry. Whitman had managed to abandon "rhyme" and still write what was recognized as poetry. Hopkins had completely submerged the rhyme-schemes of his sonnets by the use of run-on lines and a welter of alliterative and assonantal devices suspiciously similar to "rhyme" which were more important in creating pattern than the rhyme-schemes themselves. Shakespeare had been acclaimed for three-hundred years as the language's greatest poet largely on the basis of blank verse plays. It thus seemed obvious to some writers that end-rhyme might not be a requirement of poetry, and that perhaps behind the actual conception of rhyme as the correspondence of the terminal sounds of lines lay a more basic principle.

Sometime during the 1950s the American poet Robert Duncan leafed through his OED for the etymology of *rime*. The word was an adoption of O.F. *rime (ridme, ritme)* or an adaptation of Latin *rithmus (rythmus)* both of which were adoptions of the Greek $ρύθμός$ which meant "measured motion, time, proportion." According to the OED, the term "rime" was first applied to poetry in the phrase *rithmici versus* which was used to denote acentual in contrast to qualitative verse (*metra*). Apparently, as the correspondence of terminal sounds of lines was a common feature of accentual verse, the *application* of rithmus eventually became narrowed to this particular characteristic.

However, Robert Duncan decided to ignore the alleged history of the meaning of the word *rime* and re-interpret logically the application of a concept of measurement to the correspondence of sounds. *Rime* to him, then, has virtually the same meaning as its Greek ancestor $ρύθμós$: proportion as a measurable distance between correspondences, or the instinctively measurable sense of recurrence or of non-recurrence that is possible at the opposite ends of a continuum of resemblance. *Rime* could involve the correspondence of almost any two or more things: themes, images, syntactic units, phonetic units.

Rime in sound, number in sound, is derived from our possible awareness between total disresemblance of sounds and total resemblance.

Before considering the implications of Duncan's theory, one should note that it is on the surface a wishful one—that it does not agree with the best evidence available on the actual history of the word *rime*. Whereas the OED claims that the present application of rime is a narrowed version of the word used to denote measured, rhythmic verse, Duncan would want the medieval poets who first used *rime* for the correspondence of terminal sounds of lines of poetry to have had in mind its etymology and to have been considering end-rhymes as crude attempts at measured, patterned verse constructions. The etymologist and the historian would both claim that in the first "rhymed" verse the only measurement consciously attempted by the poet was in the kind and number of feet, and that "rhyming" sounds were considered embellishments separate from the attempt at "measured" verse. The long series of repeated end-rhymes in the "Chanson de Rolande" would support this position in that their rime is clearly an embellishment—a gimmick or a toy. But Duncan would feel that in the original urge to use patterns of tonal resemblance the first users of what has come to be called "rhyme" revealed a wish to provide proportions, lengths, and distances, and to make poems which were measurable constructs.

In such a consideration as Duncan's, etymology is not enough. The fact that the word rime originated rather accidentally and illogically from the Latin name for rhymed or unrhymed accentual verse, or that today it tends to mean merely the correspondence of terminal sounds, does not prevent a poet such as Duncan from pointing out that the attempt in the use of tonal rime is as much measurement as is the attempt to build lines of poetry of a set number of determined feet. When Duncan points out that tonal rime need not consist merely of total resemblance but can run all the way down a scale to complete disresemblance, and that this scale can be worked out according to a phonetic classification of vowels and consonants, he is merely intellectualizing something that poets with good ears have hitherto known instinctively—so that, as Duncan puts it, a poet will "know what he is doing."

Etymology, however, can still throw some interesting light onto a consideration of *rime*. *Rhythm, rime* (and its variant *rhyme*) both came originally from the Greek $ρύθμός$, and until the seventeenth century were spelled identically as *rithme, rhyme,* or *rhythme*. Thus a close connection between *rhythm* and *rime* must have been felt by any speaker of English before this time—a connection that could not be written off as simply as it is by the twentieth-century etymologist, as stemming from the earlier corruption of the Latin *rithmici versus*. Even today the confusing etymology of *rime* cannot prevent a thoughtful person from noting that rhythm is essentially the repetition or riming of certain stress patterns, and that regular rhythm is at the total-resemblance end of the scale of rime and irregular rhythm (what some might call the "unrhythmic" as much an impossibility as the concept of "unstress") near the total-disresemblance pole.

When word of Duncan's re-definition of rime as the measurable distance between two corresponding elements, whether they be phonetic units, stress patterns, images, or whatever, reached Vancouver in 1960, local poets immediately tried to utilize it. Most, however, were unfamiliar with the international phonetic alphabet which Duncan used to illustrate the possibilities in tonal resemblance. And of the other possibilities for rime which he suggested—theme, image, syntactic units, gender—only rimes of image seemed practical. Rimes of theme appeared possible only in long works, rimes of gender seemed esoteric, rimes of syntactical units seemed an awkward way of expressing the ideal of parallel structure. The first Vancouver poet to write a poem based on Duncan's "rimes of image" was Lionel Kearns; his poem "Subversion" appeared in the May 1960 issue of *Delta*:

> I can't stand smoking
> Vowed the reclining nude
> A smouldering cigarette
> Protruding from her vulva
> And a thin line of fumes
> Coiling around her leg.

Here is illustrated the potentially grave error that local poets made on hearing of Duncan's theory: that riming images, sentence patterns, genders, et cetera were new to poetry. And that these "new" gimmicks would merely take the place of conventional end-rhyme. Why should any rime occur at the end of a line? Merely because tonal rimes have traditionally been placed at the end of lines of English poetry, did Kearns have to place his "riming images"—"smoking," "cigarette," "fumes," and "nude," "leg," "vulva," at the ends of lines?

This poem, of course, represents a primitive stage in Vancouver's understanding of Duncan's rime. Rimes of syntactical units (parallelism), rimes of sound (assonance, alliteration, and conventional rhyme), rimes of image, rimes of gender, had been used before in poetry but had never been unified under one theory for conscious application. Now that they were, we find Kearns confusing them all with the only one he was familiar with as rime—tonal end-rhyme.

Duncan's concept of rime as being any degree of resemblance, from total to none, can be applied to any characteristic of poetry and can be used anywhere as the poem requires. Particular vowels can be permitted to recur and recur; front, mid, or back vowels can dominate a passage, round or unround vowels, and the recurrence of one of these characteristics in a later passage of a poem can set up a further pattern of resemblance. The distinctions among the consonants—voiced and voiceless fricatives and stops, or bilabials, labiodentals, alveolars, or velars—can be utilized in the same way. Also the recurrence of certain sentence patterns at key places can be used, as well as similarities and dissimilarities of stress pattern.

All of these possibilities are possibilities in rime, and, used in conjunction with Creeley's theory of organic form, can give patterned individuality to any poem. Hopkin's theory of inscape, where a poem gains the personality of a work of art through fusing assonantal, alliterative, and syntactic techniques, might well be considered an instance of good use of rime. As I mentioned before, the sonnet form of Hopkin's sonnets is often incidental; a multitude of other riming devices gives the poem its unity and conveys to the reader the sense of a crafted, measured, artistic construct.

Rime today can be used for many purposes. Rimes of stress pattern—i.e. careful interplay of degrees of resemblance and disresemblance—can be used to give mellifluous continuity that will *propel* the poem on from line to line despite burdening complexities of thought. Tonal rimes seem to me best used on heavily stressed syllables within lines to knit the poem phrase by phrase together by resemblance and/or contrast. Rimes of image work best at the level of association, providing that sense of recall—again resemblance and/or contrast—that so often strikes us in our daily living. The best rimes of image are those that *occur* to the poet, and not ones that he has searched for. These guide the poem by a natural law, as it were, of incidence or coincidence. Rimes of theme are more thoroughly in the hands of the poet. Stretching over series/sequences/years of poems, these only reveal themselves if the poet has a unifying vision of his world and his relation to it. Rime is structure; reflects order. Only so much as the poet's vision is ordered by his own sense of occurrence and recurrence, by a sensitivity to the rhythms/rimes of the natural world, will he be able to give rimes of theme.

We speak freely of the rhythm of the seasons, of the tide, of the planets, of the stars, of the life-cycle, of the menstrual period, of the wind, of the mountain stream, of the breath, or of the heart-beat. Rimes surround us, make the world meaningful, make language possible. "Without rime or reason" we say of something we cannot understand. Rime is the first assumption of scientific endeavour, is the means of the world communicating with us; it is what allows us to see proportions, meanings, structure in nature, to draw conclusions, to take measure of our world. In poetry it should have the same freedom that it has in nature. In neither can there be any fixed "rhyme schemes." The poet must have an intuitive sense of the resemblances and disresemblances possible in language—an ear for language—and must try to develop this on a conscious level so he can know what he has done and its value. Only then will each of his poems have memorable, individual, and engaging beauty and form, and be able (as Charles Olson advocates in discussing the importance of the rhythms of the human breath in poetic utterance) "to take its place alongside the things of nature."

Evidence, No. 9, Winter 1965.

Notes on the Stack

Lionel Kearns

With Duncan's absolute scale of resemblance and disresemblance and Warren Tallman talking "counting and measure" and Williams who long ago said there is no such thing as free verse, and still going back to Pound's idea of music in poetry, and knowing it in Hopkins, and then suddenly at a poetry reading having it crystalize: . . . *form* . . . is something heard, and in poetry form is "music" in the sense of non-symbolic (non-semantic) voice sound, that part of utterance which is functional without being meaningful. Of course poetry is first of all language—a poem is a linguistic act says Robert Creeley: granted. The meaning is there, as in all language, but poetry is language as such, and then some. So:

> Language is poetry to the extent that it is also music.
> Music is poetry to the extent that it is also language.

And somewhere in here there is a kind of law; call it the Law of Discourse and Song:

> In any single human utterance language and music tend to exist in inverse proportion to one another.

It follows therefore that the poet's task is to work against this law, packing his utterance as both language and music. (Now you will say that all of this is very commonplace, and I will agree, saying only that for me it had to be discovered, and I am telling you how I came to it.)

With this theory settled, I had then to get down and see what it meant. How about this "music"; how should I actually deal with it? The study of this kind of thing I found was called prosody—a word and a subject which I had always carefully avoided. And with good reason: traditional prosody is as useless (and destructive) as it is naive. I needed a new system entirely, and to get it I went to Hopkins and the linguists and the many contemporary poets who, like me, were working with a new order of prosody and taking it for granted as everyone should, but as I couldn't.

Let me put it this way: Duncan had first come up here talking of rhythm as (if I din't get it wrong) any measurable sequence of points extended in time, and this idea harkening back to Pound: Rhythm is a form cut into *time* as design is determined *space*. And so, naturally, as everyone else including a few of the traditionalists knew, the non-linguistic part of poetry, the music, the form, would manifest itself as rhythm.

But the source of this manifestation was the key point. As it happened I had been reading Edward Sapir and lo, yes, he'd spoken of it years ago: there is a part of human utterance, which is not language but which is nevertheless often present with language, that has its basis in human emotion rather than human intelligence, and becomes manifest in speech dynamics: varying qualities of stress and pitch, and in certain vocalic and consonantal contrasts and scales. In other words emotion is the source of music in poetry and will therefore determine its form. Commonplace again. Everyone knows the effect of emotion on speech, and it isn't difficult to see it as correlative, working the other way as well: just as certain emotional conditions can generate a particular rhythm, so a particular rhythm can produce emotion in a listener. Poets of course have been saying that for thousands of years: poetry is language charged with emotion.

Rhythm it was then. But I had to get this rhythm in hand. Rhythm is generated by counting, perceived by measure (Warren Tallman, if not his exact words) and both these processes, in and out, would require concrete units which would be made up of speech elements, the most likely of which would be syllables. The various traditional feet were unnatural to my poetry and speech and therefore out of the question. Williams' variable foot was a fine idea but it was, and still is, an abstraction. Everyone talks about it, but no one can actually put his finger on it. But as I was saying, I was looking for something concrete, and it finally came to me, after hearing Charles Olson reading in Toronto and then coming across the following passage in Trager & Smith's Outline of English Structure:

> Any utterance made in English ends in one of the terminal junctures. If it is a minimal complete utterance it has no other terminal junctures within it. In that case it must have one or more pitch phonemes, one — *and only one* — primary stress. . . . Such a minimal complete utterance may be called by the technical term *phonemic clause*. (49-50)

There it was: the actual foot of an organic English prosody, the same prosody used by the Anglo-Saxons, and, though it went out officially with Chaucer and the introduction of rhyme and running rhythm from the continent ("I kan nat geeste 'rum, ram, ruf'", says Chaucer's Parson, disparagingly), the prosody that came down to us in ballads and nursery-rhymes; Coleridge tried to raise it to dignity in "Christobel" and of course Hopkins found it and perfected it in his highly stylized Sprung Rhythm. Today a great many poets are using it, but for the most part unconsciously. At the time all this was coming to me I wanted something definite, a system that would attempt to correlate page lay-out and oral delivery. And so, using Trager & Smith's phonemic clause as its basic unit, I formulated *stacked-verse*:

> *stacked verse* is a system of notation designed to accommodate poetry whose rhythmic form depends upon accentual stress measure. Its basic unit is the *stack-foot*,

a group of syllables containing one primary stress and ending in a terminal juncture. In particular cases a stack-foot is preceded, followed, or replaced by an *outrider*, a group of one or more syllables ending in a terminal juncture but containing no primary stress. The terminal juncture which separates the outrider from its accompanying stack-foot is signaled by either a space of a regular juncture-signalling punctuation mark (.,?;: etc.). Stacked feet are arranged into a verticle *stack*, the accented syllables coming immediately beneath one another so that a *stress-axis* may pass through them. The beats along this stress-axis tend to be regular (isochronous) for the duration of the stack, a definite break in the rhythm coming at the end. A group of consecutive stacks using a common stress-axis is called a *stack-stanza*.

Reading stacked verse is very easy. If the reader taps his finger on the indicated syllable and observes the break at the end of the stack, he will read the appropriate rhythm into the poem instinctively.

The system works surprisingly well. I've found I could read a stacked poem in the same manner, in the same rhythm each time I tried. I began stacking some of my old poems and using the system in composing new ones, getting the rhythm right with the tape recorder and then transcribing it onto the page. In this way the poem became much easier to work on. With an authentic page lay-out I could look at it and know how it sounded. If it wasn't right I could change it ———— stress this syllable instead of that — let five syllables be crammed into one interval and two into the next. A change in page form meant a change in actual form, the sound. And when I was satisfied, the poem was finalized — it couldn't get away.

This is the only claim I make for stacked verse, that it helps me to build my poems and to keep in touch with them once they've been finished. Admittedly, the system has its disadvantages: it is a printer's nightmare. And there is Louis Dudek's point that too much direction from the poet himself tends to kill the private development of the poem in the reader's imagination. And of course, there are many poems for which stacking would prove unsuitable and irrelevant because they do not depend upon stress and juncture patterning for their effect. In my own case, however, I still find stacked-verse very useful, and I intend to go on using it until something better comes along.

Tish 16

Stack-Verse . . . a definition

Lionel Kearns

Starting from the principle that a poem exists as sound rather than print, and that the page lay-out of a poem is therefore merely a transcription of the actual form, I devised *stacked-verse* as a system of notation that would, in recording my poems, retain the rhythmic beat that is their formal core. My problem arose because I was using an accentual stress measure in which the feet vary from one to ten or more syllables. These feet end in a slight pause (the duration of which also varies) and are characterized as well by a noticeable beat which occurs on one of their contained syllables. In linguistic terminology the pause is a terminal juncture, the beat a primary stress, and the foot itself a phonemic clause or "minimal complete utterance" of English speech.

Verse-stacking means arranging these *stack-feet* on the page one underneath the other in such a way that the stressed syllables fall in line and allow a vertical *stress-axis* to pass through them. The smallest group of such feet is a *stack*, and it is important to note that beats within a single stack tend to be equally spaced in time regardless of the number of intervening syllables and pauses. This aspect of the system need not worry the reader, for if he taps his finger on the indicated syllable, he will read the appropriate rhythm into the poem instinctively. As a definite break comes at the end of each stack, it is not difficult to maintain the rhythm which lasts for two, three, or four beats, but rarely more. A *stack-stanza* is a group of stacks which share a common stress-axis, but this larger unit is arbitrary and depends on the sense of the poem rather than the sound. The only other unit in the system is the *out-rider*, a group of one or more syllables which like the foot ends in a slight pause, but which does not contain a noticeable beat. This seldom heard unit may replace a normal stack-foot, or it may precede or follow it, in which case it is separated from the foot by a space or a punctuation mark. The outrider occurs only in particular circumstances — where the natural English speech rhythm is broken up.

Evidence 6, 1962

Frank Davey

Interviewed by Elizabeth Komisar

Elizabeth Komisar: In view of your unrelenting involvement in the literary scene, in view of the fact that you've had a fairly prolific output in the last decade, you're relatively ill-known in Canada and I think that basically the reason for that is your insistence upon moving in the world of the small press—Talonbooks, Coach House, Press Porcepic. And in turn, that reflects some kind of a politic or a vision on your part. Could you explain why you continue to publish with the small presses?

Frank Davey: Oh, I think it's an issue of motivation—what you want when you become a writer. I think that a lot of people wish to become well-known and the ones who become well-known have set out with that in view. I have only wanted to be involved with writing, to write work which I felt quite satisfied with and to encourage work from other people, work with other people, make a—create a literary climate in which serious literature and a literature involved with language, literature involved with pushing literary form into new possibilities, could be created. Uh, I've never been concerned with my reputation and I have never tried to push myself onto a commercial publisher who could make a literary reputation for me.

Komisar: But that isn't to say that within the large publishing world that it's impossible to be writing experimental literature is it?

Davey: I think that inevitably you have to make some kind of compromise when you enter the larger commercial publishing world—that whether it's acquiescing to a semi-fraudulent dust jacket blurb, whether it is submitting to the kinds of promotion which the semi-mass market book requires for its success uh this kind of compromise is forced upon you.

Komisar: Let's move to another area. In the introduction of your book of recent criticism, *From There to Here*, you made several emphatic points. First of all, you stated that you weren't going to approach the various writers that you were treating on the basis so much of theme; rather, you were going to approach them from the point of view of form. And you said that ultimately only the form of a writer's work speaks to us. Could you elaborate that concept?

Davey: I think that it's frequently overlooked that when we have a piece of written literature what we have is pure form, that is, at its most basic level, black ink on a white page and we interpret that ink as having the shape of letters and those letters forming words, those words as forming various syntactical units which ultimately form sentences, paragraphs and so on. Uh, when we read a work of literature, our subconscious mind as well as our conscious mind extracts the implications of the form of those blobs of ink on the page. Too many critics talk about literature as if the content were somehow right out there on the surface, as if it had no relation to the formal elements which they must have interpreted in order to have discovered that content. The whole process of reading literature is overlooked by many critics. I find that people who read uh often subconsciously recognize far more than what the critic can bring to consciousness and identify and articulate and I want to make sure that the interpretation of literature is well founded on what the writers *actually* put on the page.

Komisar: You said that the form of the poetry reflects the social and economic realities of the time . . .

Davey: Oh! Did I say that?

Komisar: In particular, you were talking about formalists and their structured kind of poetry with reference to the hierarchies of society and all that and that's what I was hoping we could get in here as an extension of the discussion on form.

Davey: Yes. Well, there is a connection between social history and literary form. In periods where social forms are conservative literary form tends to be conservative and in times when there are large divergencies in political and social opinions, in times of unrest, then you tend to get uh wider possibilities of literary form. In the 20th century, I think this was seen very vividly in the 1950s when the poetry which was being published was very conservative reflecting the conservative, cold-war political climate.

In the 1930s, Dorothy Livesay, after writing really crisp beautiful imagist poems in the first collection of *Green Pitcher* begins writing political poems with very loose long lines uh with a very definite rhetorical repetitive structure, a greater imprecision and carelessness with words than before and overall, because of the way in which these poems drift into rhetoric and cliché, had a much less convincing tone about them. They were obviously written to an issue which she felt she had to believe in but there's no longer the sense that she believed in them as a reality in the way that she believed in those actual objects in the Imagist poems.

Komisar: What reality specifically are you talking about?

Davey: I'm talking about the Socialist-Marxist message of those poems that Livesay wrote in the 30s. They seem as things she felt she *ought* to believe in rather than she believed in. And this comes out of the form of the poem; this comes out of the fact that she uses the rhetorical line rather than the idiosyncratic line, this comes out of the fact that she uses conventional political words with a conventional, ahh, image for a political idea rather than one which comes out of her own personal experience. I think this is a *valid* indicator of the authenticity and sincerity of a poet's vision—is the extent to which he drifts to second hand wording, second hand imagery, second hand rhythms.

Komisar: Did you want to say anything more about the 50s?

Davey: There was a lot of underground poetry being written in the 50s which didn't really surface until the 60s. There was this revolutionary undercurrent that was going on which came out in the late 50s as the beat generation, the Black Mountain group or as Louis Dudek and Raymond Souster in Canada but they were not, even though they were very active during the 50s, they didn't really receive any significant public attention until the late 50s and into the 60s. The writers who received attention during the 50s tended to be conservative and I think this is because, uh, when a time is philosophically or politically conservative, it is conservative across the board and is unwilling to welcome anything that disturbs its sense of tradition and sense of convention, no matter *what* the field is—whether it be religion, literature, politics, uh, sociology, whatever.

I think the scientist in a period like this is free of it and even then the scientist tends to get channelled into conservative projects, you know, into projects which are governed by political necessity . . . that in a liberal period, in a libertarian period, the scientist tends to be much more adventurous and to go off on his own. Uh . . . ya, I think science . . . people tend to think of science as being objective but right at the point that the scientist decides what's going to be the object of his study, it is not objective it is subjective and I think a study comparing the interest, the focus of scientifc study say in the 50s with those of scientists in the late 60s — I think that would be really instructive. But it would have to be not just a few top-notch scientists but say a 100,000 scientists in North America. When I say scientists, I mean you know, uh chemistry professors who do minor research projects in their spare time — in what direction they are oriented.

Komisar: OK. Let's keep moving forward in time. In *From There to Here* you say that the current micro-electronic technology, in other words, the various kinds of media and kinds of communication that we have today are influencing current literary trends as well as trends in politics. One of the phrases that you used was that we were moving to a post-modern pre-reflective phase . . .

Davey: Well, yes. The modernist phase was dominated by the centralization of power — the centrialization of publishing power by use of large machines, centralization of political power by the use of standing armies and so on. And the writers tended to revolt against technology because they disliked the implication for human freedom of these centralized forces. This was the case of Pound, Eliot, Joyce and so on. Uh, technology recently, because it has taken the form of small gadgets, small printing presses and so on has begun to amplify the power of the private man rather than the power of large corporations, the government. It's made possible for guerilla warfare to be conducted by small groups of people against large nations. It's made it possible for small publishing operations in Canada to be successful and perhaps not to compete but to survive (which I think is important) to survive in the face of large centralizing publishing houses such as Knopf, Random House and so on. Uh, the problem which many Canadian publishers have faced has been overextension. They've taken on a scale which was inappropriate to their function. The publishing houses which have been really successful in Canada are those which have remained on the scale which the micro-technology makes economically feasible.

Komisar: You're talking about multi centres existing within Canada.

Davey: Yes, micro-technology makes it possible for every place to be the centre because from any individual through small xerox machines, small offset presses, tape recorders, etc. messages can be sent outward. And so what you get is a matrix, a network of many centres rather than a centralized world in which New York is the authority or London is the authority. That's the *big* characteristic, that's the chief characteristic of the present arts scene is that the centres are multiple and are in unexpected places *not* in London or New York or Paris. And they can be in Canada which of course is the most interesting thing from our point of view.

Komisar: A bit earlier in this interview, you referred to sincerity. What kind of moral responsibility do you feel that you must personally practise in your own writing.

Davey: Yes, I see writers as generally being divided into two groups. Those who see writing as a way to personal self-confidence or a way of gaining respect or financial security, critical acclaim, influence or power. Uh, these I do not find very interesting. They want personal advancement and are using literature as a means to an end. Uh, the ones who interest me are the ones who see the writer's role as a custodial one. Where the writer is the custodian of the language and he has a responsibility to that language which requires him to make self-sacrifices if that is what is necessary for the language to be kept pure of imprecision and literary form to be kept free of conventionality and cliché.

Komisar: Currently we have various cliques in the literary scene. No doubt each one of these writing groups would claim that they were uh writing true to their vision. What, therefore, is the test of authenticity? How would you judge a poem as being authentic?

Davey: Well, I don't know if it's just a matter of looking at a poem and asking whether this poem is authentic. There are many signs of insincerity in the writing scene. The submission to having hype, advertising flack written on one's dust jacket blurbs, the tendency for a group of writers to write hyperbolic material on each other's dust jacket blurbs which we've seen in one particular private press in Canada. There's the use of attention getting form, form which serves no other purpose but to attract public attention. There's a tendency to write of popular second hand ideas so that these ideas meet with a friendly public. There's a tendency to self-parody where a writer finds himself writing in a successful form, a form that's critically well-received and then goes on writing in that form again and again—not being willing to take any chance on pushing his writing into an unexplored area.

Komisar: What about the writer who borrows mythologies that aren't indigenous to his country or don't naturally arise out of his own environment?

Davey: Well I think the writer is able to steal from anything which will uh enable him to accurately express his vision. What I object to is . . . suddenly we get a rash of books about ecology or about uh Women's Liberation about 3 or 4 months after these have become popular on the talk shows of the country. That seems to me to be simply a rip off. The writer's obviously more interested in pushing himself rather than interested in writing.

Komisar: OK. One of the books of poetry that you've written is

King of Swords and there you've borrowed the story of King Arthur. How did you explain that as being natural to yourself and true to yourself?

Davey: Well . . . I think every writer has a fund of experiences—personal direct literary whatever—and one can only help but write out of these experiences. I suppose there were writers who had a fund of clichéd experiences which they were forced to write out of and it was authentic for them to present a conventional and clichéd vision. In that particular case, I happened to be interested in Celtic mythology uh in the Arthurian legends and many other things. When my personal experiences suddenly called to my mind resemblances with Arthurian lore, when suddenly I saw rimes occurring between what was happening in my life and what I knew was happening else-where, uh I had no alternative but to articulate these because these seemed so powerfully present in my consciousness.

Komisar: One of the people . . .

Davey: There's a very real difference between that and taking a popular idea . . . like Arthurian legend has not been a—has not been a modish thing.

Komisar: Right.

Davey: I didn't read about it in *Maclean's* . . .

Komisar: What about the other kind of poetry that you write uh simply in terms of subject matter and that's the historical poem. You've written *The Clallam*, for example, which deals with a fairly unknown shipwreck. What interests you in these obscure events?

Davey: You're asking me to analyse myself. I've wondered too what interests me in these shipwrecks. The poems come out of the fact that I *was* interested in the shipwrecks—I did not know precisely why. Uh, these were mainly unknown ships. I've never been interested in writing a poem about the Titanic or the Lusitania. These ships—I think the reason I wrote about them was because they were emblems of my personal life, my personal sense of mortality about—they fall from the surface of life, from the ocean down into the blackness—they way every event of our lives falls from the present into the past, from consciousness into unconsciousness, in the way our lives eventually end up. I think that if a critic were to read my work carefully, he would find every book I've written has been about loss—that these shipwreck poems have been emblems of my personal losses.

Komisar: OK. That for me resolves the apparent difference between the two supposed kinds of poetry you write...

Davey: There was this myth that there were two Frank Davey's—the Frank Davey that wrote about his personal life and when his personal life got too strong uh that he couldn't face it anymore—he escaped into this world of shipwreck and wrote poems about shipwrecks. My message to you is that one never does escape oneself, that when one is writing a poem about shipwrecks one is still writing a poem about oneself. *Every* experience that one has, every activity that one undertakes is subjective, reflects upon oneself. And that is the secret of form; form always testifies whether it's to what you think it's testifying or to something else. And this is what I object to about criticism that does not pay attention to form. Now the form that my uh meditations on loss took were the shipwreck poems. That testifies to my wish to evade, it's *there*—wish to evade personal experiences—but also testifies to my continual fascination with loss and my determination to work out, I suppose, some metaphysic of loss.

Komisar: For anyone that's not familiar with your writing, maybe I can say this—that you try to write as directly as possible. To what extent does that feature grow out of Olson's influence on you?

Davey: Olson had a strong influence on me when I was 21, 22. I haven't read any Olson for 5 or 6 years. The writers who have had the most influence on me recently have been the French philosophical writers, Roland Barthes and Merleau-Ponty, whose ideas about writing out of direct ongoing consciousness, out of pre-reflected consciousness, are similar to Olson's but I find uh in many ways more satisfying and more accurately, stimulatingly presented.

Komisar: Olson talks about a response—almost a physical response, an immediate response to the environment and talks about an organic vision as well...

Davey: Yes and if you have that kind of immediate response, you can't have one eye on your audience—saying, what are they going to think of this? Are they going to like my poem?

That is an irrelevant consideration.

Komisar: You continually talk about the subjective response. I could see someone misinterpreting that as basically being anti-intellectual in some ways—also you talk about post-logical writing.

Davey: Yes. I think that human imagination transcends its intellectual powers. I'm anything but anti-intellectual. However, I feel that art goes beyond and contains, transcends the intellect and that it enables us to understand a world that is not totally logical, that cannot be comprehended by logic— which can be partially comprehended by logic but which is finally post-logical, post-reasonable. We have to enter our imagination in order to understand the universe because of that sense about it. There's nothing logical about the structure of our experiences, about the structure of nature. Pardon me, there is something logical about it but that is not all. Experience is only logical up to a point then we must enter into something beyond reason.

Komisar: What would you say then, besides this attempt at fidelity to the initial experience, to the impetus behind the poem, what are the poetics for you—the poetic rules—that's a bad word—what are you aiming at in your poerty?

Davey: Ya, it goes back to Olson's statement. It's accuracy or nothing and this means that you can't be derivative. It means that you have to find the words and form that are precisely accurate to what you feel, what you have to say in a particular place, circumstance, social milieu that you're in—you've got to find the voice in your words that articulates that experience.

Komisar: Let's keep bouncing ... What do you think was the most conservative phase in Canadian Literature and then the most vibrant or experimental phase and, finally, where do you think we're at now?

Davey: Well, Canadian Literature began conservatively and remained conservative right until the time of A.J.M. Smith and F.R. Scott.

I think this is a characteristic of the literature of any colony—that it tends to seek approval from the established literary nations and especially from the literary mentors of the mother country. So that if you look at nineteenth century

Canadian literature, you'll see models are usually forty years old and even when you get to writers who are recognized as being the first writers to provide imagery that is faithful to the actual quality of the Canadian landscape—people like the Confederation poets—uh, you find that they were working out of Keats—they were working out of Emerson of all people uh who flourished in 1840 and here they are writing in the 1870s and the 80s and so on. Scott got the furthest simply because he removed himself from the literary world and went out into the wilderness. I find that out of that group, he is the least inhibited by a sense of what kind of form he ought to be writing in.

Komisar: Let's go on to what you think was the breaking point.

Davey: Oh, we went through a terrible period after the Confederation poets, you know, in the 1910s and 1920s where there was a great upsurge of nationalism in the country and of literary nationalism and of self-congratulation by all kinds of writers who belonged to the Canadian Author's Association on just how well they were doing their second-hand renderings of Rupert Brooke and W.H. Davies and Walter de la Mare. Another condition of the colonial literary nation is a choice of second-rate figures, second-rank figures, as models and that was happening in the 1920s. But there simply was *no* sense among any of those writers that they had any responsibility to originate form or to write differently from elsewhere in the world. There was a sense that, uh, style and form were matters laid down by other writers and the Canadian writer's job was to measure up to standards laid down outside—no sense that they could lead. And even when a breakthrough came with A.J.M. Smith, F.R. Scott and *The McGill Fortnightly Review* in 1926, 27, that *hasn't* changed. What's happened is that the models have suddenly become first-rate and up-to-date, but we still don't have a sense among the country's writers that *they*, just like T.S. Eliot, that *they*, just as Ezra Pound, could originate literary form— that they could write innovatively— not just from a thematic point of view but they could originate form that was specifically suitable to the material they were working in. And this was something that first rate writers in other countries were always able to do and I think that sense of responsibility to take the lead is what's been lacking in Canada.

Komisar: So when do you think that Canadian writers did take the lead, if ever?

Davey: I don't think it happened in Canada until the 1960s. Uh, you may think this is egotistic of me because I think it is the writers of my generation who did this. I don't think the writers of Richler's generation did it. I don't think the writers of Reaney's and Mandel's and Layton's generation did it, although, I think in the 60s and 70s they began doing it. I think it would be naive of me to say they began doing this because younger writers began doing it. I think the whole literary climate changed, I think that in the 1960s, Canadians did develop a sense of self-confidence which coincided with the United States' growing feeling of lack of confidence and that this has coloured the whole literary scene.

Komisar: OK, but can you talk about any particular cases in point where a mode has been successfully experimental and has been first rate literature?

Davey: Well, I think that bp nichol's is a good case in point— who began working with derived ideas in concrete poetry and in the comic strip and in Black Mountain poetry and in younger Canadian poetry of his own time. Like he was a fan of mine at a time I didn't even know bp existed. He has grown beyond that. I think that his later work, *Two Novels* and *Martyrology*, his collaborative criticism with Steve McCaffery and the TRG group—I think they are unprecedented in world literature. And these are the kinds of things that Canadians should look for in their writing—are kinds of writing which are not based on foreign models, are not looking for approval from the *New Yorker* or *TLS*, are not seeking to mimic forms of writing that have already been approved in foreign bodies of criticism but which arise specifically—arise out of the Canadian writer's own vision, his own material and the needs he perceives that material and vision to have.

Komisar: Again, I'm going to try to nail you—in which *way* is bp's writing, for example, unprecedented?

Davey: Well, I think it's unprecedented in the risks it takes. On a formal level I find *The Martyrology* is a combination of strong writing with failed poems, with banal clichéd passages which nichol obviously recognizes as such but which he includes as documents of places where he's been so that the poem becomes a record or a document of his working his way through a psychic space, a literary space and so on—and I've never seen this before in writing. I've seen Robert Creeley's *The Charm* whch is a collection of juvenalia of early failed poems which Creeley published as documents of that part of his early life but I've never seen a writer deliberately publish these failed passages as integral parts of a successful overall whole. I also think nichol's combination of genres, of concrete, comic strip, ordinary writing, the way in which he combines these is very original.

Komisar: When you're talking about using failed poems though, you're talking about integrating them into one successful whole . . .

Davey: That's right, yes. So that the failed poem becomes a document of the fact that he was overwhelmed by the material and that fact becomes important and one doesn't concentrate on the failure of the poem, one concentrates on the fact that he was going through a process of literary failure while writing the poem.

Komisar: Does it come out more on a content level than a formal level?

Davey: Well I think it comes out on a formal level but you have to extrapolate to a level of content. What it means is that *The Martyrology* has to be read as a whole—you can't just open it at random and read a page because that might be one of the failed passages which only makes sense in terms of the overall view.

Komisar: Well then, what was his process — do you mean to say that he actually had completed poems which he integrated into a larger poem sequence as he was working on it?

Davey: I don't know how he wrote it but I would see it as very similar to the serial poem where you simply continue to write whatever comes into your mind on a subject when that subject engages you and you preserve those lines in the order in which they're given and those poems in the sequence in which they're given — I think, in some sense, an obedience to the order and complexity of material.

Komisar: You were talking about your own generation of writers as uh making break-throughs and not using external modes and yet, while discussing that, you were mentioning the Black Mountain group which in fact originated in the States.

Davey: Ya, I think that what happened in our group, the Black Mountain group, was important for the first five years of our writing — for myself between 1960-65. I say elsewhere in this interview that I haven't read much Olson in the past 5 or 6 years and it's true of all those Black Mountain writers. I've got into other literary sources; I've got into different kinds of writers like anyone from Jackson MacLow, Rothenberg, Jack Spicer. Not as models but as resources on how words can be used and how forms can be used and I find myself, my contemporaries are imitating no-one and, when I say my contemporaries, I mean the people in Canadian Letters that I feel are working in the same way I am toward original form. And, as in any period like this, you tend to borrow the best and then make new use of that — new application of it. I don't think that happened before uh 1960 . . . I'll say 1960 . . . in Canadian Letters. But take the English Renaissance. There's all kinds of derivativeness there — especially on Italian models and yet what Surrey and Shakespeare and Wyatt and Sidney do is entirely new. It can in no way be considered derivative or Petrarch or Dante or whatever.

Komisar: What are you working on right now?

Davey: I'm writing a book about Louis Dudek and Raymond Souster.

Komisar: What takes you back to Dudek? He's not well known — maybe this (writing about him) again has something to do with fighting against loss.

Davey: Yes, he's a writer of fantastic integrity and he is a writer who sacrificed the possibility of a large literary reputation to the requirements of uh literary integrity. He came to a point of his life where he was very skilled in the use of complicated verse forms. He could have, in 1952, continued writing beautiful poems that were admired by the literary establishment. Uh, instead, because he believed that literature and life can not be separated, because he believed that it is immoral to extract literary beauty from the content of a literary work the way in which Ezra Pound is currently taught in Universities by admiring his form and throwing away his content, he began writing poetry uh from which the form could not be extracted from its content. Functional poetry he called it — poetry which was almost totally denotative statement where the verbal artistry is so subtle that it would be impossible for a critic to extract it. Therefore, the critics ignored him. I find that a really admirable commitment to language and I think that he's a much more important writer than anyone suspects. I think he's the first Canadian writer to conceive of the moral integrity of the writer's role to be the foremost element in his work.

Interview date: May, 1975
Transcription date: June, 1975

from White Pelican Edmonton (1975)

Tish: **A Movement**

CH Gervais

The *Tish* movement's major concern is poetics. Yet one can divide this concern basically into two themes: the relation of the poet to poetry, and the relation of the poet to 'place'.

Of the former, the Tishites would be the first to admit that they were not original or that their poetics were not even new in Canada. Frank Davey, in fact, points out in *The Tamarack Review*; "a large number of recent Canadian poets excluding the Tishites already had considerable contact with Black Mountain",[1] he goes on to name Layton, Dudek, Souster and others. The point, however, is that Black Mountain's ideas caught on more in Canada than in the United States; and that Layton, Dudek and Souster "experienced this tradition since 1951",[2] but the magazine *Tish* (founded in 1960) was perhaps the first to openly state their debt to the United States influence:

> Vancouver's *Tish* ... caught everyone unaware of Canada's previous and widespread literary entangle-

[1] Frank Davey, "Black Days on Black Mountain," *The Tamarack Review*, No. 35 (1965), p.64.

[2] Davey, Ibid., p.65.

ment in the movement...³

In tracing the statements made by *Tish*, I found that the clearest interpretations of Black Mountain's ideas arose not in letters and articles, but in poetry. Hence, the focus here will be chiefly on the poetry with occasional reference to the prose. And with this first theme — the relation of the poet to the poem — I will indicate how *Tish* interpreted (mainly) Olson's ideas, as well as pointing out both the successes and incongruities in their attempt.

Of the latter theme — the relation of the poet to 'place' — I think the Tishites stumbled upon an excellent explanation for a very predominant theme in Canadian literature, a theme which Dorothy Livesay calls the "Documentary".⁴ In studying it, I will show how it is more convincing (as far as *Tish*'s poetics is concerned) than the other.

Tish's poetry generally alludes to what Olson said in "Projective Verse" — mostly to the relationship of the poet to the poem:

> From the moment he ventures into Field Composition — puts himself in the open — he can go by no track other than the one the poem under hand declares, for itself. Thus he has to behave, and be, instant by instant, aware of some several forces.⁵

Essentially what Olson is expressing is that the poem is something of fantastic potential, and that it is up to the poet to discover what he must do with it. As far as Olson is concerned, if the poet decides to tamper with the potential poem before it declares itself, then he is, in fact, restricting its potential. Instead, the poet must act upon whatever the poem declares for itself. And in order to accomplish this, he

³ Davey, Ibid., p.65.

⁴ Dorothy Livesay, "The Documentary Poem: A Canadian Genre," in *Contexts of Canadian Criticism,* ed. Eli Mandel (Chicago, 1971), p.267.

⁵ Charles Olson, "Projective Verse" in *Human Universe and Other Verses by Charles Olson,* ed. Donald Allen (New York, 1967), p.52.

must come to the poem aware of those "several forces", which Davey re-defines as "physical-psychological-physiological".[6] Coming to the poem ready, as such, allows the poet to *see* it as it really is, not as he wishes it to be. This is George Bowering's point in "For WCW":[7]

> it is
> as it should be or
> as it is

Therefore, in regard first to the poem as something of fantastic potential, one finds most Tishites in agreement. Lionel Kearns, for instance, develops this idea in a short poem entitled "It". He describes a tree which has fallen down among other debris as "a thing...apart", something that can be "used ... or discarded",[8] it's the choice of the one who has cut it down. Kearns' inference, as well as Olson's, is that the poet too has this choice; for just as the fallen tree "declares for itself" possibilities such as mantel-piece decoration or firewood, so too does the poem declare for itself many possibilities. This is most evident in the final lines when Kearns says that the dead tree may be thrown into the fire. One may take this to mean that it can be discarded by literally throwing it away into the fire, or it can be used constructively as firewood for warmth and light. The tree by its very nature declares these choices. The poem too has such potential.

Frank Davey in "Poem-Break" shares Kearns' bewilderment and the resulting ambiguity when stumbling upon "a thing ... apart". He writes:

> Odd how one stares at a thing

---

[6] Frank Davey, "The Problems of Margins," *Tish*, No.3(1961), p.11.

[7] George Bowering, "For WCW," in *Touch Selected Poems 1960-1970*, (Toronto, 1971), p.25. All quotations from George Bowering's poems will be taken from *Touch* except those taken from *Geneve*, thus in further references only the title of the poem and page number will be given, unless otherwise indicated in the text.

[8] Lionel Kearns, "It" in *Pointing* (Toronto, 1967), p.3.

> or listens to the dull hum
> of fluorescent lights.[9]

Here, Davey, like Kearns, provides a clue to how one may penetrate that ambiguity or bewilderment. The poet in "Poem-Break" allows himself to be wide-open to things about him, and thus feels a kind of oddness, and perhaps in a sense touches the roots of experience usually overlooked. This is Olson's point all over again: if the poet makes himself open to discovery, he will indeed understand the potential (or what is called the "energy"[10] of the poem. Bowering's introductory verses to *Touch* stress this:

> Any music will touch us
> as it's power is allowed.
>
> is allowable.[11]

And Davey's "The Bandit" even goes so far as to say that if left alone, the poem will develop on its own. He emphasizes this with an analogy to weeds growing freely in his yard:

> So much
> that happens, when let happen. Left alone, there
> would still be a garden.[12]

Such an abandonment turns up in Robert Hogg's "Eclipse" as a willingness to be manipulated. Here, in a strange erotic fantasy the poet walks "into the centre of a circle of fire" where he is at once "made ... magic"[13], and where he, time and again, submits to sexual violence. In a sense, this too is Olson's idea, that the poet goes into the experience with open willingness to let the poem work its magic. For Hogg, such magic is an ecstatic purging of violence, it is self-discovery.

[9] Frank Davey, *Bridge Force* (Toronto, 1965), p.43.
[10] Olson, "Projective Verse," p.52.
[11] Bowering, "As Introduction," p.11.
[12] Frank Davey, *Weeds* (Toronto, 1970), p.9.
[13] Robert Hogg, "Eclipse," in *New Wave Canada,* ed. Raymond Souster (Toronto, 1965), p.81.

A similar action in Bowering's long poem, *Geneve*, might shed some light on Hogg's poem. Bowering begins at the centre of spiral-arranged Tarot cards (like Hogg starting at the centre of a circle of fire), and he both physically and spiritually relates to each card, entering them, and allowing their powers to make magic of him. Totally open to their decisions (as Hogg was open to sexual violence in "Eclipse"), Bowering simultaneously recognizes himself in the cards, knowing that he continues to enter each of them:

> & you know all along it's myself
> I'm talking about.[14]

Bowering's self-identification may be equated with Hogg's self-discovery, for Bowering too is purging himself when he faces up to each recognition, no matter how revealing.

But the important aspect for now, however, is not so much the idea of self-discovery, but the process by which Hogg and Bowering achieved it. The process, to put it simply, is a willing fusion of subject and object. Dave Dawson in "letters to gabriel" rather explicitly refers to this when speaking of the poet as "carver"[15]:

> he it is who makes the cut
> breaks or turns the line
> goes into the stone
> to pull
>   himself out[16]

One notices that this also takes place in *Geneve*. Each entrance into the cards results in Bowering pulling himself out. Such an action is a fusion of the poet and the card's powers, but it is also an action that can take place only if the poet is willingly open to it.

Frank Davey's interpretation, though similar, is more theoretical. He says that in order to write the open poem, one must be located where those "several forces" exist. Once

[14] George Bowering, *Geneve* (Toronto, 1971), p.8.
[15] Dave Dawson, "letters to gabriel" in *New Wave Canada*, p.40.
[16] Dawson, "letters..." p.40.

accomplished, the poet can write out of that "locus".[17] He indicates that:

> ... the only ... position from which he can (with accuracy) write ... is the one (physical-psychological-physiological) *in which ... he is standing*[18]

Therefore, it may be said that in *Geneve* Bowering locates himself in the cards, where those "several forces" thrive, and he writes from that stance. To be thus situated means to willingly submit to those forces.

It is also important to note that such a reaction may seem a passive one, but in another way it is not. Olson's distinction between "open" and "closed" verse may explain why. "Closed" verse is the sort of poetry where a writer actively moulds the poem into a desired shape, and thereby restricts its inherent potential, and consequently develops only a portion of it. In the "open" poem, however, because the poet leaves himself open to many forces, he allows the poem to develop fully. Hence, to be willingly open to the potential growth of the poem also means to be actively instrumental in making that poem; it means to actively write out of the son's belief is that the "energy" of those forces will be transferred (or fused) to the poem's—and one can identify those forces manifested in "breath" and in "voice" written right into the lines, for just as anger will show up as satire or verbal abuse in a letter, so will the poet's energy show up in the poem. But it must be reiterated that this can only come about if the poet is willingly open to both his own energy and the poem's. And this involves, Bowering says, a total break up of our attitudes:

> Breaking up
> of nations, sickness, log jam,
> mypsyche
>
> the way of the world

[17] Davey, "The Problem of Margins," p.11.
[18] Davey, Ibid.

> order,
> form,[19]

Bowering's implication is that structures should be broken up because (as he says near the end of "Breaking Up, Breaking Out") they will show nothing "till the first crack"; the first crack will be its first "gracious gesture."[20] Obviously this can apply to poetry too, for it like all restricted structures (Bowering states in "The Crumbling Wall") "requires change and must crumble to remain"[21] These allusions, not surprisingly echo Olson:

> ... the conventions which logic has forced on syntax must be broken open as quietly as must the too set feet of the old lines.[22]

Essentially what is being said here is that a break up of attitudes will result in a willingness to submit to those forces, which will, in Hogg's estimation, make "magic" of us. In the writing process, the energy we leave ourselves open to will inevitably get into the poem. It may come by way of "voice", as in Lionel Kearns' *Listen George*. His long poem breaks open the conventions forced on syntax because it is rambling and free, reminiscent of Kerouac's wordy prose and sections of Ginsberg's *Howl*. Kearns' style echoes his voice and psychological shifts in attitude more so than formalized verse, but instead lets everything flow out naturally and unaffected.

Bowering's poem "Grandfather" to a certain extent achieves this. Bowering captures his Grandfather's bible-thumping spirit in booming repetitious lines as in:

> Jabez Harry Bowering
> strode across the Canadian prairie
> hacking down trees
> hacking down trees and building churches

---

[19] Bowering, "Breaking Up, Breaking Out" p.40.
[20] Bowering, Ibid.
[21] Bowering, "The Crumbling Wall" p.41.
[22] Olson, "Projective Verse" p. 56.

delivering personal baptist sermons in them
leading Holy holy holy lord god almighty songs in them[23]

Olson's point is that a writer can discover his own peculiar rhythm in the lines that he writes. In this poem by Bowering, I think this is true; Bowering indeed does manage to get "voice" into the lines — "voice" which seems to be the result of writing totally out of several influences.

On the whole these ideas *sound* good, but I am still distrbed over the suspicion that perhaps the Tishites are contradicting what they say about poetry *in* verse. The first example which comes to mind is Kearns' poem "It"; it defines poetry within a framework, and consequently restricts it to signify one thing and not another. To counter-argue the possibility that there is no allusion to poetics is absurd, since it is more than coincidental that Kearns was writing about poetry; everything in the poem points to it — along with the fact that Tish was notoriously exigent in defining poetry. Therefore, it does seem contradictory to prescribe a fixed theory of poetics which is supposed to work the opposite effect. But on the other hand, I am not rejecting Olson's theories; I am merely emphasizing the obvious incongruity in writing an "open" poem about a strict theory of poetry.

Geneve, too, raises a point of incongruity. As pointed out earlier, Bowering reacts *openly* to the Tarot pack, and writes out of that reaction (or "locus"). Such an experience perhaps is valid for the poet — he may be able to make the magic from the fusion of himself and the cards touch him — but he fails to make it touch anyone else, namely the reader. What I mean is simply that Bowering's verses are not conducive to participation; they are too descriptive. This is especially noticeable in sections of *Geneve* where one is provided with unimaginative description of cards. For example, the verses about the "Hermit" are mere poetic speculations; nothing startling or significant is revealed about the card:

He's a Lonely Man

[23] Bowering, p.16.

>   with a long face
>   & his robes
>   ungainly
>   so far from his youth
>   he might have been
>   ....one of the warriors[24]

Obviously this language is not any different from other modes of prose description. Furthermore, Bowering's written meditations on the Hermit, though they may bring him a poetic experience, fail to provide the reader with anything revelatory.

Other *Tish* Poets

Other *Tish* poets whose works display incongruities, even more so than Kearns' or Bowering's, are many. David Cull's *3 x 4 IS* perhaps is the best one to cite. Evident in this book is the error of taking Olson too literally. When Olson said that syntax should be broken open, Cull *broke* it open to the extent that his lines make very little sense. In fact, the nearly nonexistent syntax of his poetry makes it almost impossible for a reader to get into the work. The poems are ironically "closed" beyond Olson's wildest nightmares. One can attribute this to a number of things; one, Cull breaks up the line so that words appear strung together like a mobile on the page. This is something which Bowering employs but makes effective by using the page as a musical score. With Cull's work this is virtually impossible, since there are so many unnecessary words which, for a second point, not only break any natural rhythm but also confuse the reader and lead him astray. Either Cull has not read Ezra Pound's "A Few Don'ts" or he disagrees with it. If that is the case, then how can he accept Olson's ideas which are a direct offshoot of Pound and Williams? Pound and Williams both discouraged redundancy: "Use no superfluous word, no adjective which does not reveal something"[25]. Yet a study of Cull's work will show

---

[24] Bowering, *Geneve*, p.19.

[25] Ezra Pound, "A Few Don'ts" in *20th Century Poetry Poetics*, ed. Gary Geddes (Toronto, 1969) p.515.

that he is too detailed, and that he crowds out the main thoughts of his work. As an example, "bird study in british columbia"[26], brings together irrelevant details about his Grandfather (besides, why is "Grandfather" capitalized and not "british columbia"?) much like a notebook. And like a notebook, tone and style of language shift with mood, but in Cull's case when the short and detailed tone becomes flamboyant and indirect, one begins to wonder whether there was any reason for it. Such a technique in Kearns' *Listen George* was effective because it was natural but logical; in "bird study" the change is too severe and illogical.

A final thing which I found disturbing in Cull's work is punctuation, which in most cases is misleading and not helpful, but obviously deliberate from its over-use! For example, the use of quotations without reference assumes the reader knows who the speaker is, when in fact it is rather doubtful. And the abundance of 'dashes' and 'bracketts' throughout the poems makes one wonder whether Cull really wants to say anything outright.

Jamie Reid is another whose work tends to be confusing, as well as incongruous with Black Mountain's and *Tish*'s ideas. The introduction to *The Man Whose Path Was On Fire* is indicative of the poems inside: chaotic, too private, and nearly always obstruct participation, which is a necessary requirement of Olson's theories.

Despite the fact that there are many more incongruities in the work of the Tishites, there are some poems (already mentioned) which do succeed in hurdling inconsistencies to convince a reader that such a brand of poetics is possible. Ironically, it is usually those poems which deal with much larger issues than poetry. Hoggs' "Eclipse", for example, is not merely discussing poetics but an entire theory of perception — his own — of how to react to experience, fantasy, poetry, everything. And in a like manner, Davey's *Weeds* breaks away from poetics disguised as verse because in a prolonged meditation he freely dips in and out of experience; and thereby delves into the spectrum of perception of which poetry is only a portion.

[26] David Cull, *3 x 4 Is,* (Kitchener, 1966), p. 5-7.

But as I noted at the very beginning of this paper, the theme which the Tishites handle best is one that Livesay calls the "Documentary"; and in developing it they manage to add strength to their poetics.

Essentially, the "Documentary" theme studies the relation of the poet to 'place'. It is in Livesay's words: *a conscious attempt to create a dialectic between the objective facts and the subjective feelings of the poet.*[27] As was already noted, such a dialectic occurred between the poet and the poem, and was referred to as a "fusion". I would add that the writer in *Tish*'s terms (or more specifically Davey's) writes out of those influences (both the "objective facts" and his "subjective feelings"), and thereby affects a fusion between them. But in writing out of those influences (or what Davey calls "locus"), the poet is not only making " a conscious attempt", he is in fact submitting to those forces in order to let the poem create itself. Thus, what Livesay calls the "dialectic" is actually no different from the process taking place in *Geneve*. Just as Bowering goes into the cards to pull himself out, so too does he go into the historical past with a similar intention: to let the poem create itself — but it seems more than coincidental that there is always some point of self-discovery. In "The Descent", for example, Bowering begins with the inference about his Grandfather:

> When I think of him
> ....it is me — [28]

and throughout reiterates this self-identification:

> the eyes in the pictures
> straight without desire
> -like mine
>
> it is me in
> outlandish clothes[29]

[27] Livesay, "The Documentary Poem..." p.267.
[28] Bowering, p.18.
[29] Bowering, p.18.

The suggestion from this is that with this "dialectic" must inevitably come a point of recognition. It is not so farfetched, since there is interplay of the "objective facts" and the poet's "subjective feelings". Furthermore, it is consistent with Dawson's point made earlier that the poet goes into the experience "to pull himself out". And I think that in "The Descent" this is evident. Bowering somehow becomes the image of the old pictures and cast-away articles; he seems to enter them totally and to take on their aura and fascination, just as the the spectator becomes artist in oriental art. By going deeply into the things his Grandfather has left behind, Bowering's submission is so complete that it reaches a kind of self-discovery. This process is described by Gary Snyder in terms of using one's "senses to the fullest"; he writes "sit still and let yourself go into the birds and wind";[30] it is a process by which one eventually reaches an understanding of the other by merely submitting to it.

But it should also be pointed out that as a result of such an interplay of forces, the poet manages to register some part of himself in the lines that he writes. With Bowering it is "voice" which gets into the poem. And this, incidentally, is both consistent with Olson's theories and Livesay's; for Olson states that: *Projective Verse teaches ... this lesson, that verse will only do in which a poet manages to register both the acquisitions of his ear and the pressures of his breath.*[31] and Livesay emphasizes that documentaries should be *"heard Aloud"*[32].

In any case, Bowering satisfies both in "Grandfather", successfully synthesizes and incorporates the bible-thumping spirit and enthusiasm of his Grandfather's life by bringing to the lines a fire and brimstone boom. One can read Bowerings' poem as if it were a sermon: *six years on the road to Damascus till his eyes were blinded with the blast of Christ & he wandered west to Brandon among wheat kings & heathen Saturday nights*[33]. A reader can, I am certain, read this poem with nearly the same pauses and stresses

[30] Gary Snyder, *Earth House Hold* (New York, 1969) p.120.
[31] Olson, "Projective Verse" p.53.
[32] Livesay, "The Documentary Poem..." p.269.
[33] Bowering, p.16.

Bowering intended; the reason is because the quality of the sermon has been captured; and lines as "leading Holy holy holy lord god almighty songs in them" can only be read effectively with a clipped and perhaps swift voice. And it is evident too that "Grandfather" would not be as powerful if not read out loud.

Portions of *Listen George* likewise should be heard:

Listen George Now Trains Are O.K.
From The Outside

like when you're out hiking along the track and
you put your ear down to the rail and say well
sure enough it must be this side of Troop
Junction do you think there's time to get
across the trestle which of course there
usually is though pretty soon along it comes
with two humping hissing lokies and waving
fireman and you can count the cars all of them
short hopper cars full of concentrates from
Kimberly going to the smelter at Rail or
else you're way hell and gone up the side of
the mountain and there's the train snaking
along the curve of the lake shore and maybe
it's in the late summer and...[34]

This passage should be read aloud, because its reading portrays the rapid, non-stop train's movement. Kearns does this by dispensing with periods, and relying heavily upon conjunctions — all of which results in capturing the train's rhythm. But at the same time it depicts Kearns' voice, or at least some colloquial, rambling, story-teller's. Consequently, to some extent, Kearns does get into the "objective facts" behind the story, just as Bowering becomes part of the cast-away belongings of his grandfather. Kearns gets into the energy of his story by telling it the way it sounds, by submitting to his own natural speech rhythms and the story's.

Frank Davey's use of "voice" is quite different from Bowering's and Kearns'; his is more impartial, more objec-

[34] Lionel Kearns, *Listen George*, in Imago, No. 3 (1965), p.20-21.

tive. *The Scarred Hull*, as an example, studies the relation of the poet to 'place' by a juxtaposition of actual data and short episodic portraits: both very different in tone:

> Shipwrecks
> litter this coast
> one source, Nicholson,
> listing 243 since 1803,
> plus seven hulks
> unidentified[35]

And "Jimmy":

> Taller than all
> except the teacher
> he found himself that day
> clutching the little girl's panties
> her, screaming thru the schoolroom[36]

As a total unit such juxtapositions have an over-all effect, like a film; they are documentaries of numerous activities, collages of action-life shots, journalistic reports and photographic stills. "Voice" is registered in so far as it is indicative of the form imitated (i.e. a journalist's speech).

Davey's technique is more obvious, more overt; he opens himself up to the total picture, and draws upon every episode and piece of data, since they make up the "locus" out of which he finds meaning. His presentation comes with each frame, sometimes in a particular "voice", sometimes with an image; its result is complete entry into many lives — yet the poet manages to remain incognito throughout. However, there's still the well-grounded suspicion that he has assembled this overall view for a reason, and therein lies the poet!

Generally then I think one can say that this relationship of the poet to 'place' is of such a nature that it allows the poet to participate and extend himself into that 'place' whether it be geographical or historical. And this extension may turn up as "voice" in the lines of the poem, or in some didactical way, as

[35] Frank Davey, *The Scarred Hull*, in Imago, No. 6 (1966), p.6.
[36] Davey, *The Scarred Hull*, p.19.

perhaps in Davey's *The Scarred Hull*. Whatever the result, it reflects the author's interplay with that other force. Dawson's distinction in "letters to gabriel", referred to earlier, validates this. The poet, like the carver, goes into the object to pull himself out; likewise for the one who goes into the historical past to pull out a sense of recognition. Bowering does it in "The Descent".

Thus, I think, on the whole, distinctions like these established throughout about poetics — though at times they fail in application — do fit reasonably well in to the "Documentary" theme; for here one easily can accept the idea that historical and geographical 'place' is penetrable; it is done in story-telling. It also happens in movie-theatres whatever the camera turns to, the audience accepts, says McLuhan. Therefore it should not seem too far-fetched to say that, when the poet (like Bowering or Kearns) goes into the historical past, he accepts it and takes on qualities of that experience, and equally retains some of himself in the eventual poem.

In conclusion, I might add that *Tish*'s elaboration on poetics explains much of what the process is with the "Documentary" — and perhaps can account for the upswing now in the kind of rural poems being written by Belford, Pat Lane and Dale Zieroth.

Alive Chapbook, Guelph, 1974

Poetry and the Language of Sound

George Bowering

In order for a person to one day become a painter he must one time in his young life be amazed and delighted by his own personal discovery that color is exciting, color is more than he had ever thought it could be, that the way to heaven or nirvana or the absolute control of everything is thru a hedonistic orgy of color. The poet feels a similar way about sounds, not words necessarily, but sounds, phones, allophones, phonemes, the clicking and clacking the binging and banging of sounds as they rebound about on leaving the human speech mechanism.

You will notice that I split an infinitive at the beginning of my first sentence. Without changing any words, try altering the syntax in the first eleven words before the pronoun reference. You won't be able to improve any on the sense, and the actual linear sound sequence will undergo a turn to the worse i.e.—the awkward. This is our first principle, then—let the sequence of sounds come out as the relation between your intended statement and your speech-impelling mind dictates. Delight in your miraculous ability to make sounds first, then enjoy the power you have to make sounds that people associate with the whole structural convention of the spoken language that is your greatest single inheritance. Syntax is something at your disposal, not a condition set upon the gift of language.

Then if you are a poet, if you think you are a poet, if anyone has ever told you you are a poet, put great value on your gift of speech. But in putting great value on it, dont be stingy with it. Yet at the same time dont be wasteful of it. Let us return to value later.

Now when the poet makes his great strike on the lode of speech sounds, he is having the first peak moment in his poem-making life. Personally, I think he is lucky if he makes his find quite late in life, say at twenty or twenty five. He should already have read a great deal of good poetry, and have "written" quite a lot of bad poetry. Then he can look back over a poem he had thought he'd known, and hear the sound of it, the real poem-making juice of it that his highschool teacher in English managed to suppress. Take for a random (or, anyway, not self-consciously selected) example, Hart Crane's 'Cape Hatteras', in which an American airplane runs into trouble in the sky:

> Now eagle-bright, now
>   quarry-hid, twist-
>   -ing, sink with
> Enormous repercussive list-
>   -ings down
> Giddily spiralled
>   gauntlets, upturned, unlooping
> in guerrilla sleights, trapped in combustion gyr-
> ing, dance the curdled depth
>   down whizzing
> Zodiacs, dashed
>   (now nearing fast the Cape!)
>   down gravitation's
>   vortex into crashed
> ... dispersion ... into mashed and shapeless de-
>   bris. ...
> By Hatteras bunched the beached heap of high bravery!

Now as I have seen, the only thing the highschool teacher

will tell you about sound in poetry is that it "echoes the sense." You the student would be better off if she had said nothing, or something a little more pertinent, such as "the sound echoes the temperature."

In the first place the written language is never more than an arbitrary codification of speech, which in turn is arbitrary. The sound represented by "bird" is nowhere nearer echoing the sense of that wingy creature than would be the sound "yem" if we the speakers had instead chosen it to mean that wingy creature. The sounds we have that are not arbitrary for our language, are our borrowed words (eg: "tomato"), but these are borrowed from systems that are arbitrary as our own.

Secondly, the reverse of the highschool teacher's platitude is likely closer to being an operative fact. When a teacher (or a poet) says that sound echoes the sense he is saying in effect that the poet has an intelligent statement to make, and that he considers it a feather in his cap if he can manage to force the sound of his word choice into a pattern that complements the statement. Nothing could be more lethal to the life of poetry. Taking "sense" as "meaning", we should go along with the New Grammarians (Roberts, Sledd, Hockett) in stating that meaning in speech is realized by the listener as he hears the phones that make morphemes (sound sections that differentiate meaning), as he understands the word orders, word forms, function words, and intonations, including (1) stress, (2) pitch, and (3) juncture. Hence, for example, the time-honored meaning difference between:

"What are we having for DINner, mother?"

and

"What are we having for DINner? MOther?"

We see that sense reaches us largely thru sound in ordinary speech. In poetry, which might or might not be ordinary speech, sound is the major determinant of meaning.

Another facet of sound that is dunned into young unsuspecting minds is that of onomatopoeia, both as the source of developed languages and as the special hereditary belonging of the verse maker. Usually the teacher (bless her old organizing heart) will try to establish a system of varying degrees of onomatopoeia. Full onomatopoeia is something like Whitman's:

"Hoot! Hoot!"

or

"Crack! — Crack! — Crack!"

and the program extends to the more subtle work of Keats:
"With beaded bubbles winking at the brim
And purple-stained mouth;"

The propoganda would have it that the sensual appeal here is to the senses thru onomatopoeia, the onomatopoeiac suggestion of the consonants, the aural appeal of the plosives that break like little wine bubbles. It sounds tempting as an idea, because it hastens to explain an effect already instinctively noted by the reader. But so did Copernicus. A friend and teacher of me, Mr. Ronald Baker, has come up with another answer to the puzzle of Keats' sensual appeal. Whether Mr. Baker is mostly serious or whether he is making a comment on the too-easy acceptance of high-school poetic theories, it doesnt matter too much here. He tells us to examine the passage phonetically, noticing that every consonant but two is articulated up front in the mouth, with the teeth, the lips, and the tip of the tongue. Now it just happens that it is here that the most sensitive taste buds are to be found. Then couldn't it be that what makes the sensual appeal for the reader is the matrix between the sense-reading mind and the victimized psychosomatic taste buds? I don't know. The idea sounds tempting to me, as the ideas of Copernicus used to sound tempting to the layman, as the ideas of naturopaths and chiropractors do to rural people today. In any case, it has more meat than the diluted onomatopoeia one. But I'm not buying it yet—still I respond imaginatively to Copernicus.

Which brings us to the basic point about onomatopoeia — that it is too arbitrary within each language. It is obvious that according to the simplest onomatopoeia, the imitations of animals, French roosters make different sounds from those of English roosters, and Japanese roosters crow differently from their European cousins. A barnyard trio of them would compete to wake people with a 'cocorico', a 'cock-a-doodle-do', and a 'ko-ke-ko-koh'. Why? Because the respective languages of the humans who live in their respective countries have languages just as distinctive in their sound structures. Yet one should listen more closely to socalled imitative sounds in his primary language, for instance English. Have you noticed that comic book Second World War machine guns have had their sound changed from 1944's good old *rat-a-tat-tat-tat* to the present *bud-a-buda-buda-buda* etc?

It is because we are used to seeing or hearing a certain mouthed sound being used to represent a certain real sound, that we believe in fact that it is a natural approximation. It is convention, not sincere imitation, that forms our concept of onomatopoeiac words. (And sometimes spelling: the sound represented by "bird" is often thought by people to be lighter somehow than the sound represented by "burred" —and that this is somehow related to the things signified.) If you ever heard a falling table make the actual sound of *bang* you would expect foolery afoot. But so ingrained is our acceptance of the word, that in time we have used it in nearly all the parts of speech, even as an adverbial: "We had a banging good time." In fact so unconscious do we become of irresponsible onomatopoeia that the sound originally indicated by the morpheme (and grapheme) "Ouch!", has been replaced, so that now instead of giving forth a grunt, we actually say "Ouch!" Though the Japanese would be more inclined to say "Itai!"

Now as Thomas Hardy and other anthropologists have remarked, the primitive and the artist will persist in seeking a real metaphysical association between the object and the word used to refer to it. But I sense a trend among certain American and Canadian poets to use language as sound, not as the secondary medium of verse, but as the meshing machinery of statement. Charles Olson and Robert Duncan and Jack Spicer have studied linguistics and anthropology, and have worked, for instance, with the findings of George Trager and Edward Sapir. They are aware of the esthetic and physical responses to various combinations of syllables, partaking of the relatively new attitude of formal physical study rather than notional and metaphorical description of the poetry's effects.

And Robert Creeley describes the main difference between the New Poetry and the Iowa-Yale poetry in one forgivable metaphor of his own. Some poets use language like a billboard: as Charles Olson laments

> "and words words words
> all
>   over everything"

to advertise their version of the relation of the poet to his world to

> "advertise ourselves out"

thereby placing the thing on a page *between* the reader and the countryside he wants to look at, what he took the drive for. It works by reflection, an opposite to what Charles Olson calls "projection." A projective poet uses sounds to record his own speech as a response to the poetic experience, as part of his poetic experience. The reflecting poet moves his sound *out* of his own person, attempting no record, but trying to make his speech do a job it is not culturally made for (see William Carlos Williams on the poem as machine) — thru attempting to make his sound echo the sense. You will hear your sound work for you if you choose from the sounds of life ("fish") rather than distorting them in a vain attempt to mingle sound and essential sense ("finny tribe").

T.S. Elliot, much as we malign him while we should be exposing his emulators who tried to write their own poetry in his borrowed voice, knew what he was doing with his selected sounds.

In 'The New Republic' of November 11, 1936, John Peale Bishop wrote: "Eliot, in such a poem as 'Sweeney Among The Nightingales', had shown how by controlling the sound apart from the sense the most prosaic statements could be turned to poetry." Credit Bishop with a dangling modifier and a key statement.

> "Slips and pulls the table cloth
> Overturns a coffee-cup,
> Reorganized upon the floor
> She yawns and draws a stocking up."

There is the place to investigate, in the poem itself, preferably the whole poem. Let your critical mind alone and listen to the sounds, libidinate yourself. How are the sounds working? (Fine, thank you, is an acceptable answer. And thinking of the maker Eliot, why are they working that way?

Then, if the sound does not echo the sense, and yet if it does still have an appeal for the reader, a moving appeal that winds up at the same finish line as the message has made in the syntactical progression of the words, what is the way of that appeal? How does the sound do it?

Well, how does music do it? As Ezra Pound repeats: "music begins to atrophy when it departs too far from the dance. . . . poetry begins to atrophy when it gets too far from music."

For thirty centuries estheticians have been quarreling with musicians and trying to examine the appeal of music and of the dance. And for a good deal longer than that, and all the while the philosophers have been muggling about, people have been liking and enjoying rhythmic music. Sometime you should go up to a lively pair of dancers and put the question to them. Ask them to tell you why the present sounds affect them emotionally. They should know better than anyone else.

The poet should know better than anyone else why certain phonetic events delight him or seem right to him; and he knows just as the dancers know — from personal sensate experience and patterns. If he is as true as possible to his own experience, he will be true as possible to his reader. Whether he knows the syllable means sad or wide or something indefinable, he will know it seems right (or wrong) and will capture or cleave.

Most important, the sounds he records on paper will not echo the "sense" (try and say what that is, once human voice is removed), but will echo the vocal articulation of the responding poet in the traveling moment. The poet's sound is his voice.

> "But there, within the seed, shaken by
> fear as by a sea, it wakes again! to
> drive upward, presently, from that soft
> belly such a stem as will crack quartz."

Hear that?

How I Hear Howl

George Bowering

(Poetry is a vocal art. In the following impression of Allen Ginsberg's poem, I will refer not so much to the printed versions as to his spoken version on the Fantasy LP 7005, *Howl and Other Poems.*)

I dont know how useful it is to relate a present poet to earlier poets, but I know it is commonly done, & that it can be done here. Ginsberg's sources are well acknowledged, or scrutinised by the critics & other interested parties. William Carlos Williams, Whitman, Blake, Shelley, Christopher Smart, the poets of the Old Testament, all these most immediately.

Once in the *Village Voice* (August 25, 1959) there was an article by Ginsberg called "Poetry, Violence, and the Trembling Lambs." There he made observations in slightly uncharacteristic straight sentences, that place him as a modern Romantic, as one who professes what the English Romantics professt , holding those truths in mind for the present day, this one in 1965 (1968), or possibly later:

"Recent history is the record of a

> vast conspiracy to impose one level
> of mechanical consciousness on man-
> kind and exterminate all manifestations
> of that unique part of human sentience
> in all men, which the individual
> shares with his Creator."

Then, speaking of some poets, he says they:

> "have had the luck and courage and fate
> to glimpse something new through the
> crack in mass consciousness; they have
> been exposed to some insight into their
> own nature, the nature of God."

Blake had said:

> For Mercy, Pity, Peace, and Love
> Is God, our father dear,
> And Mercy, Pity, Peace, and Love
> Is Man, his child and care.

For Blake, as for Ginsberg, the idea of God in any context other than in the nature of man at his best is meaningless; & this spirit, Mercy, Pity, Peace & Love, is dangerous & beautiful opponent to what Ginsberg calls the "mechanical consciousness," the psychic successor to the Dark Satanic Mills Blake inveighed against.

> (At this point the reader should hear
> "Sunflower Sutra")

Similarly, Shelley, the man who was ejected from university for demanding atheism, & was subsequently referred to as "pervert and anti-Christ," puts it this way, speaking to the West Wind:

> Make me thy lyre, even as the forest is:
> What if my leaves are falling like its own!
> The tumult of thy mighty harmonies

> Will take from both a deep autumnal tone,
> Sweet though in sadness. Be thou, Spirit
>
>   fierce,
> My spirit! Be thou me, impetuous one!

In the face of a great mechanistic war-centered threat to play on man's fears & suspicions, to dehumanize him in fact, the prophetic statements of Blake, Shelley, or Ginsberg, might seem optimistic, as they express their hope that the love men's souls are mutually capable of can serve to withstand & defeat the murderous impulses let loose on the world. Beat poetry, & the great surge of spiritual optimism it gave voice to, have been a remarkable answering shout of Aw Shut Up! to the delicate pessimism in post-Eliotic verse that dominated the American academy & American anthologies in the forties & fifties.

At the same time the reputation of Eliot himself has experienced a steady decline since World War II, & old gray beard Walt Whitman has begun to peer out from behind his many flourishing leaves of grass. It is no wonder that Allen Ginsberg turned to Whitman's all-inclusive barbaric yawp of optimism as well as to the visionary exaltation of Shelley & Blake. Whitman sang:

> O to make the most jubilant song!
> Full of music — full of manhood, woman-
>   hood, infancy!
> Full of common employment — full of
>   grain and trees.
> O for the voices of animals — O for the
>   swiftness and balance
>   of fishes!
> O for the dropping of raindrops in a song!
> O for the sunshine and motion of waves in
>   a song!
>
> O for the joy of my spirit — it is un-
>   caged — it darts like
>   lightning!

Ginsberg is happy to regard himself the natural son of Walt Whitman; likewise he comes athletically out of the mill country of New Jersey, & takes America as his scene, likewise containing multitudes. But the son knows a significant & painful difference wrought upon that country. Whereas Whitman could celebrate an exhuberance in the conviction that his expansive freedom he shared as a part or all of the hopeful American kosmos, Ginsberg knows his allegiance & association must be with a dream of the real America, a pocket of resistance enduring within a continent taken over by a commercial army of occupation. (A fact Blake knew about England, & expresst in his two poems called "Holy Thursday") Ginsberg's "America" is a strangely comic place, not really sinister; rather ineptly powerful:

(Reader should listen to "America")

But Ginsberg's idea of the state of the nation is not usually so indulgent. Another time he asks this unsettling question:

" Deviants from the mass sexual stereotype, quietists, those who will not work for money, or fib and make arms for hire, or join armies in murder and threat, those who wish to loaf, think, rest in visions, act beautifully on their own, speak truthfully in public, inspired by Democracy — what is their psychic fate now in America? An America, the greater portion of whose economy is yoked to mental and mechanical preparations for war? . . . When will we discover an America that will not deny its own God? Who takes up arms, money, police, and a million hands to murder the consciousness of God? Who spits in the beautiful face of Poetry which sings of the Glory of God and weeps in the dust of the world?"

Mainly the academic-slick poets, that's who. The ones who work in universities (tho not all of them, not Creeley, Dorn, a couple of exceptions), those who turn out "safe" rehashes of tepid verse turned out by *their* professors, praise the proper people in the university quarterly book reviews, & wait till it's *their* turn for a Guggenheim.[1] That is — William

Meredith at one end, & John (New Yorker) Updike at the other. A good example is John Ciardi, a curiously tough member of the safe school, a *Saturday Review* editor who exhibits a hardness & selectivity that are foreign to the Romantic poet. They close a man up so. Ciardi speaks indulgently, like a permissive but sarcastic adult, & characterizes the Beats as literary children, an idea that would not insult Blake, nor I venture, Ginsberg. Finally, Ciardi passes the Beats off as an "unwashed eccentricity." Something like the tourist lady from the Milwaukee inter-faith counsel who couldn't *bear* the odor of Palestine.

This is, of course, the famous Establishment's traditional reaction to the visionary poet. Blake was punisht by his mother for seeing a vision of the archangel Michael in a field. Yet his mother professt to being a Christian. When Shelley began publishing his poems, the Establishment pitied his wife for being forced to live with an intellectual pervert. When Ginsberg was at Columbia University he studied under Lionel Trilling & Carl Van Doren, learning about Poetry in the approved academic fashion, & learning to turn out charming verse that lookt as if it would someday qualify for a Donald Hall anthology. Then one night he had a "beatific illumination . . . during which I'd heard Blake's ancient voice and saw the universe unfold in my brain." At this point student Ginsberg wrote a new poetry, not a poetry that sought to tell of reality, but a poetry that would *make* reality, unconstrained by any non-poetical notions of "taste" or "control" — & he showed some to his mentors at Columbia. Pooh, they said, feeling as if they'd just lost a hopeful youth, that's not poetry, its hopeless raving. Shortly thereafter, the story[2] goes, Ginsberg was expelled from the university for inscribing "Fuck the Jews" on a steamy window. But why would he do that? wondered the university officials, he's a Jew himself. That bafflement has characterized the academy ever since; & the solution has always been the same: whatever is impossible to understand, reject it in case it is dangerous or a put on. Other people with the same idea are

[1] It was my turn for a Guggenheim 1965 — A.G.

[2] The story is not accurate — A.G.

220

the government & the police — hence banning of books, burning of books, & police raids on cafes & nightclubs & theaters.

Ginsberg's reply is the only one a poet & pacifist can or should make: "Who denies the music of the spheres denies poetry, denies man, & spits on Blake, Shelley, Christ, & Buddha." Christ was spat upon; so were Allen Ginsberg & Martin Luther King. But each of them replied with gentility. & this is the spirit of Ginsberg — his gentility. If there is anything to approximate Whitman's everlasting optimism & gaiety, it is Ginsberg's openness & love, always offered. Strange thing to talk about in a literary essay. His poems dont express hatred toward anyone. Even in his most famous poem, *Howl*, he does not attack the America that destroys the best minds of his generation. Instead he expresses love for the victims of Moloch, & especially as they are symbolized by Carl Solomon in the madhouse, where he has been consigned, as was Kit Smart, the 18th century poet who dared to ask people to come to God outside the official church.

(Here the reader should hear Part III of *Howl*)

2. Howl

The central image of *Howl* is the "robot skullface of Moloch," the mechanical monolith that eats the children of America. The original Moloch was just as fearful, tho not so widely powerful. This was the old Canaanite God that appealed to the wives of the original Solomon, & earlier to the followers of Moses. He was figured as a giant stone statue with arms held out & giant flames burning all round him. It was the practice of religious women to worship Moloch by casting their children into the arms of the statue & watching them burn alive, held by that mockery of affection & care. So Ginsberg's image of a present day monster, as much more terrible as the Empire State Building is taller than an ancient Hebrew statue.

(Here the reader should hear Part II of *Howl*)

(Then listen to the whole poem)

Depending on whether you are for or against Moloch, the sacrifice can mean two things. A ravenous murder of children by their self-interested parents, or a chance for the children to purify themselves thru flames & torture & death. The latter strikes close to the Christian way to paradise, or what Ginsberg calls "the starry dynamo in the machinery of night." All thru the poem, heaven & eternity are in sight, are being called upon, or bitterly regretted, so that a cynical second best stands as an ironic refuge from the world of present Moloch. In a haunting parallel to the sermon on the mount, Ginsberg substitutes for "theirs shall be the kingdom of heaven"—"their heads shall be crowned with laurel in oblivion."

Christ went on to say: "Blessed are ye, when men shall revile you, and persecute you, and shall say all manner of evil against you falsely, for my sake. Rejoice, and be exceedingly glad: for great is your reward in heaven: for so persecuted they the prophets which were before you."

These are the people seen by Ginsberg in the first broad scene of his poem: "I saw the best minds of my generation destroyed..." In seeing them, he has his eyes wide open, all three of them, & his mind opens outward, opening with long torrential lines rolled out together on an axle of sound, the words propelling one another, as in the rime & consonant leading of:

> who chained themselves to subways for
> the endless ride from Battery to holy
> Bronx on benzadrine until the noise
> of wheels and children brought them
> down shuddering mouth-wracked and
> battered bleak of brain all drained
> of brilliance in the drear light of
> Zoo

But woe betide the scholar man who says a man dont have time to see precise truth when he is lipping off this way. Let me say the great poet (& in this poem speaks he) comes to truth world thru the sounds he picks out of it. So I will mention some things I hear in Part I of *Howl*, & I say that in his rapid setting down, Ginsberg was in the happy poet experience where the true sounds of the galaxy are there with true sightings, & the man's pen is hard presst to get most he can down, in frantic pursuit.

Here I return to the "vast conspiracy to impose one level of mechanical consciousness on mankind," & the means by which the Occupation does this. The agents of the Occupation wield their control by controlling money, time, machines, institutional education, & all the means of communication.

Ginsberg goes underground against the tyranny of Time, finding some refuge in the eternity that is sanctuary of artists & religious martyrs, where Shadrach, Meshach & Abednego really walkt when Nebuchadnezzar thought he had them in his Moloch furnace. So Ginsberg's martyrs are "burning for the ancient heavenly connection to the starry dynamo in the machinery of night," the antithesis to the machinery operated by the social state.

Ginsberg itemizes the true story staggering of his martyrs who cower, get busted, purgatory their bodies, see lightning in their brains that illuminates "all the motionless world of Time." He is interested in motion, soul motion, emotion, to break thru the motionless world of Time. Time, Standard Time, Time Magazine, Time Payments, There's A Time For Everything. The face of Moloch is a clock. The martyrs (I have to call them that now) sit for hours waiting doom-crack, talk continuously for seventy hours, disgorge in total recall for biblical seven days & nights. Section I of *Howl* shows portraits of people the poet knows, caught in the eye of Time.

Finally, in one great gesture of rebellion, they throw their watches off the roof "to cast their ballot for Eternity outside of Time, & alarm clocks fell on their heads every day for the next decade." The insurgents, now, the insurgents demonstrate, & the Occupation answers by dropping bombs, clocks, the terrible measure of bombs for a decade, the weapon of Time. In retaliation the insurgents smash "phonograph records of nostalgic European 1930's German jazz" —captured Time broken loose in the smashing, the motionless world liberated for a second of Eternity; but in Eternity a

223

second is all Eternity, & a blow can be struck against the duly invested authorities.

The insurgents keep active, barreling "down the highways of the past" & driving crosscountry in 72 hours of time, looking for Eternity, a vision of Eternity, a hope. They make a seige on Denver, defy Death & Time for a moment, only to be defeated again, to go away again, "to find out the time." To try again in a bombed out cathedral where hope, "the soul illuminated its hair for a second," but a second from Eternity where the soul is; a second in Eternity is all Eternity, but shown in Time it is only a second. & Carl Solomon, hero of the poem, is torn from cathedral, thrown into institution madhouse, into the "total animal soup of time," where he still dreams freedom, making "incarnate gaps in Time & Space." He is, as Allen is, "putting down here what might be left to say in time come after death," for a time after Time, for, obviously, Eternity, when the cities will be destroyed, when Moloch will fall on his back. This is hope & prophecy. This from Solomon, from Allen, from each martyr, who is "the madman bum and angel beat in Time."

At the same time the martyrs demonstrate against the other oppressions, money & academy, prisons where not criminals but children are lockt up, bent, warpt, trained to pass thru the sacrifice fires of Moloch. Ginsberg gives a clue to what *Life* magazine (yes, where is Death magazine) calls the "Beat mystique" when he first presents the insurgents as "poverty and tatters and hollow-eyed," deviants from the control center instructions like "Clothes make the man—physical fitness keeps America strong."

Opposed to academy control of developing brains, Ginsberg proffers the direct vision, religious, hallucinatory, a flash of light, what happens in that revealed second of Eternity. So the insurgents "bared their brains to heaven," seeing "Blake-light tragedy among the scholars of war." Here is personal Ginsberg biography, as everyone must know by now, & apt—Blake is anathema to the scholar approach, he doesnt fit, he baffles the overconscious mind, & professors generally dismiss him or try to make him something he is not—politician, patriot, moron. So the young insurgents, the young in one another's arms, preferring their Blake visions, are like him, "expelled from the academies for crazy & publishing obscene odes on the windows of the skull." (Strange tough variation on Petrarchan image.)

"Crazy" still, & making archetypal protest, they leave the university & burn their money (the "heterosexual dollar"), not only a plain facts crime against the American state, but an insult to that control as sure as the other insult to the academy's programs of lassitude: "who studied Plotinus, Poe, St. John of the Cross telepathy and bop kaballa because the cosmos instinctively vibrated at their feet in Kansas."

A clear sight into *Howl*, you see, needs not interpretation, needs only listening ear, maybe rearrangement like mind that remembers qualitatively—that is, I am sure the Gysin Burroughs cut-up suggestion, done many times would also reveal here—the objects, the nouns speak out, groupt together, they speak out.

The martyrs, insurgents, wanderers now, seek out visionary indian angels, insulting[1] the professor at Columbia Berkeley Reed Iowa State University—the visionary indian angel is not caught in motionless time; if he were he wouldn't be around, alive this century. & they throw Dada potato salad at CCNY lecturers on Dadaism, making moment of gooey vision in sordid program of a prof trying to intellectual footnote chapter heading discourse organize the unorganizable—itself, the lecture, hopeless Dada that can only invite & be pointed out by a handful of potato salad on vest front. Organic communication.

As opposed to mechanistic control of machine & communication.

"Excuse me, I think my phone's tapt by the FBI."

"Then use instant soul semaphore, or like jazz."

I think the first part of *Howl* deals largely with that major concern of modern writers—that thing about communication. The heroes of the poem are broken & punisht & trained for sacrifice thru the control center's hold on the machinery of contact; & when they become insurgents they have

[1] No, ever courteous—AG

Actually, I meant that the prof would be insulted that they went to the visionary instead of to him—GB

instinctively, religiously sought (Ginsberg makes good use of the verb, "seek") communication that transcends the machine.

So they drag themselves down long straight communication streets, the city's way to Harlems, looking for a visionary connection. It is only under the communication El that they can bare their brains, looking for the heaven fix. They get busted at communication Mexican border for transporting grass illumination—the control center machines must keep their human machines in the dark. They wander in a maze of blind streets looking for heaven lightning to transport them impossibly to "Poles of Canada & Paterson." They jolt along in communication subways, tunneling away from brilliance in that above-board underground machine. They return & return to, & finally leap off the big American successful communication Brooklyn Bridge, into dirty rivers that go nowhere but down. In their prisons they wait for the light that crackt the gloom dark cell of Peter & Simon. The jukebox in the background is trapt mechanical singer of this age, & Ginsberg sees it as "hydrogen jukebox"[1] where the crack of doom will be communicated, broadcast.

The railroad in the 19th century (Whitman) pusht west to the Pacific, opening the country & closing it too, around all caught in the continent; the railroad was the communication network that made America big & was supposed to make America great. Now Ginsberg's heroes "wandered around and around at midnight in the railroad yard wondering where to go, and went, leaving no broken hearts." They are lost in America's communication center, outsiders, not even able to participate in the grand design as does Pauline of the Perils, who at least knew what was going to happen as she lay there trusst to the Union Pacific tracks— the vibrations along the rail were news.

Thru the streets of New York, Idaho, blitz purgatory, deep in subway tubes, on bridges, they are lost where men should find. They sit cold in "boxcars boxcars boxcars," racketing thru unknown snows of farmland America, prisoners of the long train in the night. Better to be inside something timeless, the Volcanoes of Mexico, for instance, volcanoes that

[1] 1965 Rock Roll *Eve of Destruction* on jukeboxes—AG

are ancient & revered as supernatural; they reach for the sky, but they have deep holes in them, where gods can enter the earth. In America the volcanoes thin out, & they are definitely not supernatural; to the American they are noted for their size, or their names as national monuments, a thing of the Time. (See Shelley on volcanoes.) "To converse about America and Eternity, a hopeless task," Ginsberg says.

At this point I want to say something about every single Ginsberg phrase in the poem—they all arrest, they exfoliate. But it cant be done, & should not. Let me touch finger to some, reader do it himself.

For instance, though, you know, you *know* where Ginsberg is & where the control center is, & who is doing what with the means of communication, when you see the martyrs "howled on their knees in the subway." The subway, how is it not the cattle train to Dachau? (This writ before we ever saw *The Pawnbroker*.) Who has not dreamed the "horrors of Third Avenue iron dreams?" But even in the shadow of the great control center communication machines, the insurgents arise betimes to construct their own holy machines of worship, to reach beyond the steel sky— "who sat in boxes breathing in the darkness under the bridge, and rose up to build harpsichords in their lofts . . . rocking and rolling over lofty incantations," doomed songs of freedom. Their songs are drowned out by the Orwell "radio of hypnotism" in the end. But outside Time there is no end. There is a place to reach. & so they reach, the martyrs, & they try to communicate in their own underground networks:

> "to recreate the syntax and measure of
> poor human prose and stand before you speech-
> less and intelligent and shaking with shame,
> rejected yet confessing out the soul to
> conform to the rhythm of thought in his
> naked and endless head."

This is the enemy of Moloch, & in Part II of *Howl*, Ginsberg howls his defiance as his fathers carry him toward the fire & gleamy eye, the final torture & death at the grim hands of the monster lurking thru Part I, where he is seen in concrete, stone, lead, iron, ugly flames. In Part II Ginsberg starts by asking: "What sphinx of cement and aluminum bashed open their skulls and ate up their brains and imagination?" Formally, the poet is working from the first line of Part I, the image of the best minds of his generation destroyed, here eaten out of basht-open skulls.

At the Chicago reading (on the Fantasy record) the poet begins Part II with a suddenly deliberate pace, after the high flight that ended Part I. By the time the fifteenth & last line of Part II is reacht, there is an exciting tension in the voice, great emotion of pain & defiance. Moloch he confronts, maybe a moment before his own brains are to be slurpt down.

As Part I was one long exhausting sentence, Part II is the natural series of noun clusters & exclamation (!) points that come from the throat of a son about to be sacrificed, the outcry that has little time. When there is little time & no place for decorum, the noun comes out: "Moloch! Solitude! Filth! Ugliness! Ashcans and unobtainable dollars!" Here Ginsberg strips his statement to essentials: "Moloch whose mind is pure machinery! . . . Moloch who entered my soul early!"

Here Ginsberg switches from the survey of the American Occupation in Part I, to first person confession & defiance. He rips thru formal logic in presentation, to the bare communication available in words direct from the soul, as adjective becomes noun, & noun becomes adjective which is noun: "Crazy in Moloch! Cocksucker in Moloch!" The control center ways of communication are removed entirely, & Ginsberg's poem at this point becomes lesson—what difference here from the abstract sludge of business jargon evasion ("due to circumstances beyond our corporate control") or evasive poetry language ("You would think the fury of aerial bombardment/ Would rouse God to relent; the infinite spaces/ Are still silent.")

"They broke their backs lifting Moloch to Heaven!" says Ginsberg of the martyrs, & he tells in four great powerful long lines, the tragedy of lost sold-out American dream gone down the choked-out American river, or again, "down on the rocks of Time!" the treacherous killer of the drifted mind removed from hope Eternity.

Part III is addresst to Carl Solomon, & now Ginsberg has

passt "thru the fire to Moloch" (2 *Kings*, xxiii, 10). "I'm with you in Rockland," he says. Rockland is name of loony bin, but this way—Rock Land—the metamorphosis of America, rock being the material of Moloch, the mountain of American machine, the "incomprehensible prison" of Part II.

Carl Solomon is addresst as a crazy Jesus, so apt, Jesus the enemy of Canaanite Moloch, & now we must think of hope, resurrection, peace, direct ascent to heaven, the connection by way of soul to the starry dynamo. This crazy Jesus has murdered his 12 secretaries, cries that "the soul is innocent and immortal," & his soul will never be returned to its body "from its pilgrimage to a cross in the void." Solomon (the wives of Solomon betrayed him to worship Moloch—this happened in the Old Testament), Carl Solomon is rebel Jesus, plotting against the "fascist national Golgotha," or Moloch again.

Ginsberg predicts victory for this sacrificial leader of the insurrection, saying they will "split the heavens of Long Island and resurrect your living human Jesus from the superhuman tomb." In fact resurrection is the prelude to revolution war, uprising of the sacrifical victims, angelic bombardments by the souls' airplanes to counter the Time bombardments of alarm clocks. The stakes are America & freedom.

> Moreover
> thou hast taken
> thy sons & thy daughters
> whom thou hast borne unto me,
> & these hast thou sacrificed
> unto them to be devoured.
> Is this of thy whoredoms
> a small matter,
>
> that thou hast slain my children,
> & delivered them
> to cause them to pass thru
> the fire for them?

Ezekial, xvi, 20-21.   *Beaver Kosmos Folio One*

Acknowledgments

Those magazines or books where the articles first appeared are acknowledged at the end of each section in this collection. They include the following: *The Making of Modern Poetry in Canada* by Louis Dudek and Michael Gnarowski (Toronto: Ryerson Press) 1967; *Tish: A Movement* by C.H. Gervais (Guelph: *Alive 26*) 1973; *Open Letter* Series 2, No.1, and No.3, 1971, 1972; *Boundary 2* Vol.III, No.1 Fall, 1972; *Evidence* 6, 7, 9, 1962, 1963, 1965; *Beaver Kosmos* Folio #1, #2; *Tamarack Review,* Spring 35, 1965, Summer 36, 1965; *Tish 1-19,* Frank Davey, (Vancouver: Talonbooks) 1975; *White Pelican* 5/2, 1976; *Vancouver Report* by Carol Bergé (New York: Fuck Press) 1963; *Western Windows, A Comparative Anthology of Poetry in British Columbia* (Vancouver: CommCept Publishing) 1977. Special thanks however go to the authors for their permission to use these individual pieces in this collection.